Finding God

A Handbook of Christian Meditation

Ken Kaisch, Ph.D.

PAULIST PRESS
New York/Mahwah, N.J.

Library of Congress Cataloging-in-Publication Data

Kaisch, Kenneth, 1948-
    Finding God : a handbook of Christian meditation / Kenneth Kaisch.
      p. cm.
    Includes bibliographical references and index.
    ISBN 0-8091-3529-9 (pbk.)
    1. Meditation—Christianity.   2. Contemplation.   I. Title.
BV4813.K4   1994
248.3′4—dc20   94-32086
                                                         CIP

Published by Paulist Press
997 Macarthur Boulevard
Mahwah, NJ 07430

Printed and bound in the
United States of America

Contents

To my son,
Samuel Kaisch

Preface

I have three purposes in writing this book. First, I wish to introduce you to the wonderful tools for spiritual transformation within the Christian tradition. We are enjoined in scripture to become like Christ, to become "sons (and daughters) of light." But there are precious few places that tell us how to effect this transformation. I hope to provide you with such a place.

Second, I want to illustrate the developmental sequence inherent in the spiritual journey. Many people try to meditate and fail, and mistakenly conclude that meditation is not for them. This is a terrible error, because God's transformation is meant for us all. One of two faults has occurred. Either they started with a practice that was too simple or too advanced, or they thought that meditation could be mastered quickly. Unlike most things in our McWorld, meditation can take a lifetime to master.

Finally, I hope to win souls for Christ through this book. I know this sounds horribly old–fashioned, but that's the sort of fellow I am. In a society that is so thoroughly focused on the glitz and glamor, someone has to call attention to the incredible riches that are waiting to be enjoyed within. For our Lord Jesus Christ makes a dwelling place in our hearts, you know, and He invites us to come and call upon Him there!

A word about reading this book: I encourage you to read through the whole book quickly at first, in order to get an overview of the spiritual journey. Then go back and begin your meditation practice, using the text as signposts to guide you on the way. The real meaning of this book cannot be unlocked and deciphered by your intellect. Your heart holds the key, and you must enter there and learn. It will take some time to unlock the full meaning you find there.

Let me also encourage you, during the time that you practice these spiritual exercises, to do so in the company of fellow–travelers, perhaps forming a small, informal contemplative community. The sharing and mutual support that you will receive in these groups will well reward your efforts here.

1

May the compassionate Christ bless you richly. May He guide you and guard you as He draws your soul to Himself. May you drink fully from the bottomless well of His love. May the longing in your heart forever find its peace.

Fullerton, California   Ken Kaisch
January, 1994

Part I
Beginning Where We Are

Let's start where it began for me. I was sitting in the fifth grade at Hunter Elementary School in Fairbanks, Alaska. Late on a mid-winter afternoon, after we had completed our assignments for the day, Mrs. Stohl asked the class a *simple* question. She pointed to the large expanse of window and asked us to look at the snow with her. "Class," she asked, "what color is the snow out there?" We looked at each other with the knowing looks of smart–aleck fifth graders everywhere and replied, "The snow is white, Mrs. Stohl. Can't you see?"

Remember now, it is midwinter in Fairbanks. The sun comes up around eleven o'clock in the morning, a disk of cheerless orange which barely clears the southern horizon, and sets around two o'clock in the afternoon. By the time school lets out, the sky is dark. The scrub spruce forest across from the playground is a gloomy black. As we looked out at the snow on the playground, she asked again, "What color is the snow out there?"

This time, we actually looked at it, with our smug, know-it-all attitudes beginning to crack a bit around the edges. "White," we all said in exasperation. "The snow is white! Look for yourself, Mrs. Stohl." She replied, "I am looking, and it is not white."

Mrs. Stohl was an exceptional teacher. Gray haired and grand-motherly, everyone in the class loved her. She was kind and fair and openhearted; in short, the very best sort of teacher. All of us felt lucky to be in her class. But what do you do when you're ten years old and the teacher you adore looks out at a snowdrift that you know is white and says, "The snow isn't white"?

As we puzzled on this in stunned silence, Linda, the quiet girl who was the artist among us, spoke up softly. "You're right, Mrs. Stohl, it isn't white. It's blue."

At that moment it was as if we were in the crowd when the little boy whispered that the emperor wasn't wearing any clothes. The silence was incredibly intense and vibrant. And then, as if scales literally had fallen from our eyes, we all *saw* the snow.

We saw that it was blue, and even many shades of blue. And

5

once we realized that it was many colors, we saw the purples, the grays, the blacks—all of the beautiful colors that adorned the snow that afternoon. And in all of our looking, we did not see any white.

What had happened to us when we looked at the snow? The snow itself was no different—it hadn't changed colors for us. We had changed. We were able, under the guidance and prompting of this wise woman to *see* the outer world as it actually was, without the distortion and protection provided by our customary webs of illusion.

I didn't fully understand what had happened, and I still have not fully grasped my teacher's lesson. But I know that as I walked home with my buddy, Gary, that afternoon in weather twenty degrees below zero, we *saw* as we never had before. There was an intense, bubbling excitement between us as we described to each other the colors, the feelings, and the physical sensations we were experiencing. It was as if each moment were the first moment of creation, and we were right there, feeling it and experiencing it for the very first time.

After awhile, the novelty of seeing with open eyes wore off. The excitement diminished. The luminous clarity with which we had seen was obscured and we forgot. We forgot how to look in this manner, and we forgot that we had, for a brief moment, been able to see clearly. We crawled back into our protective envelopes. We put on our goggles once again and walked around like everyone else, sagely nodding to one another while repeating our cultural mantras: "Snow is always white. The sun is always located up. Good guys always win. And we are the good guys."

I remembered this fifth grade incident under strange circumstances many years later. In my sophomore year of college, a fraternity brother spun out on a patch of black ice and wrapped his car around a tree. He died as the volunteer fire department tried to cut him free. For the first time in my life, a close friend had died, and the tragedy of it overwhelmed me. "What's the use of trying, if you can be cut down, just like that, for no reason?" I wondered. For the first time, I felt my own vulnerability. I walked the cold streets that night asking over and over, "Why?" "Why Bert? He had so much to offer, and he was such a warm and gentle soul. Why, God, why?" I blamed the stupidity of it on God—who else was there to blame? I walked aimlessly raging, pointlessly questioning, grieving deeply.

And in the middle of the night, on empty streets, what I took to be reality—everything in front of me, everything ordinary that I saw, the street, the quiet still trees, the sky—was peeled back as though it had been painted on a cloth and the cloth swept open like a theater curtain. I saw two angels holding the corners, with a vast space beyond. In this space, Bert appeared to me and said in his own voice and with his own words, "It's okay, Ken, you don't have to grieve so hard. I'm in a good place and I'm glad to be here. I don't want to go back. I'm okay." And with that, the angelic beings loosed their hands, the curtain fell back into place, and my conventional "reality" reappeared in front of me.

I was stunned! I stood there for minutes, or maybe it was hours. When I recovered, I slowly made my way home, no longer feeling anger or grief. In place of those emotions I felt a deep sense of peacefulness. I *knew* that Bert was okay. There was no point in holding on to my own sorrow.

That experience once again opened me to a different reality—a reality that was totally distinct and separate from everything I had called ordinary. I had never experienced anything like it before and, at the time, I did not know anyone who had experienced any-thing like it. There was no question in my mind that it was real. It was more real than what I saw in front of me. Compared to this reality that I had just seen, what I ordinarily saw and touched and tasted had the substance of a dream. This vision of Bert pointed to a dimension of experience that was so totally genuine that what I experienced around me seemed like the illusion.

As I reflected on the experience, I wondered about this thing we call day–to–day reality? What can I put my trust in? What is sub-stantial? Clearly, the visionary experience had a reality about it that was "super–real." But ordinary reality is real, too, isn't it? And then I remembered the colors of snow.

It helped to remember. "Snow isn't white," I said to myself. "Reality isn't necessarily what I believe it to be." Just because I had never been told about this kind of vision in Sunday School didn't mean that it wasn't real. I knew otherwise. I *knew* it, but I couldn't explain it or make sense of it, or even talk about it with anyone without serious risk of being taken for a nut case.

With these experiences I began to observe that reality may not be what I think it is. Watching myself and others, I grew to under-stand that we live in protective envelopes—envelopes that are self–created and self–serving. I came to see that each of us lives in an envelope of delusion, which we have wrapped around ourselves for protection. And as I looked, I came to understand that none of us really understands this; and what is more, we do not *want* to understand it. We seem to be willing to sacrifice real understanding for the illusion of protection.

Since that time, I have spent my life looking for ways out of these envelopes and into genuine living. The journey has taken me into theological studies and priesthood in the Episcopal Church. It has taken me on a lengthy exploration of the deep spiritual tradition within Christianity, finding that many, many others have walked this way before me. It has taken me into clinical work in psychology, exploring the depths of our human processes of denial, avoidance, and delusion.

I have finally understood that there is a way out of our delusional mess. There is a way to go beyond our conventional shadow–reality and into the great Reality which underlies all creation. I have come to understand that the purpose of our life is to enter into union with God. Furthermore, the vehicles that can take us into this union are the practices of meditation and contemplative prayer.

For Christians, it is not necessary to go to the Eastern religions to learn how to meditate. We have a rich, if hidden, contemplative tradition of our own. Our own tradition contains the tools we need for our transformation. It contains the tools we need to pierce the envelope of self–delusion; the tools we need to allow God to change our hearts of stone into hearts of living flesh.[1]

This book is the summary of my findings and a survey of the contemplative tools developed within Christianity. The challenge of this book is to present you with a systematic way to leave your protective envelope, should you so desire. So let us begin our journey together...

Chapter 1

Our Human Situation

Consider our human situation for a moment. We take ourselves and our experiences for granted. We seldom look inward or question who we are. We hardly ever ask, "How do I know that this experience is real?" Our vision is almost always directed outward, toward the world out there.

Even though we don't consciously realize it, everything we experience outside of ourselves is filtered by what is inside of us. Deep inside the psyche, we are constantly asking, "Does what I experience fit with my map of what I *should* be experiencing right now?" So when we look at snow, we already know that it is white. When we look at each other, we already know that this one is a friend, that one is an enemy.

We try to live in accordance with our inner maps, but these maps would have us believe that snow is always white. If these maps are faulty, though, what can we trust? What can we truly *know* about the world out there, if we don't know ourselves, our own insidious filters and biases? Indeed, what can we truly know about ourselves, because even our self–perceptions are mediated through our inner maps? Who are we, really?

Who Am I?

We might address this question by describing the many roles we assume: husband, wife, son, daughter, and so on. Or we might describe the qualities we embody; that we are courageous, loving, friendly, or bright. But these responses beg the question, don't they? These responses reflect our cultural map of what we think we should be.

We have somehow created the person who we think we should be,

9

not who we are. We have created an idealized self: a self that is wonderful, and kind, and generous, and all of the other qualities that our culture values. And in fact, this idealized self does tell part of the story. We are like all of these wonderful characteristics—to a degree. But what about the hateful mean parts of ourselves which we hide from others? The parts which only we know about?

We walk around, commonly believing that this idealized self is who we really are. But this doesn't really get at the issue. We haven't described anything about the "me" who has these qualities, about the self who adopts these various roles. Who is this "I" who comes dressed up in these roles? What is this quality of *I–ness* that lies under the cultural notion of identity? Who are you and what is your true nature underneath all of the trappings?

This is the crucial question of our inquiry here. We are asking, "What is the nature of identity?" What is the nature of this *I–ness* which each of us experiences and which holds together the disparate moments of our lives in a coherent whole? From the evidence sketched out in the argument above, it seems that we must know our self before we can truly know anything else. Not to examine the self opens us to the error of thinking that snow is always white, and other conventional clichés. We must thoroughly examine this human filter if we are to obtain any true knowledge about the world around us.

Think about this yourself—how would you describe your *I–ness*? What is that part of you that is your center, your identity? What could you say about this part of you that is the essential you?

Are you your body? Is your identity to be found in your physical sensations? Is it to be found in your emotions? Your thoughts? All of us tend to identify our self with one of these three: the body, the mind, or the emotions. We tend to see our identity as tied up with these aspects of ourself. Take bodybuilders as an example. They care obsessively for their bodies because they have identified the body with the self. But is a person's identity limited to the body? Of course not. And anyone who is not a bodybuilder understands this.

The same thing happens with the emotions and the intellect. We tend to identify ourselves with these parts, but at the cost of ignoring the whole. The body, the emotions, and the intellect are all things which the "I" has, but our essential identity cannot be found in any of these. This leaves us with our question unanswered. What is this "I" that has these things?

In addition to identifications with things inside of us, we also identify with things external to us. Unfortunately this maneuver

also avoids the issue. We identify with a job, a role, or a possession. The maneuver is this: I am important because: (check the
appropriate blank)

        ____I am CEO of General Motors.
        ____I am Joey and Sally's mom.
        ____I own a Mercedes.
        ____I play lead guitar in the most popular rock group of
           all time.

These identifications do not really tell us anything about who we
are. We still are no closer to understanding the nature of identity.
In fact, it seems as if our identifications help us achieve two
things. First, when we falsely identify with some thing or role or
quality, we relieve the anxiety that comes from not knowing who
we really are. Second, our identifications help us avoid the issue of
looking at who we are. If I am important because of what I think
or what I do or how I spend my time, then there is no need to look
any further, is there?

Our identifications are ways to avoid looking at this entity we
call the self. Thus, our identifications constitute a profound denial
of who we really are. We identify with a familiar part of ourselves,
with something that the self *has*. This precludes us from looking
any deeper into who we really *are*.

This is a profound distortion of our true nature. We spend our
lives avoiding our selves. Ponder this with me for a moment. Why
would we need to do this? What is so awful about understanding
our *I–ness*, our true nature, that an entire culture needs to avoid it
in this systematic fashion?

The False Self

If we are to have any lasting peace, we must begin to question
why we so consistently sacrifice understanding for the illusion of
protection. What has happened to us? Why would we continue to
take this ostrich approach, despite all of the evidence indicating
that ostriches get eaten alive? The answer is to be found in the
very ordinary processes of childhood development. When we look
closely, we see that a systematic process of renunciation has taken
place, through which each of us sacrifices our true nature.

A number of very perceptive psychologists have catalogued these changes as they take place during our development. Among them, D.W. Winnecott developed the notion of a "false self" that comes into being as an essential part of our maturation.[2] This false self obscures something very important within us. Winnecott's conceptual work dovetails very nicely with the more theological understanding of St. Paul.

Simplifying Winnecott's model, the false self develops in response to the socialization process. Children begin as wonderful creatures: whole, curious, trusting, and so delighted by every passing sensation. At birth they are radiant. This radiance becomes particularly noticeable around six months of age, when they complete that part of gestation which takes place outside the womb. Now they sit up and take real notice of the world. They beam at the world. The world delights them. Their radiance surrounds them in every direction.

Then we begin to learn some things that run counter to our beaming radiance.[3] We learn that parts of us are not okay. We learn that some of the things we do are not liked by those around us. We hear from our parents, as they change our diapers, that we are "stinky-poo." At first we think this is okay. We like this big smell we make. But they make faces and act toward us in unpleasant and disparaging ways. So we learn that being "stinky-poo" is not acceptable.

To keep our parents' love and approval, we work hard to cut off this part of ourselves. We learn, with much effort, to control our sphincter and to make "stinky-poo" only when we are alone. Eventually we become ashamed, not only of the "stinky-poo," but also of the body parts which eliminate these products. And by cutting off these parts of ourselves, we cut off some of the radiance which surrounds us.

Our parents, however, are not the only bad guys in this developmental story. We go to school and learn that many other parts of ourselves are not acceptable. We learn that good boys and girls are quiet in class and raise their hands when they have something to say. So we cut off our spontaneity. We learn that we don't get up from our desks unless the teacher says so. So we cut off our curiosity.[4] All the while, our radiance is progressively and perceptibly dimming.

Then we enter adolescence, that time of our greatest conformity. We learn that we have to wear certain kinds of clothing or certain shoes to be acceptable. We have to act in certain ways. We adopt certain tastes in music; certain mannerisms which are accepted as "cool." And most of the radiance that remains vanishes in our desperate efforts to be acceptable.

What we have done by means of this process of approval–seeking is to create a false self. This false self has nothing to do with who we really are. It is the product of our vain attempts to secure approval and love. Our false self changes with every passing fashion; it can be remade overnight.

This process of socialization, while giving us tools to get along in the world, also robs us of something vital and precious. This process destroys a sense of our own inner unity, our connection with God, and our connection with each other. There is, however, a positive result of the creation of the false self. By this means, we create the tools necessary for living together. We no longer can simply react to things without thinking. The false self is a mechanism which moves us into self–awareness. As the theologian Paul Tillich has indicated, we need to become estranged from God, to be a unique centered self, in order to fully experience God's love and to love Him back.[5]

Unfortunately, we come to believe that this false self is real, that this is who we are. We come to identify with the false self. Once we have identified with it, we have locked ourselves inside a self–created protective envelope. We are now trapped inside. All of our perceptions about our self and about the external world are filtered through this envelope. We have imprisoned our selves.

The false self is programmed to get the approval of other people. This is the self that says that snow is white without ever looking at the snow. This is the self that is so desperate for approval that it says whatever is socially acceptable. At the level of a child talking about snow, this kind of thinking is innocuous. But carry it forward into adult conformity. The false-self thinking that strives for social acceptance is the kind of thinking that allows manufacturers to pollute our environment, politicians to engage in deficit spending, parents to allow their children to join gangs. Any kind of thinking that ignores our fundamental needs in order to "go with the flow" is from the false self. While this can be harmless when we are children, it is often dangerous when we become adults.

This false-self programming is doomed at the outset. We created the false self to secure approval and happiness, but it can never bring us any lasting happiness or joy. What can we do that will insure that we will always get approval? The only possible way to obtain this is to change ourself for every person, to become a reflection of those around us.

The ultimate failure of the false self in securing any lasting happiness comes when we think of what success would be like under its terms. We would constantly be adapting ourselves like a chameleon to everyone around us. But even supposing that we could adapt in this way, we would have to sacrifice our own values. *We would sacrifice our self so that this same self would be acceptable.* This is a game that cannot be won. The false self system cannot give us what we seek.

We create the false self to get along in a difficult world. The false self strives to get us love and approval. The false self is predicated on the notions that our personal happiness is all–important, and that pain and suffering can be avoided. It is predicated on the idea that my self is the center of the universe. It is totally self–centered. When we stop to examine these notions directly, they strike us as silly. But unexamined, as they usually are, these notions drive us to destructive behavior.

The True Self

While we create the false self, the true self is created by God. Let us look, for a moment, at what was there before we created this false-self construct. There is a deeper and truer self that God created. This self is wonderfully formed, whole and perfect by itself. It does not need any effort from us for maintenance or life. There is no way that we can enhance this self. This is the true self, and it is God's gift to us. This is the being–ness deep within each of us. "In my own image, I created you."[6]

The true self has remarkable qualities. This is the radiant self that we notice in infants and small children. This is the self that is full of wonder and awe, the self for whom each passing moment is a delight. This is the self that accepts our dark passions, that loves fully, that is whole.

This is the self that Jesus addresses when He teaches us to pray. Jesus gave us only one prayer. When His disciples asked Him to teach them to pray, our Lord taught them to say, "Our Father, who art in heaven..." Something very important is being shown with these words. Jesus says, *our* Father.[7] That is to say, His Father and your Father and my Father. And if we all have the same Father, then we are brothers and sisters. And if we have the same Father as Jesus, then we must participate in the Divine in some very deep and special way, a way of which we are not presently conscious.

This is the key to understanding the true self. *The true self is connected to God; it is always present to God.* In mystical language, it is the part of us that receives the Presence of God, enthroned upon our souls; the part that listens to the Lord who is always whispering and murmuring in our hearts.

Every now and again, our true self breaks through the massive conditioning of the false self and surprises us. We are caught up in a beautiful sunset—something happens that we can't explain—the beauty of it takes our breath away. Here, the true self breaks through for a moment and touches us. Or we are touched by someone's love—we really feel the sweet force of someone's caring. Our false-self conditioning is momentarily disrupted, and we have a sense of going beyond ourselves, beyond the constraining limits of the false self. These are ecstatic moments. But these are only tastes of the banquet that God spreads for us. The real question becomes, "How can I go and feast at this banquet? How can I find my true self?"

These are the questions this book seeks to address. From Jesus' teaching in the Lord's Prayer, it seems clear that we don't have to add anything special to ourselves in order to have a place at the banquet. We are loved by God and accepted wherever we might be. We do not, however, typically feel as if we are accepted or loved. To experience our heritage as God's sons and daughters, we have to find a way to dismantle the false-self system. Our true self is there underneath all of the garbage with which we have covered it. What we lack are reliable methods to sweep away the garbage that obscures our true nature. These methods have been developed within the church over the past two millennia, and are called spiritual disciplines. The function of the spiritual disciplines is to help us let go of our internal garbage so that we can get to the treasure below.

Meditation and contemplative prayer are two of the more powerful spiritual disciplines. These disciplines help us disengage from the false-self programming. We disengage from the false self by learning to rest ourselves fully in God. The false self is so pervasive and so powerful that it bends everything we do to its own ends. We can dissolve its shackles only by refraining from our own doing, by resting ourselves in the Presence of the One who made us and who constantly nourishes us with love.

This notion of doing nothing in order to do something runs

counter to conventional wisdom. But reflect with me for a moment. If everything we do to get loose from the false-self system is turned against our purpose because of the false-self conditioning, what then is there left for us to do? What will be effective in this circumstance? This is our position in relation to the false-self system. Our conditioning is so powerful, our need for approval is so strong, that we are trapped within it. Our doing cannot resolve it. All the doing in the world cannot resolve it. Rather, we must learn to refrain from doing and go to that which is prior, our *being*.

Chapter 2

Breaking Out of Bondage

The good news is that there is a part of us, buried deeply inside, that is already in union with God. This is the true self, created by God. This part of us is already enjoying salvation. It is already whole and complete, and always has been.

The bad news is that we don't live in this place. We live in another, more shallow self that we created in order to cope with the difficulties of living. What we need is a means to let go of our identification with this false self. We need a realistic workable method for our interior transformation that enables us to disengage from the false self.

From our psychological analysis, it is clear that we need to change our frame of reference. We have identified with a too–narrow frame of our own creation. We need to dis–identify from this narrow frame so that we can learn God's frame of reference. And this is exactly what scripture says. Moreover, this is not just something we find only in scripture. This need has been echoed down the centuries by those saints who have walked this path before us.

In the Likeness of Christ

Scripture enjoins us to become Christ–like; to live in Christ as Christ lives in us.[8] St. John amplifies this in a nearby passage: "Anyone who loves me will be true to my word, and...we will come to him and make our dwelling place with him."[9] We are invited directly to dwell in Christ. To make ourselves like Christ. In the language of Thomas à Kempis, we are invited to imitate Christ.

Think with me about what this involves. First, we need to change our hearts; we need to love Christ much more completely than we do now. "Anyone who loves me will be true to my word." Over and over

17

we hear in the gospels that we must learn to love God and follow in the path of the Divine. This appears to be the first step.

From this action, a variety of changes follow. First, our behaviors change. As they change, our thoughts and emotions change. Even the way in which we perceive the world and ourselves will change. As we make these critical corrections, we begin to wrestle with the larger issues directly. How do we become Christ–like? How do we come to love the Lord fully?

Perhaps we ought to look at what Jesus actually did, in order to understand what we need to do to follow Him. What activities did Jesus practice, in order to realize and maintain the perception that God was within Him? Jesus lived a simple life, one that was frugal and sacrificial in nature. He was constantly going apart to be in silence and solitude. He prayed constantly, even on the cross. He prayed the psalms. He served others constantly, putting their welfare ahead of His own. He loved His followers and all people fully and completely.

As a result of these behaviors, Jesus rooted Himself in the Presence of His Father. He had a constant sense of that Presence. Because He had entered into the Divine, He was able to see from God's frame of reference. From this perspective, He constantly saw the kingdom of God in the mundane world around Him.

We must understand the significance of this. Jesus was not paying lip service to a set of abstract principles or values. He was living His life in holiness. The active Presence of God the Father was our Lord's most fundamental reality. Jesus' experience was that God lived in Him. He then shared this experience with His disciples. "Live in me," He said, "and the Father and I will live in you."

Jesus' religion is fundamentally different from Christianity as we have received it in twentieth–century America. Most of us have received a set of dry principles for living: a set of beliefs which, we are told, will transform us if we incorporate them into our lives. If this were so, if belief alone would change us, then we would not be in our present mess. I submit to you that the longest distance in the world is the distance between the head and the heart, between our intellectual understanding of something and a change in our hearts. Just believing in something does not make it so. If you are not sure about this, try believing that your skin color is green and see if you can make it so by believing. The notion is absurd.

We need to go beyond the Christianity we have received, our conventional intellectualized faith. Jesus did not give us a set of

abstract principles to be obeyed. Instead, He invited us to participate in an inside–out transformation. He invited us to welcome
Him into our hearts; to learn to dwell with Him and in Him.
Fundamentally, our Lord invites us to identify with Him: "live in
Me and I will live in you."[10] For most of us, this change is a radical
one. It is difficult to accomplish, not because the task is inherently
hard, but because we have trouble letting go of that which stands
in our way.

Standing in our way is the false self. The false self is rooted in
the notion that "I am the center of the universe." So before we can
identify with Christ, before we can love as Christ commands us,
we must first dis–identify from the false self.

We can dis–identify from the false self only by doing what Jesus
did, by practicing the behaviors that Jesus adopted. These behaviors
of our Lord have come to be known as the spiritual disciplines. They
provide us with a systematic means for overcoming the unnatural
limits of the false self and entering into the kingdom of God.

The Spiritual Disciplines

I shudder to think how you will receive these words, "the spiritual disciplines"! Our culture has terrible images for these words:
images of men in hairshirts beating themselves, starving themselves, locking themselves away from the world in tiny cells. We do
not understand how any of this is possible. These pictures are completely divorced from our intellectualized understanding of what it
means to follow Christ as Lord.

The spiritual disciplines, however, are not something terrible.
They are nothing but systematic methods for breaking through the
false self into genuine life: a life rooted in the spiritual reality of
God. The spiritual disciplines do have a destructive component.
They have to be powerful enough to enable us to break through the
false self into genuine life, powerful enough to release us from our
self–imprisonment so that we can live in freedom.

A contemporary author, Dallas Willard, has carefully examined
Christ's way of life and identified the spiritual disciplines that
Jesus used.[11] Willard divides them into two categories: the disciplines of abstinence and the disciplines of engagement. These methods can be adopted readily by anyone wishing a richer encounter
with God.

The disciplines of abstinence that Willard finds in Christ's life include solitude, silence, fasting, frugality, chastity, secrecy, and sacrifice. These methods were used by our Lord as tools for wrestling with the false self. Not only are these disciplines visible in the gospels, we also hear of them throughout scripture. Peter says, "Abstain from fleshly lusts which war against the soul."[12] We hear of these means over and over again in the writings of the saints who came after the disciples.

The disciplines of abstinence involve abstaining "to some degree and for some time from the satisfaction of what we generally regard as normal and legitimate desires."[13] These include our basic needs, such as food, sleep, sex, and companionship. They also include the derivative needs of the false self for security, comfort, reputation, and so on. These desires are not bad in and of themselves. But under the distortion of the false-self system, both sets of desires drive us without mercy. We have, for the most part, lost control of our basic desires. They own us; we do not own or control them.

The disciplines of engagement, as Willard defines them, are study, worship, celebration, service, prayer, fellowship, confession, and submission. Abstinence prepares the way for engagement. First we work to clear out the structures of the false self, then we engage in disciplines that lead us directly to the sense of God's Presence in our lives and to the true self which constantly receives that holy Presence.

The disciplines of engagement direct us to the Divine. Unfortunately, we cannot easily receive God through the false self. Since the false self understands *itself* to be the center of the world, it really cannot permit God to come into our life. The false self can, and often does, twist the concept of God to justify its own selfish ends. But this is simply another distortion of the truth. Before we can come to any true seeing, we must relinquish the false self. Thus, we must first walk the way of repentance and abstinence, exploring ways of turning from the false self. Only then can we engage God directly.

As children we were trained by everything around us to develop our false self. The entire culture moved us in this direction; we had no real choice in the matter. But as adults, when we recognize what has happened, choice comes back to us. Now we can take full responsibility for our current situation and make the positive changes that are necessary for genuine life.

One of the results of practicing the spiritual disciplines is pain. We are going after the false self, which can be likened to a cancer supplanting the legitimate functions of the true self. Just as it hurts to eradicate physical cancers, it also hurts to go after spiritual ones. This is not a pleasure jaunt; this is the literal way that Jesus walked, the way of the cross. These are the practices that He engaged in, and that brought Him into the deepest realization of His true nature. And He invites us to take on His yoke and learn from Him.[14]

As we take on the yoke and engage in the disciplines of abstinence, our pain may be immediate. For example, it is deeply disturbing to be alone, to practice solitude. When we do this without distracting our attention with radio or TV, our fears and insecurities naturally bubble to the surface. All those domains where we have trusted in our own power suddenly are called into question. When we are alone, we become afraid of even the littlest bump in the night.

We need to walk the spiritual way with a clear understanding of the pain and fear that must arise. When we walk this way, let us do so with eyes open; let us be honest with one another. Our common task is to let go of our self as the center of the universe, and to acknowledge and know God as the center. With the wonderful examples of all the saintly men and women who have walked this way before us, it is clear that this task can be achieved. We will pay a price for walking this way, however.

An Outline of the Spiritual Journey. Our journey begins everywhere and anytime. That is to say, we have already begun; everyone is already on the way. But we start moving quickly when we intentionally enter into the flow of the journey.

Our first intentional act comes about when we are motivated to begin the spiritual journey. Something happens to us that makes us take the spiritual dimension of life seriously. This is a clear starting point. As a result of our motivation, we may begin reading spiritual literature, going to church, or talking with friends about spiritual matters. We are motivated to begin, but we need to gather information first in order to understand the next step.

The next clear step is a radical change in attitude, which leads to behavioral changes. In the language of theology, we repent. We turn from our old ways of doing things, because we learn that they really don't work for us. We change our behavior, hoping to move away from the things that don't work and toward the things that do work.

Then comes a period in our lives where we regulate our behavior. We take seriously those behavioral injunctions of scripture. We try to live by the ten commandments. We try to love God with all our heart. This is a time of great struggle. If we are honest with ourselves, we have to admit that we constantly fail in even the simplest behavioral changes. The behaviors of the false self are so strong that they seem to control us, not the other way around. This is the time that we begin to take the spiritual disciplines seriously.

After we have made some headway in regulating our behavior, we are ready to begin meditation.[15] This is not to say that our behavior must perfectly conform to God's will for us to be ready. We are far from that when the time comes for our meditation practice to begin. What is necessary is that we start to take our outward behaviors seriously, and that we take responsibility for the things that are not right in ourselves. Working with our outward behaviors creates the foundation necessary to begin work on the more subtle inward behaviors.

The Discipline of Meditation and Contemplative Prayer. As we enter into these middle stages of our walk with Christ, meditation and contemplative prayer become crucial tools. They are among the most powerful and effective tools for breaking down the illusions of the false self and entering into that abundant life promised to us.

Meditation and contemplation are vehicles for effectively moving us out of our self–centered frame of reference. These vehicles move us into God's frame of reference; we learn to see through His eyes. Our lives will be transformed by these experiences so that the suffering in which we clothed ourselves falls away. There is pain, as there must be in a transformation of this magnitude. But the redemption is ever so sweet.

Through meditation and contemplative prayer, we move out of doing and into being, away from the secular into the sacred. And by means of this movement, we become the holy people we were created to be. We come into our full heritage from God; we grow into our full stature.

The charge of quietism. Some within the Christian churches view this transformative process with considerable alarm. These committed Christians may criticize the disciplines of meditation and contemplative prayer as quietism, as a passive withdrawal from the world. They view this as inherently selfish. They call, instead, for social activism, for a commitment to work for justice and peace in the world.

While these are worthy goals, this perspective misses several essential points. First, Jesus does not call us to change the world. He calls us to change ourselves, to change our hearts. How can we work for peace if we ourselves are angry and disturbed within? Meditation is a means for transforming the selfishness of our false self and living for God.

Second, the contemplative journey not only creates the peaceful soul necessary for genuine service, it also frees our energy and compassion so that we can serve fully. Look at Mother Teresa of Calcutta, for example. In all outward ways, she seems to epitomize the ideal of social service. What is not apparent to most is that she and the nuns of her order gather for contemplative prayer for several hours before they start their day of service. It is the inward transformation that gives them the power to care for the poorest of God's poor.

The inward transformation that comes from the practice of the spiritual disciplines must come before social service, if that service is to be effective and sustainable. First we change our own hearts, and only then can we work effectively to change the hearts of others.

The charge of demon possession. Others in the Christian community have the mistaken belief that meditation opens the practitioner to demon possession. Their line of reasoning is that meditation empties the mind, creating a place for demons to come in. While I will speak at length on this topic in later chapters, it is sufficient to say two things now. First, it is not possible to stop thinking, and that is not the goal of meditation. The goal is to disengage from the stream of inane chatter inside our heads. Second, the process of disengagement crucifies all that is demonic within us. It crucifies the false self, allowing the true self to emerge. So how could demons come in and possess the soul that knows itself to be truly loved by God? It is impossible. This fear comes from ignorance, not from knowing.

Both of these mistaken views miss the crucial point. The point is a simple one: our God is calling us to come back home. The spiritual journey is simply the walk that we must take to go home. The disciplines of meditation and contemplative prayer are how we move ourselves in this walk. The only really strange thing is how many people do not hear God's constant calling to them.

The Challenge

We are called by God—all of us! We are called to move beyond our limits, to move outside of the constraints which we have placed around ourselves. We are called to be something different, to be wholly ourselves. We are called to see, to hear, to feel deeply our own nature and the nature of the world we live in. We are called to be our entire self—not some facade or mockery of what we truly are. We are called to be whole people, the people God created us to be.

Each of us has felt the call to go beyond our limits, to be something different. We feel the longing when it tugs at us. We know we are something different, something greater; but we don't know what this greatness might be, or how we should respond to this deeper self. In the same way, we wonder how to respond to the deep Reality which underlies all creation, which is our God.

Because this Reality is unknown to us, it is frightening to hear this inner calling. It is even more frightening to respond to it, to open ourselves to experience what is. But most frightening of all is knowledge of the alternative. If we refuse to respond to our God, then we bury ourselves in illusion.

When we begin at our beginning—where we are right now—then we start to experience that protective envelope, that self–created bubble of illusion in which we wrap ourselves. We use this envelope in an attempt to shield ourselves from suffering. This effort is not wrong or bad. No one wants to suffer. But the way we go about trying to protect ourselves does not work. Our bubble doesn't keep out the pain, yet we deplete ourselves in futile efforts to stop the bleeding.

We start in the midst of our illusions. Deep inside each bubble of illusion there is a central core of identity—that true self that God created. By tapping into even a fleeting perception of our true self, we begin to feel discomfort with our illusions. We become aware of our incompleteness, and we are reminded, again and again, that at our deepest levels we are different from these illusions.

We begin with a dissatisfaction about the way things are—dissatisfaction with our illusions and with the false self that is grounded in them. We intuitively know we are more than these limits. At this point, we have a critical choice. We can choose to pull back and put up with our discomfort. Or we can choose to move forward, and challenge the illusions of our false self.

Letting go of our false self is like the experience of death. We have carefully constructed this edifice of the false self. We have screened from our vision those parts of us with which we are uncomfortable. Those uncomfortable parts are still there, of course, but we never allow our eyes to gaze upon them. When we try to let go of our false self, every cell in us will scream, "NO!" Letting go feels like death. And we are afraid to die. We are afraid of annihilation.

The spiritual journey is for those who are afraid of dying, but who are even more afraid of living in illusion. Together we will explore the ancient disciplines of Christian meditation and contemplation. We will explore methods which can lead us deep into our central core, which is created in God's image; methods for a systematic transformation of our deepest selves. Using these methods, we will move into a deeper perception of the Reality we label God.

We will describe the spiritual technology of meditation which has developed in Christianity. We will explore, in addition to specific kinds of meditation, the developmental character of the spiritual journey, showing what happens in the beginning, middle, and end of the journey. Ultimately, the material here will acquaint us with a language of the soul. It is a language through which we can talk clearly about personal transformation and spiritual liberation, a language through which we can talk about God in a sensible way.

So let us continue our journey together...

Chapter 3

What Is Meditation?

Because there is no fundamental separation of individual awareness from the Divine—no bottomless abyss to cross—there is nothing particularly to do to regain union with God. There are no bridges to build. No tower of Babel is necessary so that we might reach up to God. There are, however, psychological structures and belief systems to be dismantled.

Meditation is a slow and gentle way to dismantle the structures which the false self created to assert its own separateness and provide for its own security. Following Deane Shapiro, one of the foremost scientific investigators of meditative practices, "meditation refers to a family of techniques which have in common a conscious attempt to focus attention in a non–analytical way, and an attempt not to dwell on discursive, ruminating thought."[16] For our purposes, discursive thought is defined as those analytical forms of thinking which use sensory input, ranging from formal analytical thinking with premises and conclusions, to informal daydreaming with sensory–based fantasies.

In Christianity, we distinguish between meditation and contemplation. By meditation, we mean those techniques which make some use of discursive thought to go beyond the thought itself. For example, we can use thought to create an image of Jesus and to dwell on that image. This visualization is an example of what Christians call meditation. In these spiritual exercises, we use the discursive mind to create an image, and then we limit the mind to the confines of this image.

Contemplation, on the other hand, does not use discursive thought. Contemplative prayer is a radical abandonment of discursive thinking in the effort to experience what lies beyond. Because contemplative prayer is so different from what we ordinarily do, it is important first to learn the steps of meditation which lead up to the contemplation of God.

Finally, there is a bridge between meditation and contemplation, known in the Eastern Orthodox Church as hesychast prayer and in the West as monologistic prayer. This form of prayer involves holding the mind on the repetition of a phrase, while focusing the attention inwardly in specific ways. The Jesus Prayer is the best known example of monologistic prayer. Here we begin with discursive thinking, but limit this thinking in such a way that it takes us beyond thought into the contemplative dimension of being.

These meditative techniques, like colors in a spectrum, blend into each other. When we look at a specific band in a color spectrum, we quickly get to the point where we can no longer tell if we are looking at a blue–green or at a green–blue. Meditative techniques are similar. While there is a general progression in the techniques, specific determinations can be difficult to make. Furthermore, some techniques like chanting may be either a sensory meditation or monologistic prayer, depending on how they are used interiorly. An observer can't always tell from the outward signs of the practice what is going on. We need to know as well the inner operations that the practitioner is using.

Attention and Meditation

Perhaps the most important single factor for understanding the spectrum of contemplative development is the role of attention. Ordinarily, we do not think of attention as something to be noticed or trained. We take attention for granted, like the air we breathe. Because of this, we do not monitor its growth or development. Development of the attention cannot be ignored, however, if we want to move forward on our spiritual journey. It must be noticed and nurtured as the central aspect of our identities which, when properly trained, has the power to take us directly into the mystery of God.

Attention is perhaps the most important faculty of the human mind. Without a focused attention, we can do nothing. Think what life would be like if our attention bounced around like a ping-pong ball, if we were unable to focus. We could not accomplish anything. Unfortunately, most of us think that our attentional focus is satisfactory. And it is, for most of the things that we do. But it is not focused enough to enable us to disengage from the false self, and it is not focused enough to allow us to rest in God, as our Lord Jesus invites us to do.

The Dreaded Monkey Exercise. Do you think your attention is a disciplined tool that can take you where you wish to go? Try this exercise and see just what kind of tool it is. Most likely you will find that your attention is like a wild beast, running everywhere. But try the exercise and see for yourself.

The "Dreaded Monkey Exercise" has only one instruction. For the next sixty seconds don't think about monkeys. You can think about whatever you please, but don't let a single thought of monkeys come into your mind. Don't think about the ways that monkeys look. Don't think about all the silly ways they act. Just refrain completely from thinking about them. Stop your reading right now, find a clock with a sweep second hand, and do this exercise before you go on.

Most people who try this exercise report that their minds are filled with monkeys of every conceivable variety, involved in every conceivable activity. This simple experiment shows that we do not have much control over our attention. We cannot place it where we want, even for a single minute.

This lack of control can be disconcerting when we try to meditate. In meditation we quiet the mind and practice focusing our attention. As we develop our ability to focus, we prepare ourselves for the rigors of contemplative prayer. As we develop a trained and refined attention, we will be able to move into the Mystery of God.

The nurture of attention, much like the nurture of a child, involves discipline. Without clear discipline that is consistently applied, a child will never develop properly. In a similar manner, without consistent training and discipline our attention will not develop its full potential. With proper training our attention can move us into the Presence of God. Thus, it has amazing potential to transform our lives. But we are seldom moved to train our attention because we are unaware of the potential benefit.

Meditation is a series of graduated exercises which train attention. We practice meditation by restricting our awareness to a single stimulus, which may be either complex or simple. For example, we may focus attention on an image of Jesus, or on the word "Jesus" without any images or extraneous thoughts. In fact, we may use any stimulus as the focus for meditation. Each different object of meditation will have a slightly different effect on our awareness. While these effects are important, it is the *process* that is of primary importance—the process of restricting and focusing our awareness.

In practice, our attempts to focus in meditation are constantly broken by an inner stream of chatter. Each of us has an internal chatterbox that talks almost constantly. The chatterbox provides a rather inane stream of commentary that is anything but profound. For example, as I look out my window, my stream of chatter goes like this: "The green of the ivy sure looks peaceful....I wonder if I should water the yard today....I need to remember to get the plants for the north side....That reminds me, I have to pick up my shoes from the shoe repair man....And I have to call Lex and Jonathan today, too....I'd better go write this down before I forget it." So the inner monologue goes, wandering from thought to thought rather aimlessly, without focus.

As we practice focusing our minds in meditation, we gradually disengage from the inner monologue. We hear through our quieted awareness the divine voice of God. As our awareness is refined and focused, we move into deeper levels and different perceptions of God. Each of these deeper levels of awareness has a different "feel" to it; these deeper levels are not like our ordinary conscious awareness, and they are not like each other. There is an increasing sense of peace and calm as we go into these deeper levels. Our usual sense of limits disappears and we participate in all that is. And as we do this, we find ourselves experiencing the Divine directly.

Spiritual Combat

We can think of meditation as spiritual combat. The two forces that are fighting are the false self and the true self, deep within. In the language of St. Paul, the old man, consumed with its self–centered activities, is fighting with the new man who is touched by God and redeemed.[17]

This is not a casual struggle. When you begin your meditation practice, you will see just how intense the struggle can be simply to focus your mind on something. Later, as you make advances along the spiritual path, you will see how everything that we do is, in some way, participating in this struggle.

Let's take church attendance, for example. We go to church to focus on God for an hour or so. For most people, this is the only time they devote solely to God. But look at what actually happens during this hour. Look where we actually place our attention. Before the service starts we visit with our friends. We catch up with one another and the thought of God is far from us. During the service, we see people sitting in front who we want to greet. We notice that this one is attractive and that one is not. We wish that the reader would do a better job and not mispronounce all those funny biblical place names. We hope for a short sermon. We daydream. All in all, we spend very little time focused on God. So even when we think we are praying, we are really daydreaming much of the time.

This is the difficulty of an unruly attention. We think that we are doing one thing, but our false self has crept in and distracted us. What is worse, since we don't even recognize that we have been distracted, we cannot progress beyond the distraction. So we are betrayed even in the things we do with the best of intentions. We literally deceive ourselves on a continual basis without any awareness of this process. Our task is to marshal our forces and to train them to work together. Our task is to discover and transform those elements within ourselves which betray us. Our task is to disengage from the false self.

The tool that will enable this disengagement is a developed attention. With a trained attention, we can focus our awareness in God and let Him teach us. As we do this, the grasping tendencies of our false self weaken and finally wither away. We will move through a predictable series of stages in our journey, and finally come into a deep and pervasive union with God. When we finally let go of the false self and all of its subtle tendencies to make the "I" into the center of the universe, then we will find that we have always been rooted in the Divine.

The Spectrum of Meditative Practice

Over the last two millennia, our Christian forebears have developed a series of graduated spiritual exercises, designed to bring us into full knowledge of God. These exercises are designed to be practiced on a daily basis over many years. They reflect the accumulated wisdom of the church,[18] as it has helped millions to engage in the deep personal transformation of sanctification.

Let us look briefly at these spiritual exercises so that we can see how they flow into each other. All prayer begins with the practice of Recollection: remembering that God is with us. Recollection helps us develop an inward sense of the incarnation, that God is really right here and present to us. Recollection is the beginning and the end of the meditative journey. It is found, either explicitly or implicitly, in all of the meditative practices in which we will engage. So Recollection serves as a foundation that supports what we do spiritually. It undergirds all our spiritual practice.

The next part of the spectrum is the sensory meditations, which we will explore in Part III. These are the practices that use a sensory modality such as seeing, hearing, or feeling, to focus the attention. These are the practices of visualization, chant, and kinesthetic meditation. These practices have been in continual use in the church since the time of Christ, and we can even trace them back into Judaism. The sensory meditations allow us to use what is most familiar to us, our senses, to train our attention. As we use our senses to rest in God, we will find subtle changes taking place in our perceptions. We will begin to loosen the grip of the false self. God begins to break through into our awareness from time to time.

The sensory meditations are where most of us start. While many examples of these meditations are illustrated in this book, there is no practical limit to what can be done with a sensory focus. In our practice, it will be important to work through these meditations over a considerable period of time. This is not something to be rushed through; there are absolutely no advantages to rushing. Rather, the prize goes to the one who uses these practices to develop the attentional focus to the sharpest point. We need to thoroughly develop our attention so that we can let go of the false self. Pushing on to something new before we have completed the prior step will only lead to frustration and some future derailment later in our practice.

Following the sensory meditations, we will explore the practice of Lectio Divina, or divine reading, covered in Part IV. This is the meditative use of scripture, and it combines the practices of sensory meditation and contemplative prayer. Lectio Divina is a complex, fourfold method of prayer. It was originated as a method for deeply understanding holy scripture, but it can be used in other ways as well. Lectio demonstrates, in one complex exercise, the deep interconnectedness among the different practices in the meditative spectrum.

Following Lectio, we will move on to the monologistic prayers in

Part V. These prayers are short phrases which are repeated over and over again, and are very effective in training attention. As we practice them, we will move quickly into the fullness of God. There are many types of monologistic prayers that have grown up in the church. We will explore a limited sampling of these prayers. They are sometimes called "Christian mantras" but this is not really accurate. There is more going on in these practices than the simple repetition of a phrase. The repetition is the "visible" part of the practice. More important are the interior movements which constitute the bulk of the practice. We will describe these interior movements fully.

Finally, we will come to contemplative prayer in Part VI. Contemplative prayer leaves all sensory input and all discursive thinking behind. In contemplation, we simply rest our attention in God without thinking of any kind. Here we come full circle. We come back to the practice of recollecting God, but this time with the much stronger tool of a focused attention.

In contemplation, we rest our attention exclusively on God. This moves us away from the false self, disengaging us completely from its grasp. Only in contemplation can we allow God to be the center of the universe. We learn, here, to put aside the false self and its seductions. We learn directly from our God. The continued practice of contemplation will bring us into full union with God.

It is difficult to focus awareness on something without using a sensory reference point. This is why it is so crucial to develop our attention in the earlier practices of meditation. Without a strong attention, we will not be able to maintain our focus. A strong attention is the *sine qua non* for reaching our goal of union with God.

As with anything valuable, our movement toward the Divine will cost us. The price is a certain dedication: a concentrated and balanced effort over an extended period. Unfortunately, many Christians seem content to stay at the stage of behavioral change. Of those who go further and practice meditation, many will push themselves too quickly. Instead of learning fully from each meditation in the spectrum, they will go too quickly to the next practice. Because their attention is not developed enough to sustain the practice, they will fail and give up.

If you find yourself having difficulty, there is no need to give up. Simply understand that this happened because you have moved ahead too quickly. Move back to a prior practice, and take up where you left off. This will enable you to make a slow but steady advance. Remember that our God is one who loves us deeply. She is always with us.[19] Open yourself to this wonderful Presence and let yourself be nurtured.

Let's go on and explore the mechanics of meditation, so that you can begin to experience these transformations for yourself.

Chapter 4

The Mechanics of Meditation

We prepare for meditation and contemplative prayer by learning the prerequisites, such as physical posture, breathing, the length of time for our practice, and so on. These are the mechanics of meditation, which have to do with how we position our bodies and our attention during our prayer, and the issues surrounding when and where to practice. Together, these provide a basic direction to meditation practice that is essential for success in coming to know God.

1. Time and place of meditation. Set aside a regular time and place for your meditation. Choose a time and place that are quiet and free from noise. If you use your meditation place only for that activity, you will create, over time, an association which is helpful in deepening your meditation. Similarly, if you meditate regularly at the same time daily, you will benefit more.

Often it takes considerable exploration to find the right time for your meditation. Some people like to meditate early in the morning, as they arise from sleep. Others like to meditate when they come home from work. Others like the stillness of the night for their meditation. (One caution here: If you meditate just before going to bed, you may become so energized that you will have difficulty falling asleep.) Experiment with different times of the day and see what works best for you.

It is not always possible to be consistent in your choice of time and place for meditation. So do the best that you can. Set up a meditation routine that supports *your* life-style. In meditation, as in any other practice, don't set unrealistic goals, don't compare your accomplishments to your expectations, and do be sensible about scheduling your meditation given the constraints on your time. In other words, make your choices according to what is appropriate for you.

You should, however, make every attempt to engage yourself in a regular disciplined practice. Do not make excuses to yourself. Make a realistic commitment and hold yourself to that. Your false self will give you every reasonable excuse in the universe to compromise your practice. Don't listen to these excuses. Keep to a regular, realistic, daily practice.

2. Length of meditation. When you are beginning to practice, start with no less than ten minutes per session. It is important that you set a minimum length for your meditation and stick with that. When you begin to practice, you will be confronted with seemingly endless sources of difficulty. Your mind will wander and you will despair that you can ever bring it under control. You will develop an itch here or a pain there that will quickly build to what seems like an unbearable intensity. If you do not have a firm minimum time for your meditation, you are likely to let yourself be vanquished by these difficulties. What meditation provides, however, is an arena in which to do battle with these difficulties. You cannot succeed if you are constantly leaving the arena before the struggle has really begun.

Most people need about twenty minutes before their mind really quiets down into stillness. Thus, in your practice gently strive to increase your meditation to at least twenty minutes or more. This will give you time to quiet. Time spent in addition to the twenty minutes will give you an opportunity to deepen that stillness.

There is no need to set a maximum length to your meditation. You will find that there is a natural closing. You will come back to clear waking consciousness quite effortlessly as your meditation period ends. If you come back before your practice period has elapsed, however, go back to your meditation and continue to practice, focusing your awareness again for the remainder of your meditation period.

Later, as your practice develops, you will find your meditations spontaneously lengthening. This is wonderful to experience, and you should follow your own intuitive sense when this occurs. Don't push yourself to lengthen your practice, however. We have grown up with the idea that if one piece of candy is good, then one hundred pieces are much better. It is not so with candy or with meditation.

Rather than pushing yourself beyond your capabilities, learn to listen to the word of God: to that still, quiet voice within that Elijah heard.[20] One length of time is not objectively better than some other length of time. Some particular length of time is likely to be more appropriate, however, for your particular needs in meditation. No one can tell you what that is; you must learn to listen.

3. Frequency of meditation. How often you should meditate depends upon your situation. When you are starting, try meditating for short periods of time, many times a day. As you become skilled in navigating your inner world, enhance your sessions by meditating less frequently, but for longer periods. For all of us, though, it is valuable to meditate at least once a day. Two or three times a day is optimal, but not everyone will realistically be able to accommodate this schedule.

Consistency is important to contemplative development. When I first began meditating, I did not have a teacher and instead relied on a book for instruction. This book did not talk about consistency. I would meditate for several weeks, then stop for several weeks, and then start again. The problem was, I never started where I had left off. I always fell behind.

As a result of these experiences, I compare meditative development to athletic development. If you are not consistent in your exercise, your muscles lose their tone. In a like manner, if you interrupt your meditation regimen, you lose your discipline and ability to concentrate on a specific object. So to obtain the greatest gain in the shortest period of time, be consistent in your practice of meditation.

4. Posture. Kneeling is the traditional posture for verbal, discursive prayer. This is not appropriate for meditation because your knees are likely to start hurting. This distraction will pull your attention away from your focus. Instead, try a seated posture, holding your spine comfortably erect. You may use either a chair or cushions to support yourself. Of the chairs, I prefer a straight backed chair, like a wooden dining chair. When using a straight backed chair, sit with your spine erect and feet flat on the floor or with the soles touching, whichever is more comfortable. If your feet do not reach the floor comfortably, place a cushion beneath your feet, so that you have a solid position that provides adequate support.

If you are using cushions, the most comfortable are the zafu and zabuton developed in the East by Zen Buddhists. The zafu is a firmly stuffed cushion about six inches high and fifteen inches in diameter, which was developed specifically for meditation. The zabuton is a soft mat stuffed with cotton batting which protects the legs and knees from hard floors. There are several postures which can be adopted on the zafu: cross–legged in Indian style, cross–legged in half lotus position, and cross–legged in full lotus position.

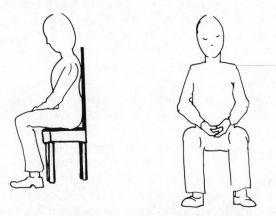

SITTING POSITION WITH CHAIR

Most Westerners have difficulty with the more extreme cross–legged postures. We did not grow up squatting on the floor, so our bodies are not flexible enough to pretzel into these postures. Even if we can get into the posture, most find it painful to maintain for any length of time. You may wish to try these postures, however. The important thing is to use the posture that is most comfortable for you.

CUSHIONED SITTING POSITIONS

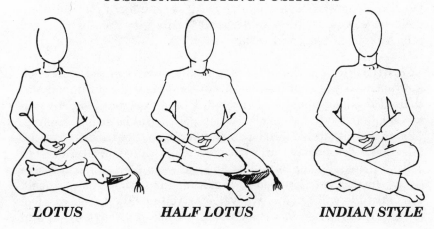

LOTUS   **HALF LOTUS**   **INDIAN STYLE**

Regardless of what position you adopt, the spinal column should be erect and straight, and the head inclined forward a few degrees. The arms hang straight down from your relaxed shoulders. Your hands are in your lap, palms open and facing up, with the left hand holding the right hand and thumbs touching. The mouth is lightly closed, with the tongue touching the hard palate just behind the front teeth. The eyes may either be closed or open. If your eyes are open, they should be focused downward and about a foot in front of you. Overall, your body should be relaxed, stable, and comfortable.

The purpose of this posture is to provide a comfortable, relaxed, and stable base for your meditation. You need to be able to hold this posture without *any* extraneous motion for the entire period of your meditation, so that you can observe the workings of your awareness, and begin to bring that awareness under conscious control.

5. Breathing. Breathe through your nose in a gentle and relaxed way. On inhalation, the belly expands outward. On exhalation, the belly contracts inward. There are a variety of practices used in meditation to control the breath, and to use the breath to influence the mind in certain ways. These exercises are for advanced practitioners, however, and are beyond the scope of this book.

6. Focusing awareness. The most important element in meditation is the focusing of your awareness. Start every meditation by becoming aware of the physical sensations you are experiencing. This process provides a grounding for your meditation. Start from what you know is real—your physical sensations. From this concrete base, you can flow much more easily into the abstract and relatively formless world within.

7. Attitude. For the purpose of meditation, you need to develop a receptive attitude of passive alertness. This is a delicate balance that each person must find through trial and error. Too active an attitude means that your meditation period will be spent thinking. This is the discursive intellect again, acting out of the needs of the false self. Too passive an attitude means that you literally fall asleep. Instead, be open to a balance between alertness and receptivity. You want to be open to that which is beyond the false self. This attitude will gradually develop as you meditate. You will feel its "rightness" when you come upon it. Once you recognize it, and have some facility in entering into it, this attitude can be cultivated apart from formal periods of sitting meditation.

8. Interruptions. Create a setting which is free from interruptions. If the telephone rings when you are meditating, ignore it, or better yet, disconnect it before you begin. Put a sign on your door if you think you might be interrupted by a visitor. If you are bothered by street noise, choose the most quiet time of the day or night to meditate. There are, of course, sounds which you cannot control, such as a barking dog or the scream of a siren. When you notice these things, simply let go of them and refocus your awareness on the object of your meditation. Every time your awareness is pulled away, gently bring your attention back to your meditation, without berating yourself.

As you sit quietly with your meditation, you will find a variety of internal distractions arising. This is perfectly normal. All of these distractions can be collectively labeled "objects of awareness": random thoughts, strong emotions, old memories, lists of what you must accomplish following your practice. When you become aware of these objects of awareness, gently let go of them, and guide your attention back to the subject of your meditation. There is no need to berate yourself for becoming distracted. There is neither merit nor virtue gained by flagellation. Berating, in itself, is simply another object of awareness. By focusing on it, you simply stay away from what you have decided to do in meditation, which is to focus your attention on and dwell in the subject of your meditation.

One of the most difficult interruptions for beginning meditators is "the Itch!" When you are meditating, awareness becomes quite acute and every sensation is experienced very clearly. When an itching sensation arises during meditation, it may be felt more vividly than perhaps any itch you have ever experienced. We are so accustomed to scratching when we itch, that we never give it a second thought. While meditating, however, the physical motion of scratching will disturb your concentration. To scratch, you move your awareness from the inward to the outward, and then you move your body. If you do this consistently, you set up an unspoken rule that mental distractions are to be ignored, but physical distractions are so important that they must be attended to immediately. This is destructive to the meditative process. Instead of giving in to the desire to scratch, refocus your attention and return to your meditation.

The same discipline is used for pain. When you sit in the same position for ten minutes or more, you may experience a twinge of pain in your legs or some other part of the body. When this occurs, stay with the meditation, and treat your pain as one more object of awareness and let it go. It is very unlikely that your pain is life–threatening or even health–threatening. So let it go, and refocus your attention on the object of your meditation.

The purpose of these mechanics of meditation is to create a stable, predictable platform for meditative practice. We are trying, in our practice, to strengthen our attention. To do so, we need to hold all other parts of our experience constant. Only then can we clearly focus our attention.

Over time, these mechanics will become second nature. You will naturally adopt the most effective posture for meditation because you will come to feel the differences between postures, thereby learning the effects that they have on your practice. In the beginning, however, prescriptions about these things are helpful. They help you set aside extraneous things so that we can begin our practice.

Let us go on and explore how to prepare our awareness for meditation practice.

Chapter 5

Grounding Ourselves for Meditation Practice

Now comes the time to use the knowledge that we have been developing. Up to this point, we have developed an intellectual knowledge base. While this is important to help us understand and prepare for the journey, this is not yet the experiential knowledge that comes from our own personal exploration. It is still in the realm of faith or belief. The time has come to move into practice so that those things that we have known by faith can lead us into the experience of God.

We have come to the place where we begin the meditative journey, our own inquiry into what is real and what is false. We will start with an exercise designed to focus our awareness and ground it in the reality of our physical sensations. This will provide the basis for almost every other spiritual exercise in our work together.

The purpose of this exercise is to help us focus, and to give us a focus that we can always come back to. In every exercise, our attention will wander. This first spiritual exercise will give us a way to focus and refocus our attention. It will provide a stable platform from which to continue our internal transformation.

SPIRITUAL EXERCISE 1
THE GROUNDING EXERCISE

1. Deal with any potential distractions, such as unplugging the telephone.

2. Seat yourself in the posture that you have chosen for meditation, with spine erect, and your limbs arranged so that they will not fall asleep if left unmoved for 20 minutes or so.

41

3. Either read the following very slowly to yourself, doing what
   the words suggest, or make an audiotape of this and listen
   to it. You should take 3 to 5 minutes to do this initially.

   Focus on the sensations in your face and head. There is no
   need to try to change them. Just be aware of them, fully
   and completely. Notice what they feel like. Experience
   each sensation as it arises and falls away.

   Notice the sensations on the skin of your face. Notice those
   places where your skin is warm and where it is cool. Just
   let yourself be aware, without trying to change anything.

   Focus on the sensations of the muscles underneath your
   skin. Be aware of the broad muscles of your forehead.
   Notice where there is relaxation and where there is tension. There is no need to try to change anything. Just
   experience the flow of sensations through these muscles.

   The little muscle groups around your eyes. Be aware of
   where there is relaxation and where there is tension.
   There is no need to change. Just be aware of the flow of
   sensation as it streams through you.

   Be aware of the sensations in the powerful muscles of your
   jaws. Let yourself flow with these sensations.

   Now let yourself be aware of the bony structure underneath
   your facial muscles. Experience the sensations which stream
   from this deep part of you. Let yourself be aware, fully.

   The sensations in your neck and shoulders. Notice how the
   flow of sensations feels slightly different in each shoulder.
   Don't try to evaluate or judge these sensations. Just let
   yourself be aware.

   The sensations in your elbows. Notice what your elbows
   really feel like. Experience the flow of sensation which
   streams through them.

Your wrists and the palms of your hands. Let yourself feel the flow in your wrists and palms fully.

The sensations in your hips and pelvic region. Let yourself experience fully the sensations streaming through you here.

Be aware of the sensations in your knees. Feel the flow of sensation here. Experience your knees as if for the first time.

Be aware of the sensations in your ankles and the soles of your feet. Feel the streams of sensation as they flow through you in these places. Let yourself flow with these streams.

4. Now bring your attention up to the region of your heart. Imagine that you are very small, and walk inside of yourself there. Go deeply into that vast inner space. Let yourself rest here for a time. There is no need to do anything here. It is sufficient simply to rest.

(To close your meditation)

5. When you are ready, let your attention come back to this place. Let the feeling return to your feet...your hands...and your face. Take a deep breath and open your eyes.

The ultimate focus of this exercise is to move us into our heart center. By "heart center," I do not mean either the physical organ or the affections or emotions. Rather, I am referring to the deep spiritual center of which scripture speaks. In scripture, "the heart symbolizes the personal center, the directing and controlling center of the self."[21] In the Old Testament, the heart means "the organ of knowledge which is associated with the will, its plans, decisions and intentions. The Bible primarily views the heart as the center of the consciously living man."[22] Thus, it is in our hearts that we begin our conscious living.

In the New Testament, the heart "represents the unity and totality of the inner life expressed in the variety of intellectual and spiritual functions."[23] The heart is where our inner life occurs. It is here that we can touch the Divine, "because the love of God has been poured out in our hearts through the Holy Spirit."[24]

It is here, in our spiritual hearts, where true prayer occurs. Because access to our heart center is so important, because it is where prayer takes place, we will refer to this center over and over again in our spiritual exercises.

As you practice this exercise, you may experience unusual sensations. This is normal. For example, you are likely to feel a kind of floating sensation. Some people find this quite pleasant, others are disturbed by it, since it suggests a loss of control. These sensations are normal for this exercise. The more intense the sensations, the deeper is your level of relaxation and concentration.

People also report various distortions of their body image. One student of mine complains that her fingers seem to turn into fat sausages when she practices this exercise. Again, this is normal. When we disengage from the false self, it no longer dictates how we feel the sensations of our bodies. We experience our sensations directly, apart from the "map" that the false self has provided. This feels different from usual and can frighten us if we are not prepared. But it is not a mark that something is going wrong. Rather, it is a signal that we are on course.

This exercise helps ground us in our physical sensations. From this solid, ongoing base, we can turn our minds to any other subject and use it as a focus for our meditation. Once we reach our interior heart center, we detach our awareness from the physical, and put it on the subject of our meditation. We will use this technique in most of the exercises below.

The Dis–Identification Exercise

As we have described, each of us is trapped within a false self which we created for protection. This false self stands in the way of our encounter with God. To know God, we must first let go of this false self. Perhaps the most direct way of beginning this process comes from the work of Dr. Roberto Assagioli.[25]

Assagioli was an Italian psychiatrist who developed psychosynthesis, a system of psychological and spiritual transformation. He developed the dis–identification exercise to assist patients in letting go of the false constructs of the self which prevented them from truly knowing who they were. As we have seen, we are separated from our deepest self, and we have become identified with a false self which is concerned with doing and having. Caught in this outward–looking frame of reference, we identify our self with that which gives us the most gratification. For example, intellectuals identify themselves with their intellects, athletes identify themselves with their bodies, and so on.

The dis–identification exercise is a useful introduction to meditation for two reasons. First, the exercise takes us within ourselves and directly confronts the outward orientation we accept as normal. Second, it teaches us how to let go of false identifications and how to experience ourselves directly.

To begin this exercise, sit comfortably in your meditative position. Then slowly read the dis–identification exercise adapted from Assagioli, or audiotape the exercise and listen to the tape. Let yourself quietly affirm the truth of these words.

SPIRITUAL EXERCISE 2
THE DIS–IDENTIFICATION EXERCISE

1. I *have* a body, but I am *not* my body.

   My body is a precious instrument of experience. All that I can experience is mediated by my body, my senses. Through my body, I come to know the world outside of me and the world within me. Through my body, I act and do things in the world. But I notice that my body may find itself in different conditions of health or sickness; it may be rested or tired, but that has nothing to do with my self, my "I." The changes in my body do not change the "I" that uses this body. I have a body, but it is only an instrument. Therefore I affirm that I have a body, but I am *not* my body.

2. I have emotions and feelings, but I am *not* my emotions.

   My emotions are a wonderful, many–colored palette that I use to *value* things and experiences. When I say I love someone, I am describing how I value that person. When I

---

say that I am angry at someone, I am describing another kind of value. I use this rich variety of valuing to order and understand my experience. But I notice that though my emotions change, sometimes swiftly and sometimes slowly, the "I" that has these emotions does not change. I notice that I remain my self: in times of hope and in times of despair, in moments of calm and moments of irritation my "I" is the same. From this, it is clear that my emotions are not myself. Therefore, I affirm that I have emotions and feelings, but I am *not* my emotions.

3. I have an intellect, a mind, but I am *not* my intellect.

My intellect is my instrument for wrestling with the world. Through my intellect, I take big things and divide them into smaller parts so that I can understand them. Then I put these small parts into a larger whole. I use my intellect to grapple with the vast complexity of things, so that I can master them. But I notice that though my thoughts change frequently, the "I" that has those thoughts does not change. I can think of a tree, but I don't become a tree. I can think of many things, but I don't become those things. I have an intellect, but it is only an instrument. Therefore I affirm that, while I have an intellect, I am *not* my intellect.

4. Instead, I affirm that I am a center of pure awareness. When I go inside my self, my "identity," I experience a vast space, open and without limit. My awareness is free to move in any direction, as quickly or as slowly as I would like. There is no limit to my movement. There is only this wonderful, vast awareness that I am...

5. Let yourself continue to explore the depths within. Take some time, perhaps five or ten minutes, to go wherever you please. If you find yourself distracted, simply bring your attention back to the vast spaciousness within yourself, and continue your journey.

(To close your meditation)

6. Let yourself begin to come back to this place. Let the feeling return to your feet...your hands...and your face. Take a deep breath, and when you are ready, open your eyes.

Sometimes, because of our deep identification with our bodies, emotions, and intellect, we are afraid to let go of those parts which we believe to be the whole of us. Mistaking these parts for the whole, we wonder what will become of us if we release them. Will our self just disappear? Will something awful happen, if we find ourselves without the partial self with which we identify?

Most people experience a great sense of freedom when they practice this exercise. After practicing this for the first time, an engineer reported:

I was afraid of what would happen if I let go of my intellect. That's all I have done for years is think. I knew you were coming to the point where I would have to affirm that I was not my intellect, and I was really afraid. What else was there? Nothing!

But the experience was so different from my expectations. It was like I was suddenly free, like I had been let out of prison. I felt so much larger and more powerful than when I had restricted my awareness to my intellect.

The dis–identification exercise addresses our fears and our self–imposed limitations directly. As a result of doing this exercise, and doing it several times in order to explore our depths, we can affirm our true selves; that at our core, there exists a vast awareness that is the source of our identity. And we will find, as we extend our explorations into this awareness, that it is inextricably inter-twined with the Divine Awareness, with God.

Like Esau in the Bible story,[26] we have sacrificed our true her-itage as sons and daughters of God for a mess of pottage, a bowl of gruel. To recognize this—not just intellectually, but out of our own felt experience—is to be ready for meditation.

Part II
The Practice of Recollection in God

I would like you to ponder with me the fundamental question that we need to answer before we begin to pray. The question is a simple one: What is prayer, really? If we strip away all the frills, all the bells and whistles, what constitutes prayer? Another way of looking at this is to examine what is the simplest thing that we can do and still be praying.

Ordinarily, we think of prayer as talking to God. Look at what this implies. First, it implies that we are focused on communicating with God. Second, it implies that God is bothering to listen to our attempts at communication. Only if these two things are taking place is there any importance to the words we use in our prayer. What happens, then, if we simply drop the words? Is it prayer if we simply sit in God's Presence?

In my experience, and probably in yours, too, some of our most stirring prayers are those which have no words, where we are *moved* deeply by God's Presence. These are rare and wonderful times when we feel so close to God. Whether this prayerful experience came about through watching a magnificent sunset or through an experience of being loved doesn't really matter. The important point to notice is that the experience didn't need our words in order to be prayer.

True prayer needs two elements; it needs our *intention* to be with God, and God's Presence. Since in Jesus Christ we have assurances that God is always with us,[27] the only thing that varies is our intention to make ourselves present to God. This intention is the basis for the practices of recollection, which we will explore below.

The fundamental basis for all Christian prayer is God's active Presence in every moment of our lives. It is this Presence that is basic to the lives of all Christians. If God exists apart from us, what good is it to us? If God does not exist right here, with us, then how will our prayers be heard? How could God possibly respond, if He is not here with us?

At the end of the gospel of Matthew, immediately before Jesus is taken up into heaven, He says to the gathering of disciples, "Know that I am with you always, even to the end of time."[28] This is an extraordinary statement. Jesus means that He is with us in

51

some way that is not ordinary and has nothing to do with physical presence. So how, then, is He present to us? Or, more importantly, how can we know if He is present to us?

Answering these questions is crucial to our faith, since Christianity rests on the presence of the incarnate God. In a similar way, all prayer rests on the assurances that God is truly with us. After all, what point would there be to prayer if there were no God to listen? Since the basis for all prayer is God's Presence to us, then the most fundamental prayers are those which focus on being aware of that Presence. These prayers are those which "recollect" the Presence of God, which call us to remember that experience and be open to it.

In the chapters ahead, I will introduce this process of recollection. I will show how recollection underlies every form of prayer, and then present three specific kinds of recollection, giving step–by–step instruction in these methods.

Chapter 6

The Process of Recollection: The Principle Underlying All Prayer

All of us have beliefs about the nature of God. Our beliefs are a very human attempt to "capture" God, to define the Divine. We list the qualities of God as if to assure ourselves that we have understood the Divine correctly. We develop dogma and theology to codify our experiences of God. But then we turn around and start expecting God to behave within the constraints of our dogma. While this human need for the comfort of certainty can be understood and even appreciated, nevertheless our needs do not constrain or limit God.

All of us have beliefs about the nature of God. But what we can say, truthfully, is that all of our beliefs about God are ultimately wrong! Every one of them. Our beliefs about God always fall short of the reality.

The Nature of the Divine

This brings us to an important juncture. If all our beliefs are ultimately wrong, how then do we come to know God? We still need some understanding of what this Being is, if only to recognize that wonderful Presence when we experience it. So, what can we conclude about the nature of God?

First, we must recognize that the way we learn about God distorts our image of God. This distortion, in turn, greatly hampers our search for the living God. Most of us first learned about God as children. When I was a child, I understood God to be a bearded old gentleman, floating in the sky on a cloud. This image of God seemed to have two faces. One face loved little children and was very indulgent; the other face would punish the slightest infraction.

I share this image with many others. As grand as it may be, nevertheless, this is not a true picture of the Divine. It is a pale reflection of what God actually is. And while this image was useful in pointing me toward God, it also inhibited my growth by limiting my understanding of the Divine. It does not matter what image we use; they all have this effect.

Second, we must learn to distinguish between experiential knowledge and intellectual knowledge. Experiential knowledge comes from direct experience; intellectual knowledge comes from the rational processes of analysis and synthesis. In regard to this distinction, St. Isaac the Syrian, a deeply spiritual man living in the seventh century A.D., said:

> Distinguish, O man, what you are reading. Can these things [about God] be known from ink? Or can the taste of honey be spread over the palate of the reader from written documents?[29]

When it comes to knowing God, intellectual knowledge has a limited scope. Intellectual knowledge may serve to get us going, like the starter motor on a car gets a much larger engine going. But we should never confuse this small motor with the larger motor which actually powers the car.

To put it bluntly, God can be experienced, but not known.

A third factor is the understanding that God is not another object to be grasped. Every person and thing in our experience, with the exception of our own self, is an object which we perceive as existing "out there." The Divine, however, cannot be experienced in this way, because the Divine is not another object. Indeed, our supposition that God can be apprehended in this way has resulted in a widespread belief that God is not important to our existence. For example, how many times have we reached out to God in verbal prayer, pouring out our woes, only to have nothing happen. "What is this?" we ask. "Does God really exist? How come He doesn't do anything about my terrible troubles?" But when we look for something to happen *outside* of ourselves, we miss the action!

Every time we reach out to grab God, we are frustrated. We grab because that is what we are accustomed to doing. If we want an education, a friend, a new job, we reach out and grab one. They are all objects to be grasped. But God is the source from which all else flows. There is a qualitative difference between the created and the One who creates. Herein lies our difficulty. How do we grasp something that is best described as "nothing," having "neither image nor form"?[30] It is like reaching out to grab a handful of air. As our hand closes around the air, the air escapes. In like manner, God cannot be grasped.

The Divine can be experienced, however. Meditation is a process through which we quiet the mind and the emotions and enter directly into the experience of the Divine. This is what our journey is about, entering into that wonderful Presence.

The Connection between God and Ourselves

While we cannot grasp God or "know" God, we can *experience* that Presence. We can experience God because there is a deep connection between us. If you will, we participate in a seamless garment that binds up, not only all human creatures, but also their Creator in a single beautiful garment.

What we experience in the deepest, most central part of ourselves is similar to our experience of God. Just as God can best be described as "nothing," with "neither image nor form," so also can our human nature—our identity—be described in these same terms. This is a critical parallel and we must clearly understand it. *Our experience of God and our experience of our deepest self are similar*. The Presence of God is to be found deep within us, in our true self. The nature of God is what we experience when we go within. This is echoed in scripture: "God created man in his image; in the divine image, he created him."[31]

This is *not* to say that you are God or that I am God. But God is *in* each of us. Further, it is this Presence that gives us our distinctive qualities—it is literally the source of who and what we are. We choose to manifest this quality or that. But the source of these qualities transcends every individual human. We can create wonderful buildings, marvelous political systems and social structures, but we cannot create courage, or wisdom, or compassion. These flow from the source of all things, and they flow freely.

For generations, the holy people in our midst have said that God is closer to us than we are to ourselves. This was their personal, direct experience; not an intellectual knowing derived from books or from wishful thinking. It was their desire that each of us come to this experience; that we, too, experience ourselves as children of God, not as beings separated from God.

Listen to what Jesus says on this matter. When the disciples asked Him how to pray, Jesus began by teaching them to say *"Our* Father," not "My Father," not "O God, who dwells at the edge of the universe outside of the created order," but *"Our* Father." Jesus' perception is that we are all created by the same spiritual Father. Thus we, too, are sons or daughters of God. This also means that we are at least half brothers and sisters—that we are part of the same family. It means that we are spiritual beings, sharing and participating in the Divine nature.

This has incredible significance for us. If we share somehow in God's nature, then we can experience God directly, simply by going inside of our own being. There is a meeting ground here, deep within each of us, where we can participate in God and where we can participate in each other. Meditation and contemplative prayer are the ways that we enter this holy place.

The Process of Recollection

The first step in this process is to dis–identify from those false or partial beliefs which have limited our understanding of God. We do this because our beliefs are too limiting. If we have limited beliefs about God, then we will experience only those parts of God which conform to our beliefs. Actually, we are likely to experience all of the Divine, but we will not recognize our experience for what it really is. So we will discard that which does not conform to our expectations.

To experience the Divine, we need to affirm that we do not know God and will never be able to fully grasp Her. Every Christian can, in good conscience, acknowledge this. Then, all that is necessary is to be open to God's Presence, without any preconceptions: open, available, and ready.

If the first step in this process of recollection is to let go of our partial beliefs about God, then the second step is to let the Lord do the work of manifesting to us. This is our stumbling block. We are so anxious and unbelieving that we want to do the work ourselves. So we hallucinate something about God, something partial. This is not what God calls us to do. We cannot by our own power make

God do anything. Our true part in this work is simply to prepare ourselves for His coming by opening up to Him directly.

Because this is so important, let me say it again. Our part, in the process of recollection, is to be open to God, to be present to God, to give our Lord our full attention. No more. There are no words to say. No beliefs to hold. Nothing to do.

The process of recollection is very simple. And, like most "simple" things, it is difficult to do. The process of dis–identifying from our ideas of God is hard because we Christians have been taught to believe in the supremacy of beliefs. How many times have you heard preachers shout, "*Believe*, and the truth shall set you free!"

In this century, the typical Christian's spiritual life has devolved simply to having the right beliefs. Yet *all* beliefs about God are limiting. Our beliefs limit what we experience. For example, if you believe that the earth is flat, you will not see its roundness, even though the evidence of its roundness is always before you. In a similar way, what we believe about God limits what we can experience about the Divine. If we emphasize the transcendence of God, we will not experience Her immanent Presence. If we emphasize the immanence of God, we will not experience Her vast transcendence.

I am not implying that you should simply chuck any beliefs you have about God. Our belief system is important. Our beliefs are a tool, among many other tools, for understanding the nature of God, our own nature, and what we are called to do. But our beliefs are only one tool among many. Compared to direct experience of the Divine, our beliefs are like bland baby food, and not the spicy rich food of real living. We need bland food when we are ill and unable to do for ourselves. But the purpose of that food is to strengthen us to go out and experience real life for ourselves. So, too, our beliefs about God are designed to help us in the beginning of our spiritual walk, and to assist us in getting to the point where we can experience God for ourselves.

The way to open to the Presence of God is deceptively simple. Open your awareness to God. Don't do anything with your thoughts; this is not a "thinking" process. Put to rest memory, sensory experiences, imagination, and reflection. Let these processes continue to flow as they will, but redirect your attention to be aware of the Divine. Simply open your *awareness* so that you can experience the Divine Presence directly, without the blinders of belief.

Many people feel a qualitative difference almost immediately, as they begin this process. Something in our awareness is changed by this process: it can be described as a "quickening" within, an energizing force around us and within us. It is as if this capacity to experience the Presence of God directly is latent within all of us. All that is needed is to *remind* ourselves to do it, and we do it naturally.

Others have difficulty with this process. Often they have in mind some idea of what God's Presence will feel like. In these cases, their beliefs limit what they experience. If they do not feel what they expect, they conclude that nothing is there. The key to the process of recollection is to let go of expectations and desires, and simply rest in God. So let us go forward and explore how we can use recollection to enter deeply into the experience of God.

Chapter 7

Brother Lawrence
and the Practice of the
Presence of God

Brother Lawrence was an obscure seventeenth century French Carmelite monk, who entered the monastery after a career as a foot soldier. He described himself as a "clumsy fellow who used to break everything."[32] Apparently his superiors agreed with his description. Because of Lawrence's apparent lack of talent and his uncanny ability to break things, he was finally installed in the kitchens, washing pots and pans.

Brother Lawrence was not upset by this placement. He resolved to use his time to be constantly aware of God's Presence. So, in this most unlikely of settings amidst the pots and pans, he opened his awareness to God. After several years, he acquired such a palpable holiness that even the abbot would go to him for advice. To understand how strange this is, think of the commanding general of an army going to a private on kitchen patrol and asking for advice on military strategy!

For Brother Lawrence, the central issue was to be wholly God's creature. He reported having read many books which presented "divers practices of the spiritual life," but these puzzled rather than helped him. Brother Lawrence summarized his meditative practice:

> I renounced for [God's] love everything that was not Himself, and *I began to live as if there were only He and I in the world* (italics mine)....[I kept] my mind in His holy presence, and recalling it whenever I found it had become distracted from Him. I had no trouble with this exercise, which I continued in spite of all the difficulties I found in practicing it, not becom-

59

ing troubled or worried when I was involuntarily distracted. I maintained this practice no less during the day than during my times set aside for prayer.[33]

Let us examine carefully this description of Brother Lawrence's method. First, there is a renunciation of all that was not God. His heart's desire was to know God and to dwell in His Presence. To attain that desire, like John of the Cross, Lawrence knew that he could not desire anything else. If we wish to get lost in this playground called creation, God will let us. But if we wish to know who created the playground, we will necessarily have to leave the playground and our delights, in order to find the Creator.

Second, Lawrence began to concentrate on God, "as if there were only He and I in the world." This does not mean that Lawrence forgot his pots and pans. But their importance diminished. Lawrence did pots and pans for a living. He wasn't trying to get someone's approval, he wasn't bucking for a promotion. He did pots because he had to, but his heart was not there. His heart was in God's holy Presence.

Third, like any human being, Lawrence had problems staying in a recollected state. His mind wandered; his emotions ebbed and flowed; his desires—for promotions, or for a sweet, or for someone's approval—flared up from time to time. When this occurred, Lawrence gently brought his attention back to God's abiding Presence, which was his heart's deepest desire. He did this without "becoming troubled or worried," and without berating himself.

While the practice of recollection finds its clearest modern expression in Brother Lawrence, it has been present in the church, in various forms since the time of St. Paul. Paul speaks frequently in his letters of putting off our old sinful nature, in which we are separated from God, and putting on our new nature in the likeness of Christ.[34] By this, St. Paul indicates that we are to live, no longer as people who are separated from the love of God, but as children with the same Father. That is, we are to live in God's immanent Presence, "praying without ceasing."[35]

Paul's understanding, that our oneness with God is more fundamental to our being than any apparent separation, is crucial for a mature theological understanding. To be aware of our unity in Christ, our oneness with God, involves a profound change of "being," a change in how we exist in the world. From this perspective, our existence, our being, is no longer for ourselves, but for God.

This change of being is possible only by dwelling in the Presence of God; hence, the centrality of this process of Recollection to all prayer and to all Christian life.

St. Paul's theme of becoming one with God was taken up by the early church fathers. Although only a few manuscripts survived from that era, those that did are powerfully concerned about reconnection with the Divine. St. Irenaeus in the second century writes: "This is why the Word of God was made man...so that man, having been taken into the Word and receiving adoption, might become the son of God."[36] St. Gregory of Nyssa offers an explanation of how this divinization occurs: "One who is a man becomes a son of God by being joined to Christ by spiritual generation....A man himself changes himself, exchanging the old man for the new....A man puts off himself and puts on the Divine nature."[37] Through a chain of saints, stretching back to Peter and Paul, and moving through Irenaeus, Athanasius, Gregory of Nyssa, and many others too numerous to mention, this idea of the divinization of humankind becomes one of the dominant strands of theology in the Eastern Orthodox Church.

In the West, however, this notion of divinization became obscured. The theological emphasis in the West focused very early on the unworthiness of humanity. Hence, Western Christians did not talk of "becoming God." They hoped, rather, to expiate their sins so as not to be cast into outer darkness on judgment day.

There are bright lights, however, even in the West. St. Francis of Assisi is one whose prayer life resulted in such closeness to Jesus that he received the stigmata, the wounds of Jesus' crucifixion. Unfortunately, Francis did not leave behind a method of prayer, and the methods that he used to enter into his ecstasies were quickly forgotten. St. Teresa of Avila, on the other hand, described a method of prayer which seems to be of the same lineage of those described by earlier mystics. This was the prayer of recollection in which the soul learns to listen to God.[38] This leads to the prayer of quiet which takes the soul into union.

It was perhaps St. Teresa's influence that directed Brother Lawrence to practice the prayer of recollection. He was a monk in the order which she reformed and he lived in the century after her death. This prayer seems to have been a gift from God to Teresa, from Teresa to Lawrence, and from Lawrence to you and me. After Lawrence's death, his letters and the abbot's written records of their conversations were collected into a small book of devotions in

1692. It is through this slender volume that Brother Lawrence's method comes to us.

The Practice of the Presence of God

The easiest way to use Brother Lawrence's method of recollection is to audiotape the instructions given below in Exercise 3 and then to play the tape for yourself. This will help you disengage from the thinking intellect and just "be." Your meditation is a "being with God," without any need to do or to achieve. If you decide to tape these instructions, read the exercise at a slow pace. When using your tape, you will need time to hear and experience what was said. The verbal part should take three to four minutes, with silence left at the end of the tape so that you can continue your inward journey. Alternatively, since the instructions are simple, you may wish to read over the exercise several times and get the sense of it in your memory. Then sit and practice.

SPIRITUAL EXERCISE 3
THE PRACTICE OF THE PRESENCE OF GOD

1. Position your body comfortably, spine erect, on a chair or cushions.

2. Ground yourself in your physical sensations. Close your eyes and slowly become aware of the sensations of your physical body. Feel the sensations as they flow through you. The sensations in your head...in your neck and shoulders...your elbows...your wrists and the palms of your hands...the sensations in your knees...your ankles and the soles of your feet.

3. Now allow your attention to collect in the region of your heart. Imagine that you are very small, and walk within...into that vast space inside of yourself.

4. As you move within, open your awareness to feel the Presence of the Divine. Feel God's Presence all around you. Within you.

---

5. Let yourself rest in this Presence. Let yourself dwell here for the time you have set apart for your meditation.

6. When your attention wanders to other things, do not berate yourself. Gently bring your awareness back to the Presence of God. Let yourself rest here.

(To close your meditation)

7. When you are ready, let yourself come back to this place. Let the feeling return to your feet...your hands...your face. Take a deep breath, and open your eyes.

How This Meditation Feels. It is difficult to learn to meditate from a book because you can't ask questions or get feedback on what you are doing. So let's explore how this meditation practice feels and the things you may experience.

As you go through the grounding exercise at the beginning of the meditation, you may begin to feel your body in a different way. The sensations in your body parts will be magnified, as you focus your awareness on each of them in turn. This is a normal part of the grounding process and indicates that there is a proper intensity to your focused awareness.

As you open to the Presence of God, you will feel a qualitatively different energy. For many, this experience is very subtle. This state of awareness and your ordinary waking consciousness may seem almost the same. If this is the case for you, you will find that, as you practice this meditation, you will be gradually able to tune into God's Presence. It will become more and more clear to you, more and more familiar to you. Often, when you tell someone to look for something new, but can't give them explicit instructions about how they will recognize this new thing, it is very difficult. In a way, it is like learning to ride a bike. You can't communicate to a person who can't ride a bicycle what it feels like. But as you develop experience, you know what to look for; you develop an understanding of what "feels right."

For those who experience a clearer difference when you begin to feel the Presence of God, you will have a sense of a slow, vibrant, deep energy surrounding you and coming from deep within you.

This will be very different from any of your expectations, yet oddly familiar. There is no familiar picture of Jesus here, no familiar words. But there is a familiar feeling with the practice, like coming home to an old friend whom you have almost forgotten.

Let yourself flow with this energy; it is the Presence of our Lord. There is no need to force anything or to try harder. It is enough to rest here, in God. Do not try to make pictures of God, simply *feel* His Presence. As you do this, you will experience a sense of calmness, peacefulness, and a connectedness to the larger whole.

Often, as people enter into the Presence, there is a sense of warmth and itching. This occurs as the muscles relax deeply. The sensation is similar to sitting on the beach in the warmth of the sun. Often, too, people report that their body image seems to change. They feel bigger or smaller. This is simply a result of the deep relaxation which accompanies meditation and has no spiritual significance.

Many people I have taught personally report an immediate sense of God's Presence. Sometimes this Presence is like a little shock, a surprise; more often it is gradual, gentle and mild. Further, there may be a sense of energy going out to this Presence, or a sense of receiving energy from that Presence. In either case, simply flow with the experience, without trying to control or direct it. There is often a sense of deep heartfelt communion in this flow.

As you gain experience with this practice, you may notice an undulating swell of intensity. Now God's Presence seems almost overwhelming, now it seems to recede a bit. This ebb and flow is natural. As you continue to dwell in the Presence, the intensity will grow. It is extremely pleasurable to experience.

Counter to this pleasure is the tendency of the mind to wander to other topics. There are few things as annoying and as persistent as this mental wandering! Do not be surprised when your attention begins to stray. This wandering is normal and expected. Meditation is what you do with your errant thoughts. When this wandering occurs, simply bring your attention back and refocus on the Divine Presence. Remember, do not berate yourself if your mind wanders, because that self–judgment is only another form of wandering from an awareness of God.

I have come to think of my conscious mind as a little child, always wandering off to find some brighter and more interesting bauble. The true treasure is not, however, outside of us. It is found by going within. Your mental wandering, rather than being a hindrance, is actually a wonderful opportunity. Experiencing your wandering mind gives you the opportunity to begin to bring your attention under control, and to develop your awareness into an instrument which can take you ever more deeply into the Divine Mystery.

Often, as you practice this or any other meditation, there is a sense of time distortion. The time that you are in the Presence will seem either very long or very short, compared to the time measured by the clock. There is often an accompanying sense of body distortion. You may experience some part of your body as larger or smaller than the rest. These distortions reflect the profound letting–go process, a kind of deconditioning which allows us to discover our true nature. As such, these distortions are nothing to be alarmed about, but rather are marks of the progress you are making.

When and Where to Practice. The value of the practice of the Presence of God is that it can be used anywhere, at any time. You can use it in your formal meditation practice—the time you set apart to go within yourself. And you can use it in the midst of daily living, going as deeply within as seems appropriate.

Several of my students find this practice helpful in dealing with otherwise unpleasant situations. They use it in the dentist's chair, in waiting rooms, and in an endless variety of ways. We each have many such periods in the day. Rather than be frustrated with these idle moments, we can fill them richly with this meditation.

Chapter 8

Other Forms of Recollection

There are several other forms for recollecting God's Presence. Like many meditations, once we come to understand the underlying process, only our creativity will limit what we actually do. One of the great advantages of recollection is that we don't have to limit our practice to formal periods of sitting meditation. We can practice recollection sitting at a desk, doing the dishes, and in all manner of activities. With recollection, we can begin the process of praying continuously, as scripture commends to us.

The next meditation, "Being Seen by God," addresses one of the problems which can arise from the process of recollection: the problem of shame. Often, because of our early learning about God, we feel an intense sense of shame when we enter into the Presence. The shame is so overpowering that we end up avoiding any but the most formal and distant relationship. But distance from the Divine is not what we were created for!

Being seen by God helps us to come to terms with our shame. As John Bradshaw and others have pointed out, we live in a shame—based society.[39] Shame pervades our sense of ourselves. At our core, many of us believe that we are inherently bad or defective. Believing this, we cannot engage in any genuine search for God, since if we find Her, we think we will most likely be rejected.

One of the most unpleasant and difficult emotions to resolve, shame wants us to hide our faces, to grow small, to disappear. Gripped by our shame, we forget that God created us the way we are. We forget that after She created us, She looked and said, "This is very good."[40] We forget that She created us with the capacity to sin, and that She, Herself, created the strong passions which can pull us toward sin. We forget that all our heavenly Mother desires is our turning from sin, that we renounce our separation from Her and from Her creation, that, like the prodigal son, we come back home again.

This meditation is helpful for everyone who experiences some shame in their life. I suspect this includes all of us. It is a very gentle way of addressing our shame, to open ourselves to God's forgiveness.

SPIRITUAL EXERCISE 4
BEING SEEN BY GOD

1. Position your body comfortably, spine erect, on a chair or cushions.

2. Ground yourself in your physical sensations. Close your eyes and slowly become aware of the sensations of your physical body. Feel the sensations as they flow through you. The sensations in your head...in your neck and shoulders...your elbows...your wrists and the palms of your hands...the sensations in your knees...your ankles and the soles of your feet.

3. Now allow your attention to collect in the region of your heart. Imagine that you are very small, and walk within... into that vast space inside of you.

4. As you move within, be aware that your Mother in heaven is watching you. Not only does She see your outside, but She also sees your thoughts and feelings. Everything about you is known by Her.

5. As God watches you, feel the love which your Mother carries for you. That you might have life, God gave Her son, Jesus. Let yourself rest in Her loving Presence. Let yourself dwell here for the time you have set apart for your meditation.

6. When attention wanders to other things, do not berate yourself. Gently bring your awareness back to the sense of God watching you. Let yourself rest here.

(To close your meditation)

7. When you are ready, let yourself come back to this place. Let the feeling return to your feet...your hands...your face. Take a deep breath, and open your eyes.

This practice of recollection can easily be done during our everyday, routine tasks. If you use this practice during your daily routine, you may find yourself stopping when you start doing some activity about which you are ashamed. When you catch yourself in this predicament, be aware that God has given you a special gift. You now have the opportunity—in this moment—to choose God directly. You have the opportunity to let go of those behaviors which separate you from the love of God.

Our Mother in heaven does not want perfection in our outward observances, the sacrifices which everyone can see. She wants our hearts, not proud and too full of ourselves, but humble and contrite. Listen to the words of the Psalmist:

> Have mercy on me, O God, according to your loving–
> kindness;
> in your great compassion blot out my offenses.
> Wash me through and through from my wickedness
> and cleanse me from my sin....
> Create in me a clean heart, O God,
> and renew a right spirit within me....
> The sacrifice of God is a troubled spirit;
> a broken and contrite heart, O God, you will not despise.[41]

Keeping God Company

Still another form of recollection, "Keeping God Company," has become one of my favorite forms of meditation. I learned of this meditation from Bernadette Roberts, a former Carmelite nun who has had unitive experiences with God.[42] She learned this meditation from a young Roman Catholic priest who kept watching one of his older parishioners spend many hours in the church on a daily basis. Finally, the young priest asked the old man what he was doing. "I'm just keeping Him company," was the response. As the young pastor got to know this old man, he found a clear and shining holiness in him. Like Brother Lawrence, the old man was transfigured by his practice of recollection.

SPIRITUAL EXERCISE 5
KEEPING GOD COMPANY

1. Position your body comfortably, spine erect, on a chair or cushions.

2. Ground yourself in your physical sensations. Close your eyes and slowly become aware of the sensations of your physical body. Feel the sensations as they flow through you. The sensations in your head...in your neck and shoulders...your elbows...your wrists and the palms of your hands...the sensations in your knees...your ankles and the soles of your feet.

3. Now allow your attention to collect in the region of your heart. Imagine that you are very small, and walk within...into that vast space inside of yourself.

4. As you move within, open your awareness to feel the Presence of God, as He sits beside you.

5. As you might keep company with an old friend, a friend with whom words are not necessary, so keep company with God. Be together. No need for words. Just feel the deep feelings running in you as you rest here with Him.

6. When you find your attention wandering to other things, do not berate yourself. Gently bring your awareness back to the Presence of the Lord. Let yourself rest here.

(To close your meditation)

7. When you are ready, let yourself come back to this place. Let the feeling return to your feet...your hands...your face. Take a deep breath, and open your eyes.

This meditation is very gentle. In the midst of a long and tiring day, give yourself permission to take a moment, close your eyes, lean back in your chair, and keep God company. As one of my students commented, "The pause that refreshes!"

I find this meditation especially delightful in a church sanctuary. Many sanctuaries have a strong feeling of holiness. Whatever the aura of sanctity might be, I suspect that it comes from many people over many years pouring themselves out in prayer and by the repeated Presence of the Lord as He has loved them. Thus, to follow the example of the old man who brings us this form of recollection, praying this gentle prayer in a church setting makes it that much more powerful.

These practices are only three of the multitude of ways that we can recollect our awareness in God. As we are now, we are broken inside and separated from God. We are scattered; our attention flies all over the map, flitting here and there like a butterfly with no direct path. Recollection allows us to collect our attention and focus it in God. Using these disciplines, we come back to our selves, to our deepest nature as children of God.

I encourage you to engage in recollection on a daily, even an hourly basis. This work, by itself, is sufficient to bring us back home to our Father.

Chapter 9

Problems in Recollection

These methods of recollection are extremely simple, but there are problems associated with their practice. The most insidious difficulty is the ease with which our attention wanders. With all good intentions, we prepare a time to meditate, sit down and make a good start, but then start wandering all over the mental landscape, making shopping lists, "to do" lists, musing about this person or that interaction.

This mental noodling is not, *per se*, particularly destructive. It is just a quick slice of our mental processing. We do this sort of thing all of the time. But when beginners sit down to meditate, they often react to this noodling with great distress. When they notice that they are wandering, they start to blame themselves. They berate themselves for the heinous crime of wool-gathering. A beginner's typical mental reaction to the discovery of wool-gathering might go something like this:

> Oh my God, I'm off wandering again! How could I do that? This is my time with God. I must surely be a bad person if I can't even keep my commitment to attend to God for five minutes, let alone the twenty which this book suggests! I guess that this meditation stuff works for everybody in the world except for me. I am soooo bad!

If we can stand back a little from our self-abuse, two things are apparent. First, we notice that this abuse is just another form of wandering. It is no better or worse than the wandering which just preceded it and for which we have been punishing ourselves. Second, we notice a certain self-indulgent quality about all this. We dramatize our "stuff"; we make ourselves out to be much worse than we really are. This is the false self again, making us out to be the center of the universe. If the truth be known, it took me years to be able to concentrate on God or anything else for twenty minutes. Reading the spiritual literature and talking to wise directors, it seems clear that my experience is not unusual. So a little bit of wandering, or even a lot, is perfectly normal for this stage of your interior development.

Often students give up on themselves or on God too quickly. Going inside, into our interior space, is a little like walking into a trackless desert, a wasteland. When, like the Israelites, we wander about in this unfamiliar territory, we get uncomfortable and even scared very quickly. "What will we eat?" we complain. "How will we find our way in this trackless waste?" "It was better to be in bondage in Egypt—at least there we got fed!" So we go back to our bondage, our familiar ways.

Blessings in Disguise. One of the many results of meditation is a deepening of our awareness. As this deepening occurs, we become more aware of our inner wounds. Typically, we do not welcome this. But if we are honest with ourselves, we realize that there are places deep in our hearts which carry hurts from long ago. We have hardened a crust over these sensitive places; we hide them from ourselves. When we notice that we cannot attend to our Creator despite our best intentions, even for a minute or two, then we become aware of our woundedness.

This awareness is a blessing, although not one of those blessings which shouts its nature from the rooftops. A wound is an opening in our surface—a cut. Through these openings, we can penetrate more deeply into ourselves; we can draw ever closer to God and His indwelling Presence.

When we greet our woundedness and seize upon it, we begin a different sort of journey. This is the journey that Scott Peck describes in *The Road Less Traveled.*[43] This is the journey that begins with our confession of sin and separation. The journey that is furthered, not by brute force or our own efforts, but by continued repentance and renunciation of those behaviors which keep us separated.

Repentance is the process of turning from our sin, from those actions that separate us from God and from our deepest self. Continual repentance is crucial to the success of our spiritual journeying. We cannot move forward if we constantly hold on to the things that hold us back.

As we move into the Presence of God, into the Divine Mind,

there is a profound letting go. Typically, we grasp and hold onto things because we are afraid. We use things to protect us. Even our thoughts are things which we hold for their protective value. "Poor people deserve to be poor" is the kind of thought which allows those with wealth to protect their sense of themselves. But the erosion of our spirit which this holding onto engenders is ultimately toxic to us.

Even in the simple exercise of recollection, we may begin to experience these problems. One option, when we have trouble, is to abandon our meditation practice. Abandonment comes out of our fear, our felt sense of inadequacy despite all of our Father's assurances. If we continue to wrestle with these problems, we will also experience the blessings which they conceal.

The Importance of the Practice of Recollection. The practice of recollection underlies all Christian prayer. The practice of recollecting God is therefore central to Christian meditation and contemplation. On the face of it, the practice is extremely simple. Anyone can do it. It can be done anywhere and any time. This method is the distillation of almost 2000 years of Christian contemplation. It focuses the practitioner on the heart of all contemplative method—how to enter into God's holy Presence.

The apparent simplicity of this meditation conceals a deep complexity. We will, in our journey through this book, explore other forms of meditation for which recollection is simply implied. The practice of recollection comes explicitly to the fore again in the contemplative practices which we will explore later. It is the fundamental basis for infused prayer, the prayer which the Holy Spirit gives to us. Thus recollection, with its humble exterior, conceals a wonderful and rich blessing in its interior.

Part III
The Sensory Meditations

In the previous section, we plunged together into the Divine, throwing ourselves into that wonderful Presence, and exploring the chaos which lies within each of us. We began our spiritual exercises there because recollection is the bedrock upon which all prayer is based. While it is necessary to start there, only a few will be comfortable resting there for long.

We are not comfortable with recollection because our attention is, at this stage of development, almost uncontrollable. Without graduated training in meditation skills, we can't focus very long. At this early stage of interior development, the problem of controlling attention may seem overwhelming. It is terribly frustrating to intend to sit with God and then find ourselves everywhere else. This happens to everyone, despite our best intentions, but it is cold comfort to know this.

The problem with recollection, in these early stages, is the formless quality of the practice. We are used to dealing with "things"— tangible somethings that we can see and touch and feel. The Presence of God may not be tangible in these beginning stages. It may be wispy, vaguely present when we start our meditation and then disappearing. Of course, it is not God that disappears; it is our attention that is wandering. But from our perspective, we will wonder a lot where She has gone!

Because of the formless quality of recollection, it is easy for our attention to drift. There are two reasons for this instability. First, our attention is like the ninety-eight-pound weakling at the beach, with bullies kicking sand in his face. It is not yet strong enough. To be successful in meditation, we literally have to forge our attention into a tool capable of sustained use. We do this by means of practice, just as with anything else. When we practice meditation sufficiently, we create a strong tool that can move us into the Presence of God and rest there.

The second reason for inattention is the sin which pulls at us, the concerns of the false self which distract us from our true nature. Look closely at the kinds of distractions that pull us off course. We are likely to find various lists of things to do, things forgotten, memories of past encounters where something was left unresolved. Let's look at this carefully. Why do we make lists? If we look closely, we will probably find that we are trying to remember to do things so that we can get approval, either from someone else or from the critical part within ourselves. The underlying message is, "You are not good enough unless you do everything right." How different this is from God's message to us: "You are my beloved children, and to you I send Jesus, the Christ, the Savior, to cut you down from your cross."

In meditation, we begin to go below the surface of the mind. There we encounter all of the old emotional programs which keep us believing that we are essentially unloved and unlovable, that we are bad, that no one wants to be with us. Once we stop the chatter of our conscious mind, these programs come into awareness. In the past, we have always acted as if these programs were true—ultimate statements of our deepest reality. In meditation, however, we simply observe these programs without buying into them or following them in any way. We just notice that they have arisen and go back to our meditational focus.

When we first start encountering this, it is sometimes devastating. Quite often people weep when this arises, the power of these old programs is so great. Fortunately, other Christians have walked this way before us. They found ways of using the senses to develop a strong and stable attentional focus. Because we are all familiar with using our senses—you are using your eyes right now to read this— we can start on known ground. From this known base we gradually build a bridge out into the unknown, toward the Divine.

The focus of this section of the book is learning to use our sensory apparatus to forge a stronger tool of our attention and to use that developing attention to move deeply into the Presence of God. Let us, then, continue...

Chapter 10

The Spiritual Use of the Senses

Our senses are the primary means by which we gather information. What we know about the outer world has come to us through our five senses. We use our senses to go out to the world, to experience the world, and then to represent that outer world within ourselves. Much of our stream of inner chatter has arisen from this process. We see an apple; we ask ourselves if we are hungry, checking the kinesthetic cues; we remember our past experiences of apples like this one, accessing memories of taste and smell. From this information we make a decision about whether to eat the apple. We use this simple compare–and–contrast process many times every minute, without even thinking about it.

Early mystics in the church found that the sensory processes could be harnessed for spiritual use. The best known examples of this are the techniques for visualizing things in our minds. We know this today as "guided imagery" or "guided visualization," techniques often used by pastors and psychologists.

Perhaps the greatest set of visualizations ever produced are the exercises of St. Ignatius of Loyola.[44] Ignatius, while recovering from battle wounds, developed a series of visualizations on the life of Jesus that is still being used today. So powerful were his *Exercises* in transforming the false self that a monastic order came into being around Ignatius, as men wished to learn his techniques and to change their lives as he had been changed.

The original purpose of these sensory techniques was not only to gather information about inner realities, but also to strengthen attention into a more useful tool for inner work. With visualization, for example, we close our eyes and imagine a visual image. For spiritual purposes, a religious image of some sort is often used, perhaps a cross or an image of Jesus or Mary. Focus on the image is maintained as long as possible. Of course, some other thought regularly grabs our attention and moves it away from the visualization, but when this is noticed, we simply refocus back to the spiritual image.

The process of visualization naturally inhibits the attention from wandering. Our conscious mind can only hold seven bits of information in our attention at a time.[44a] The process of visualization loads our awareness with all seven bits. If you can imagine your attention as a wild horse who follows his own fancy, then the process of visualization is like loading that horse with so much weight that all it can do is stay on the road where the path is smooth.

So far I have talked about the sense of sight, but the other senses can be used in a similar fashion. We can use the auditory sense modality by chanting. The kinesthetic sense can be used in a similar way, focusing attention on the kinesthetic sensations that stream through our bodies. I have even heard of the senses of taste and smell being used in meditation. Before a workshop, participants were given a small cup of raisins, which were promptly gobbled down without awareness. After learning to be aware of their inner world, and the flow of sensation streaming through them, they were given one raisin, and instructed to let it sit in the mouth, and to eat it slowly and mindfully. When you eat raisins without awareness, they are nothing to write home about. But try eating them in this contemplative way!

When we fully occupy the attention, loading all seven bits with information, a very important shift occurs. No longer do we exert conscious control in the same way as before. When all seven units are busy, there is no attention left to "be conscious" of what the other six bits are doing. So at the moment of full engagement, we shift from a doing/active mode to a being/receptive mode. In this receptive mode, we reconnect with the deeper and larger true self and we enter into the Mind of God.[45]

This process of "loading" in meditation is similar to what happens when we learn how to ski. When we start to ski, we try desperately to be actively aware of everything that is happening. The ski instructor says to watch which edge of our skis is biting into the slope, where our weight is, the position of our skis, our poles, the other skiers, the natural obstacles such as trees, and so on. Of course, when we try to do all of this our mind overloads because more than seven things are going on here. We forget to attend to something crucial, and we fall down a lot.

Later, we stop trying so hard. We stop resisting our falls. We let go and simply enjoy what we are doing and where we are. In a word, we become receptive. We allow our consciousness to be overloaded and we relax and let go. Then, magically, we stop falling. We "fly" to the bottom of the slope, and a sense of limitless freedom arises. We have entered into the Mind of God. The freedom that we experience, the sense of limitlessness, is what we experience in God.

By overloading our attention in this way, we facilitate a shift into the Divine. We enter into a different state of consciousness. In our ordinary waking state of consciousness, we are incapable of any true awareness of God. In our ordinary waking state, we are not aware of God's Presence; we are not aware of our intimate connections with all other people; we are spiritually numb. But when we change our state of consciousness by opening up in a receptive manner, then we can enter into the Presence of the Divine, and into limitless freedom and peace.

Charles Tart, a psychologist who has researched states of consciousness for the last twenty years, has come to some interesting conclusions about what we experience in our ordinary waking state. Based on his research, he says that we live in a "consensus trance"; that what we actually experience every day is not reality, but our collective agreement about reality.[46] Dr. Tart describes consensus trance as being induced by the process of enculturation. As we learn to be "normal" in our culture, we suppress who we are at our deepest levels. We abandon our true self and create a false self that parrots what everyone else says. We walk around saying to each other and ourselves statements such as, "Snow is always white," "the good guys always win," and "we are the good guys."

The cost of this is stupefying. We learn to act like robots. We walk around with characteristic fixed body movements, gestures, and mannerisms. We develop fixed attitudes that may have nothing to do with reality. We develop distorted ideas about the world we live in. We "see" through many filters and blinders, in order to conform our raw perception to the accepted norm, to the consensus trance.

Consensus trance is great for going to work, for washing the dishes, and for many other tasks, but it is not good for all things. For example, the consensus trance is not good for driving a car—when more than seven things go on at once, so that ordinary consciousness can't keep track of them. Consensus trance is not good for doing surgery—if your surgeon is not in an altered state, focusing very carefully on the operation, then your physical well-being is in jeopardy. Ordinary waking consciousness, in fact, is not good for anything that requires great concentration. It is too susceptible

to distraction: attention cannot be focused sharply, so we are frequently pulled away from that on which we want to concentrate.

For the purpose of contemplative development, ordinary waking
consciousness is very limited. The collective trance in which we
live does not admit an awareness of the Divine. We cannot experience the Divine by means of this kind of awareness. Admittedly,
we can learn many things about God in ordinary waking consciousness. This is the form of awareness prevalent in most Bible
studies and, unfortunately, in most prayer groups. We can go to
school in ordinary waking consciousness, and we can learn things
"about" God. *But we will never experience God directly from ordinary waking consciousness.*

Let me put it in another way. Which would you rather have: the
words "chocolate ice cream" written on this page, or a bite of chocolate ice cream melting in your mouth? Which would you rather
have: the words "God loves you" as they are written here, or the
direct experience of that love?

Altered states of consciousness—which are simply different from
ordinary waking consciousness, neither better nor worse—
are necessary if we want to *experience* our God. They are the road
we travel to get from our sinful, separated state into the state of
union. While all religions use altered states widely, it has become
fashionable in Christendom to deny that we use altered states, and
to denigrate them in others. This is a travesty! The holy eucharist—
also called the Lord's supper, and holy communion—is shared by all
Christians and is a carefully constructed method for leaving our
ordinary consciousness and entering into altered states. All prayer,
even prayer with words, attempts to move us into altered states.

The important thing is to realize what we are doing. If we want
to experience God, it is important that we not consciously deny the
means to achieve that experience. We will make too many missteps
if we engage in this massive sort of denial. We must acknowledge
the road that we walk upon, value it, cherish it, and walk within its
confines. This process is likely to bring us to our destination much
more quickly than wandering all over the countryside.

Chapter 11

The Process of Sensory Meditation

Sensory meditation uses the senses in order to concentrate attention and to enter into an altered state of consciousness, thus facilitating an experience of the Divine. We will examine in detail the processes behind each of the modalities of sensory meditation, in order to illustrate how they work. But let's face it, when we talk about leaving behind our ordinary waking consciousness, most of us get a little apprehensive. If we understand the process, however, much of our fear will evaporate. We have used these processes all of our lives. Meditation is simply the conscious use of an ordinary tool that we have employed since we were children.

The Process of Visualization

Just underneath our conscious awareness, there is a stream of images that flows constantly. This image stream seems to be a "summary mechanism" in the unconscious mind. This is how the unconscious summarizes the data that it receives and packages these data for the conscious mind to use.

People vary in their ability to perceive images. A few create eidetic images, which are picture-like, correct in every detail, even the smallest. These are the people who can memorize a page by looking at it once. They don't really memorize like the rest of us, they just look—that's all it takes. Most people can visualize with varying degrees of sharpness or fuzziness. I am ordinary in this regard. Sometimes I get a very clear image, with every detail standing out clearly. Mostly though, I get fuzzy outlines, and it is only through great concentration that the image gradually clarifies. About seventeen percent of the population cannot visualize at all.[47] In all of the meditation books, and in all of the instruction that I have received, this very important fact has never been addressed. If you happen to be one of these people who cannot visualize, please do not spend much effort with visualization. All that will happen is that you will get terribly frustrated, feel inadequate, and quit. Instead, simply skip ahead to the material on auditory meditation. The ability to visualize, like most other abilities, is part of the incredibly rich natural variation that the Lord built into His universe. Just like the natural variation in adult height, hair color, intelligence, artistic ability, and just about everything else you can think of, so too there is variation in the sensory modality through which you receive the bulk of your information.

Of great importance is the way that this process of visualization can connect us with the deep unconscious without strenuous effort. During the process of visualizing, we are in touch with our unconscious naturally. In this altered state of consciousness, we can process more information than the usual seven bits, because we are using a tool that is more powerful than the conscious mind. By using the fullest extent of our mind, we have entered into the limitless Mind of God.

Hence, the importance of visualization. It is a method for quickly receiving a great deal of information about the divine realities. And because visualization stirs up the emotions, this information is not just of the cognitive sort. At its best, the information derived from visualization includes both cognitive and emotive components. It is experiential knowledge. We experience, through a limited medium, the living God, the reality of the Ultimate. The information gained here is far more useful than book-learning about God. Although intellectual knowledge is a useful precursor to experiential learning, book-learning can never substitute for the direct experience of God.

Visualization, and all of the sensory meditations, allow us to retain a measure of rational control during the meditation process. Many people are afraid that they will be swallowed up and never come back if they enter into an altered state. While we long for union with God—we long to know intimately and to be known—we are also afraid. The sensory meditations allow us to test the waters with safety.

When we start to visualize, we become aware of that part of consciousness which simply sits back and observes the process. We don't have to set up this mechanism, it just naturally occurs. This watcher-self is our tie to the outer world. In visualization, our rational controls are mostly suspended, but are still in place if we need them. We enter into another world and participate in that world to our fullest extent. The watcher-self serves as our anchor in these initial stages, while we check out the territory within ourselves. If something awful comes up—and we all fear that something will—then the watcher-self will bring us back. I have never known of an instance where the meditator was unable to come back to the outer world.

Later, as you progress in your meditation, you will learn to let go of even this watcher-self. You will have built up enough trust in the process through your own experience, that the watcher-self will be unnecessary for your sense of safety. Then you will be able to go even deeper into God's Presence.

The Process of Auditory Meditation

The process of auditory meditation is similar to visualization, but instead of a visual stimulus, an auditory sequence is created. Often chant is used in this process. Most people, when they listen to Gregorian chant, find themselves transported to another place—a place of deep inner calm and holiness. The genius of Gregorian chant is the splendid marriage of word-meaning with music. The music emphasizes the words and evokes internal states quickly. Other auditory sequences can also be used. Tones can be generated internally, hymns can be sung, and so forth.

To my knowledge, a thorough study of auditory meditation has never been done. Because most people process most of their information visually, the auditory world has been neglected. Thus, those who are primarily auditory in their information gathering have had, and will continue to have, some difficulty in finding material that is suitable for their spiritual development.

This is truly a great loss, not only for those who are primarily auditory, but also for the rest of us. The auditory modality quickly accesses the deep unconscious and induces an altered state. If you have any doubt of this, then examine the glazed look on the eyes of the nearest teenager who is plugged into a set of headphones. Furthermore, you don't have to be in the seventeen–percent group to have this happen. I am primarily visual, but I find that auditory meditations have a profound effect on me. Often they are much more powerful than the visualizations I use.

There are wonderful stories in the history of the church about the power of chant. St. Joseph of Cupertino, a Roman Catholic of the seventeenth century, used to fall into ecstasy and levitate while chanting mass.[48] This happened not just once or twice, but so many times that his superiors forbade him to attend public mass because his levitation was disruptive of everyone else's equanimity. We see from this that chant is a powerful vehicle for inner change, useful in both the beginning and advanced stages of spiritual growth. Thus, chant is not a tool to be denigrated or overlooked. We need to understand it better so that we learn how to use it well.

One advantage of auditory meditation is its power to stir up the emotions. It is hard to sing without being moved emotionally. Music grabs us emotionally and shakes us. Here we begin to harness our emotions, our passions, to our search for God. This makes for a much more powerful meditation. Auditory meditations thus have an extraordinary utility in moving us out of our conventional reality and into the Mind of God.

In addition, auditory stimuli have a compelling quality that visual stimuli do not often possess. We can ignore visual stimuli quite easily, just by looking away. But try to ignore the sound of a jackhammer or the sound of a crying baby: it is extremely difficult. Thus, because of this compelling quality, auditory meditations are very helpful in focusing attention and maintaining that focus.

The church has widely used the techniques of visual and auditory meditation throughout its history. In recent centuries, however, with the neglect of the contemplative tradition, the church has not always recognized what it was doing when it employed these methods. As a result, there have been few spectacular examples of saints using these forms of prayer in modern times.

One of the unfortunate qualities of ignorance is that we don't know the value of what we have. If we don't know what we are doing with these methods of prayer, we typically quit before we derive the benefits of the practice. It's like building a car by hand, carefully making the engine, the drive train, and fitting everything together so that it works, but then not driving our newly created machine. With auditory meditation, churchgoers often develop the technique, but seldom use it properly.

The Process of Kinesthetic Meditation

If the process of auditory meditation has been neglected and poorly understood, how much more so has been the neglect of kinesthetic forms of meditation. Kinesthetic meditation focuses our attention on bodily sensations. Because we all have these sensations, they have an immediacy and a vividness that is very powerful. We don't have to construct a visual image or an auditory sequence. We simply focus our attention on the stream of physical sensation that naturally occurs within us.

As I have searched the spiritual literature of Christendom, I have seen allusions to kinesthetic forms of meditation in the desert fathers and others, but I have not yet come upon a complete description of a formal practice of kinesthetic meditation. The first spiritual exercise in this book outlines the beginnings of such a formal practice. I will develop this further in chapter 16.

The Spectrum of Practice

It is important, perhaps vitally so, that the student of meditation understand that there is a continuum of meditative and contemplative practices. These practices are sequenced in a developmental order. It is necessary to do the beginning work before you can successfully grapple with the more advanced exercises. As a result, the material presented in this book is graduated, from introductory practices through advanced work.

This does not mean that you might not be ready now, on your first reading of this material, to begin with the more advanced material. I have met a number of people who have found ways other than meditation to disengage from their internal stream of chatter. These people are able to maintain an attentional focus that is sufficiently strong to move directly into the contemplative exercises. They have already moved through the developmental sequence for which these spiritual exercises are designed. But most of us need to begin with a sensory meditation and practice here for a time in order to strengthen our attention.

In childhood development, it is not better to be quicker. Babies grow at their own pace. Their bodies develop, their perception develops, their thinking abilities develop; all according to an inner blueprint that guides their growth. There is no rushing in this process. Development unfolds in its own time.

So, too, with meditation. We need to begin where we are in the spiritual spectrum. We cannot progress to the next stage of development until we have fully completed the former stage. So it is useful to understand something about this developmental sequence at the outset. The spectrum of meditative practice looks like this.

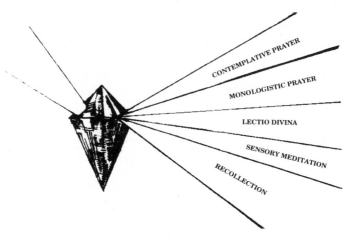

As we explore each of these practices in the chapters ahead, I will describe the signs that indicate when you are finished with a particular practice and ready to embark upon the subsequent method. It is helpful here to consult with an experienced spiritual director or a group of spiritual friends. On this journey, we cannot see ourselves clearly until we reach the end.[49] Others, however, often see us much more clearly than we ourselves can. Their counsel can often speed our journey.

In our culture, there is an unfortunate tendency to want to have arrived yesterday. Hence, we have a tendency, in doing meditation, to try to promote or to delude ourselves into believing that we are ready for a more advanced practice, or have achieved a higher state than is actually true. The danger is that, when we do this, we move out of the strong and deep stream of God's movement and into a little eddy that goes round and round and no place in particular. None of us begins meditation to reach this sort of circular end.

The Inner Experience of a Sensory Meditation

Let me describe what a typical sensory meditation might be like. If you are trying to learn meditation from this book, it is helpful to have some sense of whether you are on target or not. Too often, people who make a good beginning quit just as they are making progress. This can have devastating effects in several directions. First, you give up on these practices and thus you resign yourself to never knowing God directly. This is a terrible waste. Second, you are likely to denigrate contemplative practices and those who engage in them. This makes it less likely that others will be interested or motivated to try them. Both outcomes are unsatisfactory and destructive. And both can be prevented with adequate guidance.

Let's say that you begin with a visualization—a very typical place to begin. Unlike most folks, you resolve to start in a simple way, so you get a plain cross, hold it in front of you, focus on the visual aspect, and then close your eyes and create that visual configuration in your mind. Initially, you have great difficulty: you cannot maintain the eidetic image that occurs after you shut your eyes for more than a second or two. You wonder, as you meditate and afterwards, if you are some sort of visual cripple: everyone else can probably do this easily, you think.

But you persevere over a period of weeks or months, and finally you notice that you can maintain the eidetic image for longer and longer periods of time. In meditation, you say, "Wow! I've been doing this for the last thirty seconds," and you begin a process of self-congratulation. In this self-congratulation, the image vanishes. So you kick yourself, "You fool! Look what you went and did. You finally get some success and then you screw it up." If your early upbringing left you vulnerable to this critical inner dialogue, you will continue to kick yourself. In the process, all thought of your meditation has been left behind. You are lost in an old emotional program which, once it has begun, is hard to notice, let alone stop. These old programs are what most of us thought was "normal." So you get up from your meditation disgusted.

What has happened here is typical, good, and very useful for spiritual development. We have not "wasted" the meditation time, although most novices might say so. Rather, in our meditation the old emotional tapes from our false self have surfaced. Our challenge is to focus on the object of meditation and not to attend to the old tapes. They will play on and on; they will provide ever more seductive scenarios to try to engage us. These scenarios are fantasies from the false self. They keep us locked in our old, painful ways.

Many people stop here. They try meditation, and then, when the practice is successful in revealing the old tapes, they *misinterpret* that event and believe they have failed. In fact, they have just begun to be successful. *Meditation is the process of wrestling with our mind.* It is seldom easy, and success is measured more by the intensity of our struggles than by inner calm. The inner calm does come, but only after the struggles.

So let's say that you persevere with your meditation. You steadfastly resist the pull of your old tapes, and continue to focus on the image of the cross. Your ability to hold this image in mind increases slowly, almost imperceptibly. As you gain facility with this, you become aware of other data passing through your mind. Nothing as intrusive as the first eruption of the old tapes, but more subtly, like images ghosting across a screen in the back of your mind.

As your concentration improves, your awareness expands. It doesn't feel like it is expanding, but in fact, it is. You become more and more aware of this other, more subtle data flow. Then you find yourself increasingly distracted by these data. You probably say, "I'm failing! I have spent all this time in meditation, but once again I am overwhelmed by thoughts and images!"

Once again, we are not failing, but succeeding. Our awareness is no longer limited to "gross objects of awareness." We are now sensitive to a data stream that has been there all along, but because we could only perceive on the gross level, we never experienced this more subtle data stream.

Like the first wrestling match with the gross objects of awareness, we are now engaged in another wrestling match. We will have a series of successive matches, each at a more subtle level of awareness. We may feel like a failure at the outset of each of these levels. But take heart, and resist this feeling of defeat. The Lord is with us, and He guides us with love and gentleness. Our task is simply to take courage and to follow where He leads.

Chapter 12

The Practice of Visualization

Visual images for Christian growth are present everywhere in our culture. No matter where we look, there are images of the cross, the archetypal Christian image. Even heavy-metal rock-and-roll performers display crosses prominently all over their bodies, albeit for reasons other than spiritual edification. Religious pictures abound. How many different pictures of Jesus have you seen in the last month? There are so many images—from the virile, smiling young blonde who has such an affinity for children, to the austere and foreboding judge, to the Hispanic or the black figures—it makes the head spin.

What has been missing is a coherent teaching on how to use these visual images for spiritual growth. In this section, I will show you how to use this wonderful capacity to visualize to move more directly into the Presence of God. To facilitate our movement, I have divided the practice of visualization into three modes. The first mode is used to develop and strengthen our attentional focus. The second develops the receptive component of awareness. The third mode helps us internalize the entire process, and brings us into God's Presence in a more focused manner.

The First Mode of Visualization

Using the first mode of visualization develops our ability to focus attention in one place. The process is simple, but not easy. We begin by taking a *simple* image, such as a plain cross or a circle, and we learn to hold that image in our mind. We place the image before us, gaze at it for a moment, and then close our eyes and picture it inside. When the interior image fades, we open our eyes and gaze at the image again to refresh our memory. Then we repeat the process.

This method provides us with a means for quickly developing a focused attention. Without a strong attentional focus, we will have enormous difficulty in progressing in meditation, so the time spent here will be rewarded later in our journey. This part of the journey, however, is not particularly exciting. It is somewhat like washing the dishes night after night—rather boring. Like dishwashing, however, this practice is necessary. It helps us to sharply focus attention, the *sine qua non* for future progress.

SPIRITUAL EXERCISE 6
VISUALIZING A SIMPLE IMAGE

1. Position your body comfortably, spine erect, on a chair or cushions. Place the image you wish to use in front of you. It should be extremely simple: an unadorned simple cross, a picture of a circle, or something similar. For this exercise, the content of the visualization does not matter, only that it be simple and easy to hold in awareness.

2. Ground yourself in your physical sensations. Close your eyes and slowly become aware of the sensations of your physical body. Feel the sensations as they flow through you. The sensations in your head...in your neck and shoulders...your elbows...your wrists and the palms of your hands...the sensations in your knees...your ankles and the soles of your feet. Now bring your attention up to your heart, and let it focus in a steady way there.

3. Open your eyes and focus your attention on your image. Study the image for several moments. Memorize it. Then close your eyes, and visualize that image in your mind. See the image inside your mind exactly as it appears to your gaze.

4. When the image clouds or fades, do not berate yourself. This kind of self-talk is simply another distraction. Simply open your eyes and gaze at the image again. When you have refreshed your memory, close your eyes and move within, visualizing the image in your mind.

5. Continue this process for the period of your meditation.

(To close your meditation)

6. When you are ready to finish your meditation, open your eyes and come back to the room. Let the feeling return to your feet...your hands...your face. Take a deep breath, and reorient yourself.

This process is an exercise in concentration. It is the most effective and direct exercise that I know to forge attention into a useful tool. If you have trouble keeping an attentional focus with some of the later exercises, you will find it useful to return here and spend time practicing this exercise.

Intensifying Your Practice. As you gain facility here, there are further intensifications of concentrative development that you might explore. When you find that you can hold the image in mind without any distractions for ten seconds or more, then go on to these other exercises.

For the first intensification of this practice, visualize the object without repeated looking at the physical form. Simply create the image in your mind, remembering it in every detail. Practice holding it in attention, and when you are distracted, gently bring your attention back and re-create the image. One benefit of this practice is that you will never be without something appropriate to meditate upon.

Once you have gained facility with this first intensification, do the second. Holding your image in mind, rotate it through space until you have another view of it. To manipulate a mental object of awareness in this fashion takes much greater concentration than simply holding the image in awareness.

This third intensification is not one that we can control or attempt. It is the gift from our God of infused prayer. If you are given this gift, you will see with your inward vision the essence of the object that you are concentrating upon. For example, if you are visualizing a simple cross, the pure essence of that cross will emerge from the actual cross you have been visualizing. It is as if you see into the very heart of the material object and can now discern its true identity. This gift is a rare occurrence, and happens only after a long period of concentration, and the development of the first two intensifications.

Most people do not develop the three intensifications mentioned here. They get frustrated or bored, and go on to other practices. The value of this intensified concentration, however, is that practice here will be rewarded by greater progress in the later stages. If you are just beginning meditation, however, the most important fact is that you root yourself in a practice that you are comfortable in doing repeatedly. If this first mode of visualization seems too boring for you, do not worry or fret. You are not alone. Go on to the visualizations described below.

The Second Mode of Visualization

The first mode of visualization uses a concrete object as the springboard for learning to create and hold an internal image in our mind. The second mode uses a more abstract springboard: words. In using this mode, we will generate a visualization that is driven by external stimuli, but produced internally. The visualization will involve complex pictures that change over time.

In all probability, you have already experienced this mode of visualization many times. Perhaps, in your earlier encounters, you did not realize that this is a tool which you can use for spiritual growth. The most prominent church use of this mode of visualization is in the sermons that you hear. As an Episcopalian, I am used to long intellectual sermons that ramble and have trouble coming to a point. I have even preached a few like that myself. So I will always remember a Baptist preacher, Jim McClendon, whose entire sermon was a retelling of the story of Jesus at the well with the Samaritan woman. "You can feel the pressure of the sun," he said, "the heat is like a dead weight pressing on you. The smell of the dust, hanging in the air. The bright, unremitting sunlight. You have been walking since dawn. It is past midday now, and your muscles feel like lead. And up ahead, you see the well outside the gates of Samaria. You think about the cool water—the blessed relief. Your pace picks up."

As the preacher continued, he drew a word picture that placed me in the scene. I closed my eyes, and I was there. I "saw" Jesus at the well of Samaria. I "felt" the power of His Presence. This was different from my usual imagining; the images were much more complete here. This Baptist preacher opened a door for me that helped me move more fully into Christ's Presence.

Since that experience, I have many times felt the power of great evangelical preachers as they re-create the gospel stories. Using the power of words, they paint a picture with images, feelings, sounds, and smells—all of the sense modalities. They help the listener to experience first-hand the holy Presence of Jesus.

We seldom recognize that these preachers stand in the long spiritual tradition of visualization within Christendom, which goes back to the earliest roots of our faith. Jesus Himself drew word pictures to teach His followers. All of the great stories that He told use clear images that have power for us even 2000 years later. "The kingdom of heaven is like a man who, while plowing his field, came upon buried treasure."[50] How many times have we heard this? Just these few words and I can "see" this plowman. Like him, I too search for that treasure that is buried inside, in our hearts. I, too, look for that spiritual wealth that Christ gives us.

Beginning from these roots, Christians have always used teaching stories. We activate the imagination and visualize the story. We imagine, i.e., we hold in the faculty of our imagination the spiritual reality that we wish to experience. Visualization has always been a part—even the best part—of storytelling. Later this practice of visualization was formalized as a spiritual tool. The Benedictine monks developed visualization into the practice of Lectio Divina which I will describe in Part IV. Other practices arose using visualization which I describe in this chapter and the next two.

In this modern day, we are cut off from our early roots of imaging. Unfortunately, this tends to make our practice less powerful for us, because of the inner doubts that we harbor. Perhaps, after all, we are just "imagining" a God, and not really experiencing anything except our imagination. Thus, instead of following the signposts erected by those who have journeyed here before us, we are constantly asking if this is truly the way to God. God help us, because our doubts paralyze us. In our modern world, we have been taught that only the things outside of ourselves have any reality. If we image something within, we doubt that it has any reality or power. We dismiss the image and the practice on the grounds that we are simply imagining this. "It is really just an illusion, and all that you do with this practice is fool yourself." So we cut ourselves off from the artesian waters that bubble up inside of us, the living water of God.

This criticism, that we are simply hallucinating something, misses the real power of the faculty of imagination. The Empire State Building, and every other thing that human beings have intentionally created, began in the imagination. In perfect truth-fulness, you could say that imagination created the Empire State Building. Furthermore, somebody had to "imagine" the house you are living in, the car you drive, the clothes you wear. On closer examination, you will find that real life for us starts on the inside and moves out into the world. Using visualization simply makes us aware of this truth.

This second mode of visualization uses words to evoke inner pictures, sounds and feelings, in order to make the spiritual realities more present to us. The best word pictures are not limited to the visual; they include elements from all of the sense modalities. Sensory words are used to evoke an immediate reality in the listener. The internal picture does not have to be crystal clear to be effective. In fact, most people do not "see" inside with this kind of clarity. It is okay if the picture is fuzzy; what is necessary is that we have a felt sense of the words.

The tool of imagination is very powerful. The practices of visualization allow us to use this powerful tool for spiritual growth. The following exercise taps the power of visualization to take us into the Presence of Jesus. Rather than reading the text below while trying to meditate, you will find it more powerful if you tape the exercise, or have someone read it to you slowly.

SPIRITUAL EXERCISE 7
VISUALIZING GOSPEL IMAGES

1. Position your body comfortably, spine erect, on a chair or cushions.

2. Become aware of the physical sensations which flow through you. Close your eyes and experience the stream of sensation that courses through your physical body. No need to change them. No need to judge them. Simply let yourself feel deeply the multitude of sensations that cascade through your body. Gently focus on the sensations in your head...in your neck and shoulders...your elbows...your wrists and the palms of your hands...the sensations in your knees...your ankles and the soles of your feet.

3. Now open your mind and let yourself picture this story...
Last night, you heard that Jesus—the one everyone calls
the Messiah—has come to town. It was late, after dark,
and your friend didn't know where He was staying. But
this morning, you resolve to search the community until
you find Him. So you hurriedly eat a bit of bread to take
the edge off your hunger, and walk out your door.

The streets don't smell so bad in the morning. The cold
keeps the smell in check. Your eyes range down the
alley—it can hardly be called a street—twisting between
the houses. All built of the same red sandstone and mud
as yours. All low, with a few windows covered by rags.

You search. You walk to the center of town to the syna-
gogue. You heard that the rabbi likes to teach there. Only
a few others are about, a few of the young ones like yourself. You stop and ask them. They don't know either; they
are here for the same reason that you are, to hear the
rabbi teach. Nobody seems to know in whose house He is
staying. There is a fear that ripples through you, "Maybe
He isn't here after all." You walk again through the town.
Quickly.

As you walk, you see a knot of people down by the lake.
"Maybe they know." You walk toward them. They all seem
to be facing the lake. "That is strange; I wonder what is
going on down there." As you approach the fringes of the
group, you see that they face a man, who is speaking to
them.

He seems ordinary-looking enough. "Could this be Him?
His voice is one of authority...but I am too far back to
make out the words." So you worm your way forward. And
the man says:

"The reign of God is like a buried treasure which a man
found in a field. He hid it again, and rejoicing at his find
went and sold all he had and bought the field."

The words seem to burn into your heart. "Isn't that what I have been looking for all these years? The buried treasure deep within? This rabbi says that you have to go buy it. It is worth everything I have, certainly. I would gladly sell all if I just could find that treasure. Where do I find this inner gold, rabbi?" you ask inside. "Where do I look?"

And as you say that, He looks at you—LOOKS straight into your soul. Like He knows the trouble in your heart. And He says, "Come follow me. Take my yoke upon you, for I am gentle and humble of heart."

4. Respond to the Lord in whatever way you feel called to do. Let yourself go in your imagining, and see what happens.

5. When you find your attention wandering to other things, do not berate yourself. Gently bring your awareness back to this scene. Watch your Lord who says to you, "Come follow me." See what He asks of you. Let yourself rest here.

(To close your meditation)

6. When you are ready, let yourself come back to this place. Let the feeling return to your feet...your hands...your face. Take a deep breath, and open your eyes. Take a moment and look around the room to reorient yourself.

As you practice this exercise several times, you will notice two changes taking place. First, your attention will begin to have a stronger focus. It won't jump around so much. As a result, your meditation will deepen and become more rich over time. Of course, you may still have some trouble maintaining attentional focus. This will be with you until the end stages of the journey. But over time, you should notice a perceptible strengthening. If this focus seems to deteriorate, go back and practice Exercise 6, visualizing a simple image, until you can hold a visual image in mind for ten seconds or so without distraction.

The second change is that we move from an active mode of awareness to a more receptive mode. In the active mode, our attention ranges outward from us, in an active, acquisitive manner. As we begin the practice of turning inward in spiritual pursuits, we first use this active mode of awareness because that is the tool with which we feel most comfortable. In the course of our practice, however, this active mode will gradually change, seemingly of its own accord. We will find ourselves learning to be open and we will begin to trust in our meditation.

In the face of God's doing, our doing counts for very little in this spiritual work. Ultimately, it is God who does the work within us. We simply prepare the place for Him, according to His directions. Hence, we need to be aware of and develop this receptive component, because this stance will help us move more quickly into alignment with God's will. This is part of the paradox of deep spiritual work: we move most quickly by not doing.

The Third Mode of Visualization

Initially in our visualization practice, we used a visual stimulus to assist us in making an internal image. Then we went to a word picture that was prompted by external stimuli. Finally, in the third mode, we produce a visual image that does not depend on any external stimulus, but is entirely generated from within.

The third visual mode uses an internally generated image in the manner of a story. The three components of this mode are: 1) total reliance on internal generation of the visual stimuli; 2) a complex, and dynamic picture; and 3) placing ourselves as the central character in the flow of action. The process of meditation becomes more internal, our attention becomes more focused, and our emotions are stirred up.

As we come to this stage of visualization practice, we can begin to take full advantage of the power of the imagination, and harness it fully to work toward spiritual growth. Depending on our needs and our inner wounds, we can visualize the different aspects of God's nature. We can "see" God as Father, as Mother, as Friend, as Lover; all of the aspects of the Divine are available to us. Here we begin to open to the infinite nature of God.

I typically use this mode of visualization for inner healing. All of us carry scars from emotional wounds which we have received. These scars protect hurt places that are buried deep within our unconscious. These hurt places keep us from knowing God's love fully. At a certain point, our emotional wounds literally inhibit our spiritual growth. How can I know God's love, when I am deeply angry at someone? While our anger may hurt the other person, it certainly hurts us. Before we can progress very far spiritually, we must resolve our psychological wounds. The inner wounds that we carry, all of the emotional scars from feeling unloved and unlovable, need to be resolved. Fortunately, there is a way to use the visualization process to further this.

In recent years, psychologists have learned a great deal about the role of the inner child in carrying old trauma into the present. Since Transactional Analysis identified the child ego state that is in every adult, a number of therapeutic methods have arisen to heal the wounds which the inner child carries. Following Morton Kelsey's lead,[51] I use the third mode of visualization as a way of using the spiritual power of Christ to address the hurts that the inner child carries.

SPIRITUAL EXERCISE 8
EXPERIENCING THE POWER OF CHRIST'S LOVE

1. Position your body comfortably, spine erect, on a chair or cushions.

2. Ground yourself in your physical sensations. Close your eyes and slowly become aware of the sensations of your physical body. Feel the sensations as they flow through you. The sensations in your head...in your neck and shoulders...your elbows...your wrists and the palms of your hands...the sensations in your knees...your ankles and the soles of your feet.

3. Now allow your attention to collect in the region of your heart. Imagine that you are very small, and walk within... into that vast space inside of you.

4. As you move within, it feels like you are walking down a long dark tunnel. You see a dot of light in front of you, marking the tunnel's end. You move toward it...As you leave the tunnel, you find yourself on a small rise, overlooking a beautiful mountain meadow. The grass is green

and lush. You feel the warmth of the sun on your skin. The stir of the breeze. A sense of calm arises in you.

5. Take a moment and explore your meadow. Let yourself wander over by the stream. Put your hand in and feel the coldness of the water. Lie down and listen to the birds. Let yourself go.

6. As you continue to explore, you notice a large rise with a spreading oak tree on its crest. There is something about this place that intrigues you—you feel attracted by it. So let yourself wander over there.

   As you draw closer, you notice that the pull seems to increase, like some palpable force which beckons you hither. You notice that there is someone seated under the tree, someone dressed in white. As you get closer, you can see that it is a man, with a very warm and welcoming look on his face. There is something about him that is compelling.

   And then you realize that this is Jesus, your Lord.

7. You slowly approach, feeling the multitude of conflicting emotions which arise within you. He stands and greets you, welcomes you in His arms. As He does so, all of the hurts, all of the confusion and the pain come welling up from inside you. He sees and understands. He does not reject you, but sits down and holds you.

   Feel His arms around you. The loving-kindness which flows from Him. The warm feeling of acceptance and love with which He enfolds you. Take the inner hurts which have plagued you and show them to your Lord. Ask Him for healing. Let yourself rest here for a time...

8. When your attention wanders to other things, do not berate yourself. Gently bring your awareness back to Jesus and let yourself rest here, enfolded in His love.

(To close your meditation)

9. When you are ready, come back to this place. Let the feeling return to your feet...your hands...your face. Take a
   deep breath, and open your eyes.

This exercise is simply one example of what we can do with a
Christ-centered meditation. There are a number of additional
things worth exploring. For example, as we get comfortable with
Christ in this way—a sort of silent holding and healing—we may
ask Him to guide us in other ways. We can ask Him questions; we
can ask Him to take us on a journey that will disclose those
actions of ours that keep us from more fully realizing His love. We
can ask Him to introduce us to the Father, to the Holy Spirit.
What we can accomplish here is limited only by our imagination.

I often ask the Lord to hold the child that is within me. That
hurt little boy inside of me often has needs that I cannot fulfill.
Jesus, the Son of God, does not have the limitations that I do. Let
yourself explore the boundless love that is accessible to you
through this meditation.

Some may wonder if using imagination is a valid way of moving
into God's Presence. Perhaps all that happens here is simply an
imagining, a fantasy; something that has absolutely nothing to do
with the Divine. Perhaps this is just a sophisticated way of fooling
ourselves.

In spiritual work, this kind of concern comes up frequently,
since we cannot "see" with our physical eyes the goal of our journey. The disciples also had these concerns, so we stand in good
company when we wonder in these ways. Jesus responded to these
concerns by inviting the disciples to look at the fruit of the work.
By the fruit we know the tree. By the results of the practice, we
know whether the practice has validity in moving us toward God.
When our hurts, however slowly, begin to heal, then we know we
have been with the Divine Healer.

Visualization is a powerful modality for our spiritual growth. By
means of visualization, we can explore aspects of God that are
inaccessible to the discursive intellect. By means of visualization
we can heal inner wounds that keep us from enjoying fully the love

of God. There are tremendous spiritual riches to be mined, using the tool of visualization.

By no means is the material above the last word on the spiritual uses of visualization. For a deeper exploration than is possible in this introductory work, I would refer you to *The Spiritual Exercises* of Ignatius.[52] Before you turn to Ignatius, however, practice and develop these three visual modalities. Use the richness of the sensory equipment which God gave you to see the giver of these gifts. Look beyond the gifts and see the giver...

Chapter 13

Visualizing Aspects of God

There are a multitude of applications for visualization. Many spiritual problems or dilemmas that you may face can be resolved by using this tool properly. To assist you with the application process, and to indicate some of the kinds of problems which visualization can address successfully, I have applied the tool of visualization to several issues below.

God as Father/God as Mother

Some people cannot relate easily to God as Father as a result of the many painful experiences that they had with their human fathers. For them, a huge barrier inhibits any flow of feeling. In these cases, the separation between the soul and God is formidable, like some vast abyss.

When I began the meditative part of my spiritual journey, in my twenties, I was so angry at my father that I even had a hard time saying the Lord's Prayer. I was not about to pray to any Father that treated me as harshly as I perceived I had been treated. A wise old priest suggested that I might be better off thinking of God as my Mother in heaven, until I came to better grips with my anger at my father. I did so and was able to continue my spiritual journey. At a later date, I was able to resolve my feelings toward my father, and since then have found great power in the notion of God as Father.

We are created in God's image, "in the divine image He created them, male and female He created them."[53] Although most Christians, and the Jews before them, have consistently interpreted God as Father, erasing the feminine qualities of the Divine, scripture says differently. In the Divine, there is both male and female. This suggests that both sets of qualities are accessible to us and important to us. I would encourage you to explore them with the following meditations.

**SPIRITUAL EXERCISE 9
GOD AS FATHER**

1. Position your body comfortably, spine erect, on a chair or cushions.

2. Ground yourself in your physical sensations. Close your eyes and slowly become aware of the sensations of your physical body. Feel the sensations as they flow through you. The sensations in your head...in your neck and shoulders...your elbows...your wrists and the palms of your hands...the sensations in your knees...your ankles and the soles of your feet.

3. Allow your attention to collect in the region of your heart. Imagine that you are very small, and walk within...into that vast and wonderful space inside of you.

4. As you move within, let your awareness be open to the Presence of God, your Father. You may see Him as a huge figure, seated on a throne; as a person, much like yourself; or without shape and form. Let yourself be open to the Divine Father...see how He manifests Himself to you this time.

5. As you stand in His Presence, feel the qualities which flow from Him. The deep father-love, that is now firm and demanding, and now nurturing and healing.

   Feel the directness of His Presence. The firm and strong purpose. The "I-will-not-be-thwarted" aspect of the Father. Feel the Father's purpose for you: what does He expect of you? What is His will for you?

6. Let yourself rest in the Father. Tell Him about the pain of your living. The frustrations. Ask for His guidance. Be in Him.

---

7. When you find your attention wandering to other things, do not berate yourself. Gently bring your awareness back to the Father's Presence. Let yourself rest here.

(To close your meditation)

8. When you are ready, let yourself come back to this place. Let the feeling return to your feet...your hands...your face. Take a deep breath, and open your eyes.

I have been fascinated by my students over the years, and their stories of what has happened to them in this meditation. For each one, with each particular set of hurts, God has manifested Himself differently. This is the Holy Spirit working in each of our hearts to heal what has been wounded or broken. If we can sit with our wounds and bring these to our heavenly Father; if we can sit with our pain and reveal it to God, then healing takes place.

Sometimes, of course, we cannot bear the tension of this. It hurts too much to uncover this old pain and to sit with it. It hurts too much to go to a heavenly Father who wears the face and manner of our hurtful human father. In these cases, it is important to go into psychotherapy and address these issues. Having a therapist guide you, step-by-step, and accompany you as you explore the pain will make it easier to resolve this old trauma. There is no shame in getting help. Our journey is too painful to walk alone. That is why we have each other. And why God sends us His Son.

God as Mother

There is a different "feel" to a mother's love. It has different qualities. It feeds us in ways that are quite different from a father's love. We know that to be whole persons, we need both parents. Likewise, to be spiritually whole, we need to receive love from both aspects of the Divine. The church has often used Mary, the Mother of God, to focus and carry the feminine aspect of God into the hearts of believers. It is not insignificant that Mary is often accorded more importance than the Father in the Roman Catholic and Eastern Orthodox churches. Many Protestants, unfortunately, are entirely cut off from this aspect of the Divine. The feminine face of God is more accepting, more gentle. There is a different quality here, a different kind of nurture. I would encourage you to explore this nurture directly with the following meditation.

SPIRITUAL EXERCISE 10
GOD AS MOTHER

1. Position your body comfortably, spine erect, on a chair or cushions.

2. Become aware of the physical sensations which flow through you. Close your eyes and experience the stream of sensation that courses through your physical body. No need to change them. No need to judge them. Simply let yourself feel deeply the multitude of sensations that cascade through your body. Gently focus on the sensations in your head...in your neck and shoulders...your elbows...your wrists and the palms of your hands...the sensations in your knees...your ankles and the soles of your feet.

3. Allow your attention to collect in the region of your heart. Imagine that you are very small, and walk within...into that vast and wonderful space inside of you.

4. As you move within, let your awareness be open to the Presence of God, your Mother, the Divine Feminine. You may see Her as a huge figure, seated on a throne; as a person, much like yourself; or without shape and form. Let yourself be open to the Divine Mother...see how She reveals Herself to you.

5. As you stand in Her Presence, feel Her warmth, acceptance, and nurture. Feel the qualities which flow from Her. The deep mother–love that enfolds and soothes you, wiping your worries away, enabling you to come more fully into Her Presence.

Feel the closeness of Her Presence. Be aware of the softness rooted in Her underlying strength. The compassion.

The relatedness that you feel with Her and with all creation through Her. Feel Her purpose for you: what is Her
desire for you? What does She want from you? What is Her
will for you?

6. Let yourself rest in the Mother. Tell Her about the pain of
   your living. The frustrations. Ask for Her guidance. Be in
   Her.

7. When your attention wanders to other things, do not
   berate yourself. Gently bring your awareness back to your
   Mother's Presence. Let yourself rest here.

(To close your meditation)

8. When you are ready, come back to this place. Let the feeling return to your feet...your hands...your face. Take a
   deep breath, and open your eyes.

You may have quite different reactions to these two aspects of the
Divine. Note the differences. What does this say about you? Are
there hurts from a human parent that come up during your meditation that need to be resolved and healed? If this is so, go to the
image of God as the opposite parent and ask for assistance and
guidance. So if you have differences with your human father that
you cannot seem to resolve, go to God as Mother, and ask Her help.

Often when you do this, you will not get a verbal response. The
inner figure of God may simply sit and be with you. Alternatively,
the Divine may move and take you some place. No matter where
the Divine takes you, go there. Even if you are afraid, go there and
see what happens. Leave only when the action ceases and you
have some deeper understanding.

Sometimes when you ask, God will speak to you directly. In my
experience, this is relatively rare. More often, there is a felt sense of
God communicating with you—as if God has written something in
your heart that you know is there, but you can't quite make it out. It
may be that you cannot bear to see what is there at the present
time. So simply take what you experience, and attempt to live it.

We need to adopt a flexible stance toward what arises in meditation. People often get carried away by their wishful imaginings,

imaginings that have nothing to do with the Divine Reality. Sometimes we get sidetracked into areas that are counterproductive to spiritual growth. We need to develop a spirit of discernment as we progress on the journey. A useful tool here is to remember our original intention with these spiritual exercises: to know and be with God. Not to be special, not to have special and exciting experiences, but simply to be in the Divine Presence.

God as Friend

God comes to us in many ways. The Divine is not limited to Father or Mother. In each different way that God comes, a different facet is revealed to us. One of the ways which is most useful to us is that of friend or guide. Often, what we need spiritually is not so much the comfort and love of a parent. We simply need friendship and guidance—a wiser older brother or sister to take us a little further down the road. The story in the gospel of Luke about Jesus' appearance to the disciples on the road to Emmaus[54] is one example of this incarnation of our Lord.

Using this modality is especially important after we have made our initial beginning in the spiritual journey. In the beginning, most of us need the strong nurture of a parent. We are so broken, our hurts are so deep, that only the strong love of God as parent can mend our souls. After a time, we need a different kind of nurture.

There are many parallels between our development as children and our spiritual development. Just as a child depends first on his parents, and then moves toward his peers, so it is also in the spiritual journey. The following exercise is designed as a guide for this kind of work.

SPIRITUAL EXERCISE 11
GOD AS FRIEND

1. Position your body comfortably, spine erect, on a chair or cushions.

2. Ground yourself in your physical sensations. Close your eyes and slowly become aware of the sensations of your physical body. Feel the sensations as they flow through

you. The sensations in your head...in your neck and shoulders...your elbows... your wrists and the palms of your hands... the sensations in your knees...your ankles and the soles of your feet.

3. Allow your attention to collect in the region of your heart. Imagine that you are very small, and walk within...into that vast and wonderful space inside of you.

4. As you move within, imagine that you are walking down a country lane. Feel the uneven surface of the dirt and grass under your feet. The warmth of the sun on your face. Let yourself gaze upon the green meadows and the deep blue of the sky. And up ahead, you see someone else walking. You notice that you are gradually catching up.

5. As you draw near, this person stops and turns around, waiting for you. The stranger's face has a pleasant look, and your heart is filled with a surge of joy that you can't explain. You walk together for a time in silence. You feel the qualities which flow from your traveling companion. The deep friendliness and acceptance. Your companion doesn't demand anything of you. It is sufficient to be together.

After a time, you begin to talk about your life—your trials and joys, your doubts and troubles. Your companion listens quietly, perhaps asking—with a questioning look—for more information. You find yourself pouring out your heart. It feels wonderful to let go of the burden you have carried.

Feel the comfort of this Presence. The absolute reliability. Feel the inward support and caring. If you wish, ask your traveling companion for guidance and advice. Your companion may or may not speak, depending upon your own readiness. If your companion speaks, listen closely, and resolve to follow in these suggestions.

6. Let yourself rest with your spiritual companion. Let yourself *be* in this Presence.

7. When you find your attention wandering to other things, do not berate yourself. Gently bring your awareness back to your traveling companion's Presence. Let yourself rest here.

(To close your meditation)

8. When you are ready, come back to this place. Let the feeling return to your feet...your hands...your face. Take a deep breath, and open your eyes.

This meditation is open-ended, inviting continued exploration. Like most of the exercises in this book, it is not sufficient to do it once or twice. Each exercise needs to be repeated daily over a period of weeks and months for maximum effectiveness.

The Use of Icons and Other Holy Images

From the very earliest times, human beings have made representations of the Divine. Within Christianity, however, there was an initial resistance to making any images of God because of the influence of the second commandment not to make graven images. Around the fourth century, Christian representational art began to be seen in the Eastern churches, and several bishops, notably Eusebius of Caesarea, speak in their letters of icons of Christ, the Virgin Mary, and the apostles.

Icons have traditionally been used in the Eastern Orthodox Church as objects of devotion. The Greek word for "icon" means "image." This is the same word that is used in the first chapter of Genesis in the Greek Bible, when God made humanity in the *image* of the Divine. This word is used by St. Paul when he says that Jesus Christ is the image of the invisible God.[55] Icons, therefore, are further examples of the principle of incarnation. They are symbols which point to the invisible reality of the sacred. Thus, they are also a means by which we can make contact with that Divine Reality.

Icons are often described by those in the Eastern Orthodox churches as "doors" which open onto the Divine. Images speak very directly to us. They bypass intellectual and discursive thought, and speak directly to the heart. Thus, icons are a door which not only allows us to experience the Divine; they also can be a door into the depths of our own hearts.

There is a stillness deep within each of us. Below the noise of thoughts and desires, there is an inner stillness which opens onto the Divine. When we come upon this stillness, we begin to explore God's work in humanity. St. John of Damascus said that "the Word made flesh has deified flesh."[56] This transfiguration of humanity is found, not in someone else, but in our own flesh, our own hearts. Icons are one of the several doors through which we can come to experience this transfiguration.

Thus, icons are to be experienced; not only in a visual sense, but also through your heart. Let yourself stand before an icon and open the door to the sacred reality, which stands just beyond the image. It is as if a membrane separates these two strands of reality, the secular and the sacred. The icon is the open door which allows you passage, which allows you to see that other reality immediately.

While the use of icons for prayer, and the theology which guides their use, is somewhat foreign to those raised in Western Christianity, I would invite you to explore this ancient method of meditation. In my experience, I have found this use of images to be very powerful.

SPIRITUAL EXERCISE 12
USING ICONS IN MEDITATION

1. Position your body comfortably, spine erect, on a chair or cushions. Position the icon in front of you, so that you can look easily at it. You may have it on the wall, or hold it in your hands.

2. Ground yourself in your physical sensations. Close your eyes and slowly become aware of the sensations of your physical body. Feel the sensations as they flow through you. The sensations in your head...in your neck and shoulders...your elbows...your wrists and the palms of your

hands...the sensations in your knees...your ankles and the soles of your feet.

3. Now allow your attention to collect in the region of your heart. Instead of going fully inside, as we usually do, open your eyes and gaze into the eyes of the image of your icon. Maintain the center of your attention in your heart region.

4. Let yourself feel the sacred Reality that shines through the figure in the icon. Don't "try" to do this. Simply rest your attention in this reality. Open your heart to this Reality, and rest your attention there.

5. When you find your attention wandering to other things, do not berate yourself. Gently bring your awareness back to the image and the sacred Presence. Let yourself rest here.

(To close your meditation)

6. When you are ready, let yourself come back to this place. Let the feeling return to your feet...your hands...your face. Take a deep breath, and look around yourself.

Because not all of you will have immediate access to an icon to practice this meditation, an illustration is provided of an icon of Jesus Christ.[57] This icon was produced in Constantinople in the sixth century and currently resides at St. Catherine's Monastery in the Sinai desert.

In addition to formal meditation, there are several other ways in which you can use icons for spiritual development.[58] For example, you can collect religious images that provoke you to develop certain spiritual qualities in yourself. St. Seraphim of Sarov is a favorite saint of mine. St. Seraphim was a Russian of the nineteenth century, a man of deep prayer and powerful spiritual discernment.[59] Seraphim exemplifies purity of intention. By means of his prayer, he moved deeply into unitive states with God. He performed many wonders and brought many to a deeper experience of Christ.

To cultivate those qualities in myself, especially the quality of pure intention, I have a number of icons of Seraphim: one hangs above my desk now as I write, and one hangs in my office. I use the icon to remind myself of where I am spiritually, of where I could be with the effort of a Seraphim, and to provoke myself to develop a clearer and more pure intent.

All that is necessary to use icons or other holy images in this way is to take your own inventory and identify those areas in which you are spiritually weak. Then search the history of the church for those who have gone before you who were especially strong in these areas where you are weak. Look for icons of these saints and place them in your living space. When your gaze falls upon the icon, make a rule that you reflect on the qualities of that particular saint, no matter what you are doing. In this gentle way, you will cultivate these qualities in yourself.

Unfortunately, we have a tendency to habituate to visual images rather quickly. We buy the most wonderful picture in the world, hang it in a prominent place, and within a year we do not see it anymore. Because of this tendency, I have found it helpful to rotate the religious images around me. This keeps the practice fresh. In this way, some aspect of the Divine is always "new" to me. This seems to provoke a greater depth than when I leave the sacred image in the same place forever.

Our spiritual journey is not something that should be reserved for special times or special places. Our spiritual journey is at the center of our life, whether we know this or not. So it is useful to look for ways to integrate our journey into God with our everyday experiences. Images provide a simple way to begin this integration.

Chapter 14

Visualizing the Spiritual Journey

Now that you have learned the basic techniques of visualization, it is time to introduce journey meditation. Journey meditations are a relatively recent addition to the spiritual armament. They have their roots in the teaching stories of Christ, and are related to Carl Jung's method of active imagination[60] and Roberto Assagioli's method of initiated symbol projection.[61] In journey meditation, you visualize going on a journey of some sort. Much like *The Pilgrim's Progress*,[62] the journey serves as an allegory for your own spiritual journey. You provide yourself with a basic structure for the journey, and then you gently look for symbols and images which will spontaneously arise as you travel within. These symbols can be viewed as devices from the collective unconscious which will aid you in deepening your spiritual life.

Most often, our inner journeys will assist us in identifying and resolving emotional hurts which have blocked us spiritually. Let me give you an example of this process from my own life. For a long time I was unable to release the anger I carried toward my mother. I believed that she did irreparable harm to many of those closest to her. While I felt that I had overcome the hurt she did to me, I was angry for those who had not resolved the pain they received from her. This resulted in a certain hardness of heart within me. This inner hardness kept me from progressing spiritually. For a long time, I could get so far and no farther in my spiritual practice. I was inhibited from the unitive states; I would go right up to them, and something that I couldn't recognize would hold me back.

In a journey meditation, I asked God for a guide who could help me with this problem. He provided a wise old woman, who served as my inner guide. She took me to an ugly, many-headed reptile that was absolutely revolting to look upon. Before I could go on, I had to kill the beast. Everything I tried proved ineffective: spears, guns, even the atomic bomb! Finally, at my wits end, I appealed to my inner guide. She said that I must embrace this horrible monster. Barely holding in check my tremendous disgust, I did so. As we embraced, much of the bitterness and rancor that I had held came pouring out of me. As it left, I found that I was embracing my mother.

This was the start of much inner work to heal this old wound. When I had finished, I was once again able to make progress in the spiritual life. What Jesus teaches about binding sins is true. I found that the words of the Lord's Prayer, "Forgive us our sins, as we forgive those who sin against us" were literally true. The task, for those who would progress spiritually, is to find what we are holding onto, and to make a decision to release that pain. Only then will we, ourselves, know the fullness of God's love.

Journey meditations provide a vehicle for this identification and release. Because these journeys are often somewhat involved, it is best to have someone read the following exercises to you very slowly, or to tape record them.

SPIRITUAL EXERCISE 13
THE JOURNEY UP THE MOUNTAIN

1. Position your body comfortably, spine erect, on a chair or cushions.

2. Become aware of the physical sensations which flow through you. Close your eyes and experience the stream of sensation of that courses through your physical body. No need to change them. No need to judge them. Simply let yourself feel deeply the multitude of sensations that cascade through your body. Gently focus on the sensations in your head...in your neck and shoulders...your elbows...your wrists and the palms of your hands...the sensations in your knees...your ankles and the soles of your feet.

3. Now allow your attention to collect in the region of your heart. Imagine that you are very small, and walk within... into that vast space inside of you.

4. As you move within, it feels like you are walking down a long dark tunnel. You see a dot of light in front of you,

marking the tunnel's end. You move toward it...As you leave the tunnel, you find yourself on a small rise, overlooking the foothills of a great, snowcapped mountain range. There is a footpath in front of you, leading into the mountains. You follow it up.

5. As you walk, you are aware of the bright sun shining, and the warmth of it on your skin...The smell of the pine forest around you...The incredible beauty. You become aware of the effort you are making as you climb. The thinness of the air as you breathe more deeply. You notice that the path is getting smaller and more difficult. Finally, you are up above the tree line. You pause for a moment and then go on. Your path leads you up to the high places and into the cliffs. As you turn past a huge boulder, you see here the path ends. There is a cave up ahead. The path ends here.

6. As you approach, you see that the entrance to the cave is blocked by an ancient, iron-studded door. You push the door with all your strength, and it grudgingly opens. You enter, lighting a torch from the pile by the door. The cave takes you downward. You go through vast caverns—so large that you cannot see their end. You go through winding tunnels. Anticipation builds. You keep going down; it seems like forever.

7. Finally, in the distance, you make out a light. This is it! What you have struggled all this way to find. You approach slowly now. You can see that the light comes from an entrance-way on your left. You pause before you look, gathering your courage. Then you turn into the door and look. Take a moment, and see what is there.

Go into the space and begin to explore what is there. If there are people or creatures, go and interact with them. What do they have for you? Perhaps there will be a wise old soul who can teach and guide you. Perhaps a fierce beast that represents some inner passion. Let yourself explore...

---

8. When you find your attention wandering to other things, do not berate yourself. Gently bring your awareness back to your journey.

(To close your meditation)

9. When you are ready, let yourself come back to this place. Let the feeling return to your feet...your hands...your face. Take a deep breath, and open your eyes.

This guided visualization can be done many times with benefit. To spark other adventures which will change the content of the journey, you can vary the locale. In addition to the mountain and cave imagery, I have found that going into a primeval forest, into the depths of the ocean, and into heaven or hell can be useful.

These visualizations are not particularly helpful in facilitating the development of attention. Rather, their power lies in taking you into the unconscious to explore the inner pain that blocks you from going deeper. If you will, this is a kind of spiritual psychotherapy.

The following exercise was given to me by another psychologist, Dr. Ronald Jue, the former president of the Association for Transpersonal Psychology. Dr. Jue developed this exercise to help his clients access the inner resources that they need for deep spiritual work. This exercise is very powerful, since it accesses the deep inner wisdom of the true self. It gives us a method for tapping this resource in a conscious way, so that our strength can minister to our weakness.

SPIRITUAL EXERCISE 14
THE JOURNEY FOR INNER ASSISTANCE

1. Position your body comfortably, spine erect, on a chair or cushions.

2. Ground yourself in your physical sensations. Close your eyes and slowly become aware of the sensations of your physical body. Feel the sensations as they flow through you. The sensations in your head...in your neck and shoul-

ders...your elbows...your wrists and the palms of your hands...the sensations in your knees...your ankles and the soles of your feet.

3. Now allow your attention to collect in the region of your heart. Imagine that you are very small, and walk within...into that vast space inside of you.

4. In this space, deep in your heart, imagine that you are standing on a sunny ocean beach. You can feel the warmth of the sun on your skin. The cool ocean breeze as it streams over your body, the smell of salt in the air. You watch the sea gulls as they hover and swoop. And as you look into the sky, you see another bird, high up, that seems somehow to draw you. As you watch, the bird descends, gradually growing larger. You become aware that this is no ordinary bird. It is huge. And it comes to ground on the beach in front of you.

5. The bird looks at you—it seems intelligent. And it moves its head as if to say, "Come on. Get on so that we can go. You are wasting time." So you climb on his back, grab hold firmly, and you are off. The bird soars into the air, his strong wings taking you high above the clouds. And above all there is a sense of knowing that this is right for you. You are going to your destiny.

6. After traveling over the ocean for hours, you notice that you are descending. Your bird has begun to circle an island. It is a lovely tropical island, an old volcano rising from the center, forests all around, and an unspoiled white beach surrounding the entire island. There is no evidence of habitation. Your bird lands on a beach. You get off, stretch, and see a path leading into the rain forest. The bird indicates that you should follow it.

7. You walk through the forest with a deep sense of awe. The trees tower above you, and there is a reverent stillness. It is very tranquil. As you climb toward the mountain, you come upon a large meadow. There is a very old church

here, now beginning to fall into ruin. There is a sense of mystery and power about it. You approach it carefully, and walk around the outside, looking at it. Finally, you enter.

8. You stop for a moment as your eyes get accustomed to the gloom. There is something about the altar that draws you forward. You approach slowly. There is a growing certainty that you should be here, and as you approach, a Voice gently says, "You are in need, beloved child, so I have gifted you with three articles of power to help you in your spiritual journey. Use them wisely." As you come to the altar, you see that there are three things on its surface: one to the left, one to the right, and one in the center. Take a moment and look at each item. Let each item coalesce in your consciousness. Then look at the next item, and the next. You do not need to know how to use the item now, just identify it.

9. When you have identified all of the items, go back to the first. Let it speak to you. What is its purpose? How does this article want to be used? If the answer is not clear after a time of receptive sitting, then go on to the next. Usually, however, what you should do with the item will be clear to you. Take the power that is released by this knowledge into yourself. See yourself using this power in your everyday life. See yourself growing stronger and more confident, so that you are able to withstand the rigors of the spiritual journey. See yourself as whole.

10. When you have understood all of your articles of power, return to your bird, and go back to the mainland. Take with you the knowledge and power you have gained. As you land on the beach, thank your avian guide for his assistance.

(To close your meditation)

11. When you are ready, come back to this place. Let the feeling return to your feet…your hands…your face. Take a deep breath, and open your eyes.

The first part of this meditation is a voyage into the unconscious to ask for the assistance that can always be found there. The second part is to make sense of the items of power, to understand how they are to be used. From time to time, you may have trouble either seeing the articles on the altar, or understanding their use. If this happens, don't be hard on yourself. Gently come back to this process again and again until you understand. The value of these spiritual exercises is: 1) to help you develop vivid imagery, and 2) to identify and address the psychospiritual roadblocks that interfere with your deeper development. These exercises are useful in identifying and resolving some of your emotional dilemmas.

Our old emotional wounds are roadblocks which inhibit our progress on the spiritual journey. As we move forward, it is necessary to balance our healing of these inner wounds with the cultivation of attention and a receptive attitude. Our healing is a gift from the Lord Jesus. The cultivation of attention and receptivity are tools which we must develop for further progress.

A Meditation on Dying

The primary element which keeps us from progressing spiritually is fear. We are afraid. Our Lord Jesus recognizes this, and when He returned from the grave, His first words were, "Fear not."[63] What we fear varies from person to person, but the results of fear are identical in each of us. We are afraid, and so we either run from our fears, or we paralyze ourselves and cannot approach them. Think of all of the fears that we have had about meditation. Although we may long for a unitive experience with the Divine, most people are deathly afraid of what will happen in that moment.

Common to us all is the fear of dying. Even those bold people who confidently assert that they are not afraid of dying have a fear of dying. It is useful to contrast this with the attitudes found in the early church. Did you know that the saints' days that we celebrate commemorate not the birthday of the saint, but the death day? The day of death is called their "birthday into eternity." This is such a profoundly different attitude from our own that it deserves our exploration.

This ancient Christian attitude toward death came from being part of a believing group that regularly faced death. From the knowledge developed by experience and faith, early Christians learned not to fear death in the ways that we do today. One of my favorite saints is St. Polycarp, bishop of Smyrna, who was martyred on February 23, 155 A.D. Polycarp was an old man of 86 years, who had been a Christian all of his life.[64] His roots go back to the times of the apostles, and it is said that he knew St. John and learned from him directly. Polycarp was a man of such transparent holiness that all in the community loved him.

In one of the periodic persecutions of Christians, Polycarp was arrested and brought before the Romans in the arena. The police who arrested him were so taken by his holiness, his calm demeanor, and the palpable feeling of spiritual power around him that some of them felt badly and encouraged him to escape. When he refused, he was brought to the arena. There the chief of police begged him to make the incense offering to the emperor. Polycarp refused and was brought before the proconsul. In front of an arena of people howling for his blood, the proconsul demanded that Polycarp "curse Christ."

Polycarp replied, "Eighty–six years I have served Him, and He never did me any wrong. How can I blaspheme my King who saved me?" And then, so there could be no mistake, Polycarp went on to say, "Listen plainly: I am a Christian. If you desire to learn the teaching of Christianity, appoint a day and give me a hearing." (Imagine saying that to your judge and executioner!) Then the proconsul threatened the bishop with wild beasts. Polycarp expressed no fear, and said, "Call them." But because the beasts had just eaten, they would not make good sport, and so the proconsul decided to burn Polycarp. After the wood was gathered, Polycarp walked onto the pyre without assistance, and told his executioners not to bother nailing him, he would stand there to be burned, "For He who grants me to endure the fire will enable me also to remain on the pyre unmoved, without the security you desire from the nails." So he stood there in the fire until he died.

This approach to dying is radically different from our own. There is a freedom found here in Polycarp and many of the other early Christians that we need. A freedom that allows life to be lived to the fullest and relinquished without care. To obtain this freedom, it is useful to meditate on your own dying. As you do this, you will begin to uncover the underlying certainty that Polycarp knew.

SPIRITUAL EXERCISE 15
MEDITATION ON DYING

1. Position your body comfortably, spine erect, on a chair or cushions.

2. Ground yourself in your physical sensations. Close your eyes and slowly become aware of the sensations of your physical body. Feel the sensations as they flow through you. The sensations in your head...in your neck and shoulders...your elbows...your wrists and the palms of your hands...the sensations in your knees...your ankles and the soles of your feet.

3. Now allow your attention to collect in the region of your heart. Imagine that you are very small, and walk within...into that vast space inside of you.

4. As you move within, imagine yourself on a high cliff, near the top of a tall mountain. Let yourself stand on the edge of the cliff and feel the sun warming your skin...the breeze on your face and tugging at your hair. Let yourself feel the exquisite joy of living. Feel your own aliveness. Feel your connectedness with everything: the ground beneath you, the air you breathe, the birds soaring on the wing. Let your awareness open and feel your Father in heaven as He watches you. Wrap yourself in His Presence.

5. Now move to the very edge of the cliff. Take a deep breath, feel your aliveness, and step forward, off the cliff. Feel yourself falling, the wind pulling at you. Feel your fear. The sensations as your flesh meets rock below, the breaking of bones, the tearing of flesh. Feel your life slipping away from you.

6. Stay concentrated on your experience as you die. Do not run from it. After a time, you will notice that you are still here—your identity still exists. So pick up what remains of your self and go to the next cliff which is a few steps away. Stand there on the cliff's edge and feel your life. The good-

ness of it. The aliveness. And take the step forward again and fall to your death. Once again, feel the life leave you. Stay with the experience and see what remains.

7. Repeat this process over and over, until the fear leaves you. Notice that there is always a part of you that survives your dying. Feel the purity of that essence—that essential "I" which endures.

(To close your meditation)

8. When you are ready, come back to this place. Let the feeling return to your feet...your hands...your face. Take a deep breath, and open your eyes.

This visualization is useful in addressing our fear of death. I believe that the fear of death lies at the root of many, if not all, of our fears. I have found that as we resolve the root problem, the derivative problems disappear of their own accord. Clearly, this meditation is not meant as an instruction to test your own mortality. Do not, I repeat, do not go jump off of some actual cliff to see what will happen to you. This is an inner exercise, aimed at your spiritual growth by means of resolving the root fear from which we all suffer. As such, this spiritual exercise can be practiced beneficially over and over again.

A "Good" Meditation or a "Bad" One?

We have explored together the spiritual practice of visualization and how we can use it for our own spiritual development. But how can we tell if we are doing it right, working from a book. How do we know whether or not we are really "getting it"? How do we know whether our meditation is really effective or not? Trying to distinguish between a successful meditation and an unsuccessful one is a tricky proposition. Oftentimes, when you feel like you have had a terrible meditation, this is when God was most present to you. Since our capacity for self-deception seems endless, how can we distinguish whether we are on the right track?

Assuming that you have not had much experience in focusing your attention to the degree required in meditation, you will go through fairly predictable stages as you begin. First, you will be confronted with your inability to control and focus your attention. This will likely prove frustrating. You simply assumed that your mind is under your own control. You have never stopped to see how the mind is driven by things other than your conscious will. Seeing this is often deeply troubling.

As you continue your meditation practice, you will gain some rudimentary control of your attention. You will find that you can focus for three seconds without a distraction, then five seconds, and then ten. You will then congratulate yourself and your congratulation will be the sign of having lost your focus. Sometimes it seems like even when you win at this, you lose! As your control over the attentional focus increases, you will find yourself going "deeper" or "higher." You don't really go anywhere, of course, but it feels as if you do. These directions are metaphors that represent a qualitative shift in awareness. My preference is for the "deeper" metaphor, since this more clearly locates the Divine within us. Emmanuel—God is with us! As you go deeper, you will find periods of great clarity arising. Often, there will be a sense of endless space all around you. The usual limits of ego-identity and body-image seem to disappear. In this state of awareness, many people see colors; others, a profound darkness.

When these periods of clarity arise, be still. You have entered into the Mind of God. You will find that you naturally want to be still and be. Follow your heart here. These periods are the springboards to infused prayer, which the Lord Jesus will give you at a later time in your practice. The attainment of these experiences may take you several months or several years, depending on your previously developed skill in concentration and the seriousness with which you approach these spiritual exercises. Each sex has a particular gift in this process. Women will tend to progress more quickly than men because men like to explore a lot. Men tend to go off on "inner adventures" that are very entertaining, but not always productive spiritually. On the other hand, men are often gifted with a more intense focus than women. The real controller of progress is your intent and skill in practice.

A "bad" meditation must be looked at closely. Most typically, what people call "bad" was really a meditation in which there were lots of distractions and a difficulty in controlling attention. You had to really "work" at your meditation. You came away from it tired. But is this really bad? Often these are the most productive periods of meditation. I know that they don't feel productive, but you were face-to-face with the very elements which keep you from knowing God's love. You had the opportunity to wrestle with them and pin them to the ground. Is this really bad?

At this stage of your development, there are two kinds of meditations that are not spiritually productive. The first kind is the meditation that doesn't happen. Your regular period for meditation is 6 a.m. but you decided to sleep for a few more minutes. This is not spiritually productive. Yet you will find that you compromise your growth many times for reasons as trivial as this.

Second, there is the meditation that is really a kind of mental noodling. You intend to sit in meditation, but your mind turns to some interesting topic or another and you process this topic instead. This may be very interesting to you, but it is no different from any other kind of discursive thinking. Further, because you did it when you were supposed to be meditating, you are likely to get confused and think that this is what meditation is really about. This kind of mental noodling turns you off the track and into a dead end; it is not spiritually productive.

Most people, in these early stages, consider their distractions to be terrible. These distractions are not terrible, of course; they only seem terrible because they appear to lie between us and what we want. In fact, our distractions are the most efficient mechanisms that our Father in heaven could devise to prepare His children to know Him.

Let me illustrate with an example from another kind of development. To create his muscular body, Arnold Schwarzenegger had to pump tons of iron. Over and over again, he worked with the weights, using the resistance of the weights to build up his muscles. So it is with those who meditate. Our "weights" are the distractions. We push against these distractions and build up a stronger and stronger ability to focus our attention. Without the distractions which resist our efforts, we could not build up our attention. And without a strong attention that is capable of sustaining an awareness of God, we cannot develop spiritually. Although I say this with mixed emotions, thank God for our distractions!

Chapter 15

The Practice of Auditory Meditation

The auditory and kinesthetic meditations appear quite different from visualization on the surface, but actually they share the same basic technical demands. Each of the three sensory meditations uses one of the senses as a tool for concentrating attention. This attentional focus is then aimed at God in such a way that we learn to rest our attention in the Divine. And then God slowly and gently works the transformation in us.

The Process of Auditory Meditation

The process of auditory meditation is similar to that of visualization. The difference is that we use an auditory sequence for our meditation focus instead of a visual sequence. Over the long history of the church, the primary method for creating an auditory stimulus has been chant. The music of the chant is selected to evoke internal states quickly. The music also serves to emphasize the words, by marking them out through auditory means. We can use this combination to quickly enter those states of consciousness where God can be perceived. As you will see, other auditory sequences can also be used. Tones can be generated internally, hymns can be sung, and so forth. We will explore these in depth later in the chapter.

Truly amazing things have happened to those who have used chant to draw closer to the Divine. We spoke earlier of the story of St. Joseph of Cupertino, an Italian saint who died in 1663.[65] Joseph used to levitate while chanting mass and the litanies. In the beginning, he was an ordinary sort of man who wanted more than anything to be a monk and devote his life to God. Once in the monastery, however, he continually got into trouble because he couldn't do anything right. He was even worse than Brother Lawrence, since he couldn't even wash the dishes properly; he kept dropping them. He was so awful that he was kicked out of one monastic order and had to try a second.

During his second try, Joseph was put forward by a relative to become a priest. Joseph, however, was not a bright man. He could never remember his lessons. He became the patron saint of students after an incident that occurred during his examination for the priesthood. He was supposed to be quizzed on the meaning of scripture, but he had been able to remember only one passage. Due to God's infinite blessing, that was the passage chosen by the examiner for him to expound. He did such a good job with this passage that his examiner did not test further.

After some years of prayer and austerities, without much spiritual direction, Joseph began to levitate. When mass was being chanted, he would regularly fall into ecstasy, and then would rise into the air with a loud shout that appeared to be spontaneous. Joseph would fly to the altar and be suspended there for a time, and then he would fly backwards to his place in the congregation and regain the floor. When asked what happened, Joseph spoke of visions that he had seen of Christ's action in redeeming the world. As Joseph grew older, these visions taught him many things about the nature of Divine Reality, so that he often confounded those who had theological degrees. That this bumbling indifferent student exhibited such a striking increase in knowledge was yet another sign of God's grace to Joseph.

You can imagine the consternation that this caused among Joseph's brothers and his monastic superiors. And once word of these levitations spread among the populace, great crowds tried to get into the church to see the holy man. The situation got so out of hand that some of Joseph's fellow monks became envious, and denounced him to the Inquisition. Joseph was examined by the Inquisition and found without fault. He returned to the monastery in Assisi and remained there for several years. Then the press of the crowds grew so great that he was assigned to successively more remote monasteries. Finally, he was forbidden by his superiors to say mass in public, to join in any of the solemn processions, or to take his meals in the refectory with the other monks. He died in ecstasy at the age of sixty.

Contemporary readers of these old reports of the supernatural tend to scoff and make light of them. We talk about the credulity and naivete of these ignorant people, and so forth. In Joseph's case, however, the observers were not naive, nor were they ignorant. They included, among others, several popes, a Lutheran prince who was carried by Joseph into the air during a levitation (and who subsequently converted to Catholicism), and the Inquisition. We must conclude, from this array of sophisticated and reliable observers, many of whom wanted to disprove that Joseph levitated, that Joseph did indeed levitate.

The story of St. Joseph of Cupertino indicates the potential power of chant to transform us. While St. Joseph engaged in other practices besides chant, it was during chant that he would fall into ecstasy most often. It is useful, therefore, to look carefully at what happens within us during chant. When we chant, we concentrate our attention on the words and music, loading consciousness in a way that facilitates movement into another state of consciousness. We feel physically the vibration of our own voice (and those of others if we are chanting in a group) thrumming in our bodies. Our attention focuses on these phenomena, and we begin to loosen our tight hold on our intellectual controls. We begin to respond out of a deeper part of our mind than the conscious ego. The vibration resonates within us and carries us within. We begin to enter into the chant, becoming the words and the music—the pure vibration resonating through space.

When the chant comes to an end, we will find that we continue to vibrate and to resonate. It is as if the chant continues within us on a more subtle level. There is an amazing stillness, but not a dead sort of stillness. There is a living, vibrating quality to it. Our intellect is stilled. A great sense of peace arises, as we rest in this stillness. The old intellectual need, that scurries around trying to find ways to control the world, relaxes and comes to rest. The vibration of the chant has soothed the underlying hunger, the need for assurance and love. In this confidence, we rest in love. We can simply sit and be still, and be with our Creator.

The First Mode of Auditory Meditation

The analog to visualizing a simple image, which is the first mode of visualization, is the generation of a simple tone. We begin by listening to a simple tone, like a bell tone which rings a single sustained note. We then take this inside our awareness, and generate the tone within ourselves. If you process information primarily in the auditory mode, you will find this tone generation a simple matter. If you do not have this facility, you may wish to use a single bell tone to get started. Use the sustained tone as the stimulus object upon which to concentrate. When the tone fades, or when you become distracted, simply renew the inner tone within yourself, using the auditory equivalent of imagination.

SPIRITUAL EXERCISE 16
SIMPLE TONE GENERATION

1. Position your body comfortably, spine erect, on a chair or cushions.

2. Become aware of the physical sensations which flow through you. Close your eyes and experience the stream of sensations that course through your physical body. No need to change them. No need to judge them. Simply let yourself feel deeply the multitude of sensations that cascade through your body. Gently focus on the sensations in your head...in your neck and shoulders...your elbows...your wrists and the palms of your hands...the sensations in your knees...your ankles and the soles of your feet.

3. Generate a simple tone, a single sustained note. Do this either by ringing a bell (or sounding a piano key with the sustain pedal, etc.) or by imagining this tone within your mind. Rest your attention on this tone. Concentrate here.

4. When your attention wanders to other things, gently bring your awareness back to the tone. If the tone has faded, regenerate it, listen for awhile, and rest in it.

(To close your meditation)

5. When you are ready, come back to this place. Let the feeling return to your feet...your hands...your face. Take a deep breath, and open your eyes.

This exercise is included for those who process most information in the auditory channel. The primary utility of this exercise is to strengthen your attentional focus, so that your attention becomes a stronger, more useful tool. Like the first visual mode, however, this exercise is not the most exciting to practice. While valuable, many may prefer to skip this exercise. If you find that you have trouble keeping a concentrated focus, however, you may wish to come back and practice this mode.

The Second Mode of Auditory Meditation

This mode uses simple monotone chant to intone a single word. It is very plain, repetitive, and all of the frills of chant are stripped away. From a technical point of view, any word can be used, but I would suggest a word with religious connotations such as "Holy," "Alleluia," "Amen," or the like. Make sure that the word is not associated with a visual picture. If you use the word "Jesus," for example, you are likely to make and concentrate on a picture rather than on the sound. This practice, while valid, is a combination visualization-and-auditory-meditation, rather than an auditory meditation, *per se*. While in practice you may combine these various modes in one meditation, for learning purposes I have chosen to present them separately, in a pure form.

During your chanting, you will find that your body vibrates as you chant your word. This vibration is a powerful way of stirring us up, at very deep levels. As you feel these vibrations through your flesh, sink into them and let them move you. You will find, as

---

SPIRITUAL EXERCISE 17
SIMPLE CHANT

1. Position your body comfortably, spine erect, on a chair or cushions.

2. Ground yourself in your physical sensations. Close your eyes and slowly become aware of the sensations of your physical body. Feel the sensations as they flow through you. The sensations in your head...in your neck and shoulders...your elbows...your wrists and the palms of your hands...the sensations in your knees...your ankles and the soles of your feet.

3. Choose a word from the religious vocabulary that has no visual connotations, such as "Alleluia," "Holy," "Amen," or the like.

4. Chant aloud your word for approximately five minutes. Very slowly chant this word, over and over, in a monotone. You may vary the tempo, phrasing, and pitch as you please. Let yourself explore...*BE* this word. Let it resonate within you. Do not worry about getting it right. Be still and let the word work in your soul.

5. When you stop chanting, sit in the stillness that surrounds the word, and let yourself resonate with the stillness. Open your awareness and feel the Presence of the Divine. Feel God's Presence all around you...within you.

6. Rest in this Presence. Let yourself dwell here for the time you have set apart for your meditation.

7. When you find your attention wandering to other things, gently bring your awareness back to the Presence of God by chanting silently in your heart. Let yourself rest in the chant for a few moments and then be still again.

(To close your meditation)

8. When you are ready, let yourself come back to this place. Let the feeling return to your feet...your hands...your face. Take a deep breath, and open your eyes.

you become familiar with this, that chant has the power to move us quickly into the deep stillness of God.

This is an especially powerful tool when practiced in a group. In OneHeart, the contemplative community in which I practice, the leader keeps time so that the rest of the group does not have to keep looking at a clock. The leader signals that it is time to stop chanting by stopping, and gradually the group hears this and the chanting stills. The silence that remains is so powerful that it shakes us. During this process, each one is better able to let go of our own small intellect, and enter into the stillness that is the Mind of God. The experience is awesome.

Whether you do this alone or in a group, this meditation is very powerful. This tool enables those with restless minds and wandering attention to create some focus and attentional stability. It is as if the sound itself carries you outside of yourself. While you may still feel somewhat distracted during the actual chanting, you will find that when the chanting stops, the silence is compelling. It is here that those with restless minds may find peace most easily.

The Third Mode of Auditory Meditation

The third mode of the sensory meditations intensifies the internally generated stimulus by adding complexity. The auditory rendition involves the use of complex liturgical chant, such as the Gregorian or Eastern Orthodox chants,[66] to focus attention and to place consciously that attention in God. The use of chant has a venerable history in the Christian church. From numerous references in the gospels, it is clear that Jesus used the psalms extensively. They formed His "book of prayers," to the extent that when He hung dying from the cross, the words of Psalm 22 crossed His lips: "Lord forgive them, for they know not what they do."

The psalms are metrical prayers. The meter in the psalms indicates that they were designed for oral recitation. Most probably, this recitation would be chanted, since, in the days before microphones, chanting was used to amplify the voice.

Various styles of chant have arisen in the church. The style most familiar to Western Christians is the Gregorian style, given definite form by Gregory II in the mid-600's. Under Gregory, the very plain chant of the Romans took on a distinct Byzantine ornamentation. As pope, Gregory decreed that all churches in Rome would use this new form of chant in their liturgies. The Western churches, who looked to Rome as the storehouse of Christian knowledge, then adopted Gregorian chant and it spread widely throughout France, England, and Germany. During a monastic reform in the early ninth century, Gregorian chant was widely disseminated among the monasteries and has been used in this context ever since. This is especially notable, since the monasteries have been the primary arena for spiritual transformation throughout most of the history of the Western church.

Other forms of chant besides the Gregorian mode can be equally powerful, if less common to Western listeners. The chant of the Orthodox churches is especially powerful and moving, with the dialogue between a deep bass cantor and choirs singing at a higher pitch. Some of the settings for the mass that have come out of Africa are also deeply moving.

Chant marries words with music in a way that settles the discursive intellect and penetrates deeply within the psyche. The words of the chant carry a certain amount of intellectual content. Because the chant is repetitious, however, the questing, grasping quality of the intellect is first run into the ground with boredom, and then ignored. We can only repeat the same words for a limited period of time before the discursive intellect is bored.

The music provides an element which somehow moves the meaning of the words within us. There is an old saying that when we sing, we pray twice. We cannot sing with just a part of ourselves. Song activates both the emotions and the intellect. I suspect that it activates and opens the spiritual dimension within us as well. As a result, the music provides an entry into the deep psyche, bypassing many of the problems that we have with the intrusiveness of the discursive intellect.

This deeper movement changes how the intellect deals with its environment. When I chant, my mind tends to move into a more receptive mode. Rather than actively scurrying around trying to "get it," the intellect receives the words, ponders and reflects on them in a receptive fashion, and integrates their meaning into the psyche. Chant fosters a quicker stilling of the roaming, discursive mind and engenders an open receptive quality.

In order to give you a taste of this delightful and powerful form of chant, I have adapted the Kyrie into a simpler form than Gregorian chant. The Kyrie is an ancient prayer of the church which originated in Syria in the fourth century. It is a brief petition for divine mercy, often used in the liturgy. The Kyrie, in ask-

---

SPIRITUAL EXERCISE 18
KYRIE ELEISON

1. Position your body comfortably, spine erect, on a chair or cushions.

2. Ground yourself in your physical sensations. Close your

eyes and slowly become aware of the sensations of your physical body. Feel the sensations as they flow through you. The sensations in your head,...in your neck and shoulders...your elbows...your wrists and the palms of your hands...the sensations in your knees...your ankles and the soles of your feet.

3. You are going to chant the Kyrie for the next five minutes. Chant slowly, over and over. Let the sounds of the Kyrie resonate within you. The words are simple:

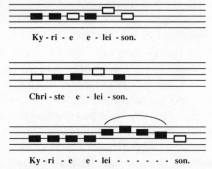

Ky - ri - e   e - lei - son.

Chri - ste   e - lei - son.

Ky - ri - e   e - lei - - - - - - son.

4. Gradually let your chant come to a resting place. Sit in the stillness that surrounds the chant, and let yourself resonate with the stillness. Open your awareness and feel the Presence of the Divine. Feel God's Presence all around you...within you.

5. Rest in this Presence. Let yourself dwell here for the time you have set apart for your meditation.

6. When you find your attention wandering to other things, gently bring your awareness back to the Presence of God by chanting silently in your heart. Let yourself rest in the chant for a few moments and then be still again.

(To close your meditation)

7. When you are ready, let yourself come back to this place. Let the feeling return to your feet...your hands...your face. Take a deep breath, and open your eyes.

ing God for help, sets God at the center of our lives and works in subtle ways to move us from our false self identification.

Other examples which use these principles of chant include the chants developed by the Taize Community in France. Recordings of their chants are widely available.[68] You may wish to purchase them, and learn some of the simple ones such as "Ubi caritas," "Veni creator spiritus," and "Veni sancte spiritus." These chants have the additional advantage that they are sung in Latin, which further thwarts the discursive intellect. Another way of participating in chant is to purchase recordings of Gregorian chant, and listen to them during your meditation periods. To achieve some spiritual benefit, open your heart to the Divine in a receptive manner. Do not pay attention to the stirrings of the discursive intellect. Let yourself rest in God.

Finally, there is hymn singing. Hymnody is an outgrowth of chant, but not one that is particularly suited for moving us into altered states where we can experience the Divine. Hymns differ from chant in that they march along in metered time, 4/4 or the like, rather like an army: tramp, tramp, tramp, tramp. The resulting clunky quality is different from chant, which is not metered. Chant moves with the rhythm of breath—it floats in the air; where hymns march aggressively on the ground. Because of this metrical quality, hymns do not work as effectively as chant as a meditative means.

This is not to say that hymns are not useful. They are a much easier form than chant for congregational singing, and they do stir up and involve the emotions in your prayer. In addition, the hymns with which you have become familiar have made a home in your psyche, and they will nurture you from time to time. A colleague states that phrases from hymns often come to her in times of trouble, bringing exactly the right consolation or suggestion for action. She has learned to trust this wonderful capacity of her psyche, and from time to time bases decisions on these unconscious promptings from her hymns.

One way of using hymns for meditation is to take a line or a short stanza and turn it into a chant, repeating it over and over again. Here you can use a simple monotone for your chanting or create a melody of your own.

Like visualization, auditory meditations are powerful tools which take us into the Presence of God. Like visualization, the auditory meditation can be divided into three distinct and increasingly complex modes. We will go on now to examine how to use a kinesthetic focus for Christian meditation.

Chapter 16

The Practice of
Kinesthetic Meditation

Kinesthetic meditation is a neglected area in contemporary Christian practice. There is very little physical or kinesthetic involvement in the existing prayer traditions in most branches of Christianity. Kinesthetic meditation is the process of focusing on the kinesthetic sensations of the body as the object of meditation. Since our bodies are given to us by our Creator, and since we are created in God's image, there must be something divine about the body and the nature of our physical being. Yet, with few exceptions, this arena has been largely neglected by those Christians who have walked this path before us.

I suspect that this neglect stems ultimately from traces of the gnostic heresy in the second and third centuries which have lingered on in the church. The gnostics had a firmly dualistic view of the world. They postulated an infinite abyss between the world of spirit, which was pure and holy, and the world of matter, which was dark and disgusting. If you were on the spiritual path, salvation could only be found by rejecting the body and focusing solely on that divine spark which was within you. Thus, everything that had to do with the body was seen as bad, and something for those on a spiritual path to reject. Unfortunately, this heresy crept into the Western church in subtle ways, and has continued throughout most of our history as an emphasis on the mortification of the body.

For most Christians in this country, the body is popularly understood as something evil or bad, a source of temptation that will lead us away from the Divine. While we prize the intellect, and focus mightily upon developing it, we neglect our bodies and the physical sensations that flow through them. If our intellect is where light shines for us, then our body is the part that is enfolded in a dark shadow. Given the sacred heritage of our bodies, "in His own image He created them," this oversight is tragic and mistaken.

The use of kinesthetic foci for meditation is more developed in other religious traditions. In Buddhism, for example, the Theravadin school developed *vipassana* meditation.[69] Here the practitioner focuses on the rising and falling away of physical sensations. This is used to train attention for deeper forms of contemplation. Christianity, however, does not have a clear parallel to this practice.

In spite of this omission, I will organize Christian kinesthetic practices into three modes, as I did with the other forms of sensory meditation. While the body of kinesthetic practices is presently small, the division into modes suggests ways to increase the scope of these practices.

The First Mode of Kinesthetic Meditation

In the first spiritual exercise in this book, I presented a format for grounding yourself in the physical sensations. This is, fundamentally, a kinesthetic meditation. In each of the succeeding spiritual exercises, I have given an abbreviated version of this kinesthetic meditation, because it helps to ground you in what you know is real, your body, and also helps to focus your attention. Thus, if you are practicing the exercises as you read, you have been employing kinesthetic meditation for some time now. Rather than repeat the exercise here, I would refer you back to the first spiritual exercise on page 41.

This exercise can be done by itself, with the same kinds of benefits that accrue from a visual or auditory meditation. For those whose primary mode of apprehending knowledge is kinesthetic, this exercise will probably be the preferred method of sensory meditation. Like the first mode in both visual and auditory meditations, this exercise focuses on a stimulus that exists apart from your perception of it.

The Second Mode of Kinesthetic Meditation

The second mode of kinesthetic meditation involves focusing on internally generated feelings that are driven by outside stimuli, and the development of complex and dynamic sensations. These meditations can take several forms. The more familiar form uses gospel stories in a clear parallel with the second mode of visualization. Here, you process a story from the gospels or some other suitable literature, with a kinesthetic rather than a visual focus. You may wish to go back to exercises seven through eleven to practice with a kinesthetic focus.

The second kinesthetic form of this mode involves a repetitive movement of the body before God. In times past, the church used prostrations before God as a way of meditative prayer. Today the most widely used kinesthetic practice is making the sign of the cross on ourselves. In the exercise below, we show how to use this repetitive motion of signing ourselves with the cross for meditation.

Since most people do not usually process information by using the kinesthetic mode, developing this mode serves as an easy entrance into an altered state of consciousness. As such, we can readily utilize it for the purpose of experiencing the Divine. There is a certain wry sweetness here. Like Jesus, this sensory modality is rejected by most people. Yet both can so easily serve as a cornerstone in our efforts to know God and follow His love more closely.

The following exercise was taken from Russian Orthodoxy.[70] It involves crossing yourself while gently swaying back and forth. This exercise uses the whole body as a focus for our intention to draw closer to the source of all love. It is an invitation to explore using our body and its sensations to move us into the Presence of God.

SPIRITUAL EXERCISE 19
SIGNING THE CROSS

1. Stand in a comfortable relaxed manner in the space where you usually meditate.

2. Ground yourself in your physical sensations. Close your eyes and slowly become aware of the sensations of your physical body. Feel the sensations as they flow through you. The sensations in your head...in your neck and shoulders...your elbows...your wrists and the palms of your hands...the sensations in your knees...your ankles and the soles of your feet.

3. Now allow your attention to collect in the region of your heart. Center your attention in your heart and experience your body from this location. Extend yourself out through your heart, and experience the rest of the world from your heart center.

4. Put the thumb and first two fingers of your right hand together, making a trinity. Maintain this configuration during the time of your practice.

5. Rock your torso gently backward a few inches, while bringing up your right hand and touching your forehead.

6. Now rock slowly forward and bring your right hand down to your lower belly.

7. Now rock gently backward, and bring your right hand up to your left shoulder.

8. Now rock gently forward, and bring your right hand up to your right shoulder.

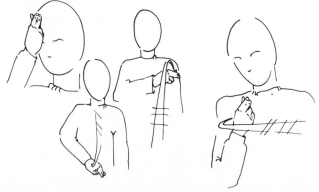

9. Repeat the operations in steps five through eight. As you do this, focus your attention on the region of your heart. Open your heart fully to receive God's Presence. The sign of the cross over your body is the outward symbol of a deeper acknowledgment that you are God's. Open yourself fully, and give Her your allegiance. Receive the blessing inherent in the cross and take it within your soul.

---

10. When you find your intellect wandering and becoming distracted, gently focus on the feelings of placing yourself mentally in front of God and acknowledging Him as your Lord and Savior.

(To close your meditation)

11. When you are ready, come back to this place. Let the feeling return to your feet...your hands...your face. Take a deep breath, and open your eyes.

This practice is often unfamiliar to Western Christians, especially Protestants. Nevertheless, it deeply embodies the focus that all Christians share, that Jesus is our Lord—the One who is in charge of our lives. This practice can allow us to feel, in a new way, the giving over of the false self in our search for that which is deeper, more true, and more enduring.

The Third Mode of Kinesthetic Meditation

There is a wonderful story[71] recounted in the sayings from the desert fathers from the fourth century. A monk went to Abba Joseph and asked, "Abba, as far as I can, I say my little office (i.e. his set form for daily prayers), I fast a little, I pray and meditate, I live in peace, and as far as I can, I purify my thoughts. What else can I do?" Abba Joseph stood up and stretched his hands toward heaven. His fingers became like ten lamps of fire and he said to him, "If you want, why not become totally fire?"

Abba Joseph illustrates two things with his actions. First, he shows forth the fruits of prayer through the transformations that have occurred in his body. Through his deep contemplation of God, he has purified himself and entered into union with the Divine. Thus Joseph participates, in a limited way, in the resurrected and incorruptible body of Jesus Christ and is showing forth the fruit of that labor to a brother who is advanced enough to benefit. The second, and more important thing for us, is that Abba Joseph shows us not only the fruit, but also the means by which this was accomplished. You will find, if you meditate for very long, that you will have periods in meditation in which you will generate an immense amount of heat through your body. This is one of the signs that you are going deeply into prayer.

When this occurs, you should not be alarmed, but neither should you rejoice. The rejoicing would simply pull you away from your prayer, and dilute your concentration. Rather, let the experience happen within you. If there is something that you can do which seems to facilitate the production of this inner fire, do so. This fire is a purifying fire which gently consumes the emotional pain which separates us from God. It literally burns up our sin.

This incident is one of the few recorded in the history of Christian spirituality which refers to a kinesthetic focus in deep prayer. To accomplish his epiphany, Abba Joseph focused on the sensations in his body and invited the other monk to do the same. Since the body and the kinesthetic sensations that flow through the body are important to us, it is reasonable to assume that there are other forms of kinesthetic meditation that have been developed during the long history of Christian spirituality. However, they have not been featured in the literature of Christian spiritual practice.

SPIRITUAL EXERCISE 20
OPENING THE HEART TO GOD'S LOVE

1. Position your body comfortably, spine erect, on a chair or cushions.

2. Become aware of the physical sensations which flow through you. Close your eyes and experience the stream of sensations that course through your physical body. No need to change them. No need to judge them. Simply let yourself feel deeply the multitude of sensations that cascade through your body. Gently focus on the sensations in your head...in your neck and shoulders...your elbows...your wrists and the palms of your hands...the sensations in your knees...your ankles and the soles of your feet.

3. Now place your attention in your heart. Let all of your attention gather there. Become aware of the feelings that flow through your heart. Within the heart of every man and woman is a living flame of love, placed there by the

One who created us. Let yourself feel this flame as it leaps in your heart. Feel the warmth of it. Rest in this warmth.

4. Feel this warmth as it spreads through your chest. It is not "your" warmth; it is given by the Divine Presence for your enjoyment. Let this warmth slowly spread throughout your body. Up into your neck, your face, your head. Into your shoulders, down your arms, into your hands. Feel the energy in your hands like hot fire. Down through your torso, your hips, your genitals. Into your legs, your feet. Until you are all aflame.

5. Flames leap up in a constant motion. They consume the flammable gases that are released by their action. Feel what feeds your fire. Both the holiness of God's action and your own sin feed this fire. On your part, offer up the whole of your sin, your separation to this purifying flame of God's love. The separation you have felt today, and yesterday, and all the yesterdays before that. Offer it up as your sacrifice to God.

6. Let yourself rest in these feelings. When you are distracted, gently bring your attention back to the flames within and focus here again.

(To close your meditation)

7. When you are ready, let yourself come back to this place. Let the feeling return to your feet...your hands...your face. Take a deep breath, and open your eyes. Take a moment and look around the room to reorient yourself.

There is so much that we have inside of us that keeps us away from the deep love of God in our hearts. Usually we turn away from this love and busy ourselves in other things. We spend our time and attention to develop our careers, raise our families, and enjoy the blessings of this wonderful creation. As rich as these things might be, there is no lasting satisfaction in any of them. We are hungry, and we have such a hunger that only the ever-present love of God will fill us.

Yet, despite our hunger, we continue to busy ourselves in things that cannot satisfy us. What a joy it is to begin our journey home! What a joy it is to offer up all of those things that separate us from the love that we most desire. What a joy to feel that precious love!

Chapter 17

Reflections on the Process of the Sensory Meditations

As you practiced the spiritual exercises above, you began to experience how many different ways you can come close to God. And this book does not pretend to be exhaustive in cataloging the sensory meditations! Truly, volumes could be produced simply to describe meditations on each of the senses. My purpose was to sketch an introduction for you, so that you can experience for yourself the spiritual richness available in our Christian tradition.

It has been said that every inch of the spiritual journey has been charted by those who have gone before us. Every stone, every pothole, every detour and dead–end. Our forebears have gone before us on this great highway. We have their reports, and their promises of the rich land that they have gone to dwell in. We have their encouragement, to journey there ourselves. This book could be considered a catalog of the vehicles which can take us on part or all of the journey.

There are some important limitations, however, that we must note. No spiritual practice is suitable for all people at all times. The sensory meditations have their limitations and these must be properly understood if we are to use them appropriately for our spiritual growth.

First, no words or images or sounds or feelings can ever define God or contain the Divine. These many tools can point to God; they can help us experience some aspect of the Divine. But that is the limit of their effectiveness. Remember, none of these techniques is an end in itself. They are simply vehicles that can take us a little farther down the road. They all point beyond themselves to the deep Reality that underlies all things.

One of the major uses of the sensory meditations is helping us release the constraints that we put around our awareness. We hold ourselves so tightly, barely admitting anything new. We are like children, hiding under our security blanket. We peek out through a tiny hole at the vast and unknown world. We allow ourselves to see and experience only a fragment of the riches out there. In so doing, we actively prevent ourselves from experiencing God. Let me give you an example of how this works. Most of us have been touched by deep emotional pain of one sort or another. We had parents who could not love us enough, or who taught us values that limited our growth. These situations resulted in our grasping onto our security blanket in ways that narrow our vision to a little peephole. We falsely think that this narrowed vision protects us.

The practice of the sensory meditations provides a forum for working through much of this. For some, these practices may release a flood of pain. If this pain is overwhelming, or if you have difficulty in processing and resolving this pain, consult a psychologist. With the right therapist, psychotherapy can be a great complement to spiritual growth. Therapy allows you to process quickly these old emotional programs that hinder you, so that you can move on to the deeper contemplative practices.

You will find that there is a complementary quality between meditation and psychotherapy. As you meditate, the old pain that blocks your spiritual growth will begin to surface. This can be overwhelming at times. I have had students who have stopped meditating because of the old pain that surfaced as a result of their meditation practice. With some, forgotten memories arise during meditation. With others, the meditative process loosens the grip of repression so that these painful memories come up during the course of daily routine.

If this happens to you, do not be afraid. There is nothing to fear, since these are just *memories*. There is no new pain here that you need to avoid. Rather, the surfacing of these memories is God's gift to you. This process allows you to resolve the old pain that keeps you holding on to your self so tightly. It provides a vehicle for you to relax and trust the Divine more and more fully. How wonderful it is to be free of the load that you have been carrying! How much freer your steps...how much clearer your perception.

At the beginning of my adult spiritual journey, I used the sensory meditations exclusively for about five years. During this time, I also went into psychotherapy to resolve some of the hurt that arose. The process of resolving the old emotional programming that says "I am no good" is, for most of us, a lengthy and worth-

while undertaking. Let me commend it to you as a central part of
your spiritual work.

Gaining Control of Your Attention. Another utility of the sensory meditations is that they enable us to refine our attention into
a usable tool. It is so distressing, when we start to meditate, to
find that we cannot keep our attention focused for more than a second or two without some distraction pulling at us. The sensory
meditations provide us with the means to address this deficit.

This is usually not a pleasant experience. The process of refin-
ing the attentional focus is like wrestling with an opponent who
seems much bigger and stronger than you. You struggle and struggle. Only after great effort will you find yourself gaining strength.
In this struggle, there are no superheroes who fly in and save the
day. Everyone who wrestles in this arena gains strength only slowly. Nevertheless, we do gain strength in the process. I am now in a
position, after many years of effort, where I can sit in meditation
and enter into deep stillness within a few seconds. So your effort to
persevere here will bear fruit. You simply have to keep practicing
regularly.

Understanding the Time Frame for Results. The meditation
process often seems to be a slow one. We live in an age of instant
gratification, with instant food, instant sex, instant everything.
Everything about our era conditions us to believe that we can have
whatever we want right now. And so, when we struggle for a long
period to add a whole entire second to our meditational focus, the
cost seems to outweigh the benefit.

Look at the complexity of what is happening in meditation,
though. We are not only gaining attentional focus, but are also
releasing our subtle patterns of conditioning. We are releasing our
old pain, our dysfunctional patterns. We are letting go of our deepest fears and distrust. While each of us wants to release all of this
quickly, are we really ready to do this? Are we ready to stand
naked, without our usual defenses? Are we ready to toss aside our
security blanket and see the world as it really is?

The truth is, we *want* to be ready for this, but we are not. The
regular practice of meditation will help us slowly to gain strength
to be able to do these things that we want and that are so important to us. There are, however, no shortcuts. We have to take the
first step before we can go on to the second; and the second step
before we go on to the third. The meditation process takes time.

The Dangers of Self-Promotion. This brings us to the conundrum inherent in a book like this. I am laying out a clear progression of inner states and the techniques for achieving these states. Thus, instead of this knowledge being the province of a few seasoned teachers who have traveled this road, the knowledge becomes accessible to everyone who takes the trouble to read this book. And unfortunately, I am writing in the land of fast food and instant gratification of every desire.

There is a real and substantial danger in trying to promote ourselves as we work through these practices. We all want union with God, but we will get there only by doing the hard work of putting one foot in front of the other, over and over again. We will not get anywhere by taking a few steps and then believing that we have arrived. It is clear that I cannot go from Los Angeles to New York by walking ten steps in an easterly direction, and saying, "I think I am there now." No matter what we think, New York is farther away than ten steps. Unfortunately, the interior distances do not have clear exterior reference points that everyone understands and can verify. So we have a tendency to think we have progressed spiritually further than we actually have.

Let me show you what can happen when you try to self–promote, with a story from my own spiritual journey. Many years ago, after a period of great inner striving and exerting tremendous effort, I pushed myself to the very point of achieving the first unitive state. As I sat in meditation one day, there arose the understanding that all I needed to do was to give the last assent and I would enter into union with God. And immediately following this understanding, a great fear rose up in me that pulled me back, seemingly against my own will, from giving my assent.

I hope you can understand this! I was right at the point of achieving what I most wanted in all of the world. Right at the point of achieving what I had worked for over the past ten years. I was utterly horrified when this fear arose, grieved beyond what my words can convey when I found myself retreating. How could I be saying "No" to God, when I had worked so hard to say "Yes"?

What had happened was that I promoted myself before I was truly ready. I ignored some of my deep emotional programming. I fooled myself into believing that I had resolved it all or that what remained had no real importance. I went on in my inner work as if this old programming did not exist. As a result, the fear that was engendered by that programming surfaced and it dragged me backward. Out of this experience of my own, and from watching others in similar circumstances, I caution you about spiritual promotion.

When Are You Ready to Go On? If self-promotion is dangerous, how can you tell if you are ready to go on to another practice? The best way is to consult with an experienced meditation teacher or a spiritual director who has experience with meditation. Such a teacher will discern where you are and guide you to your next step.

A second way of ascertaining readiness to move on is to work with a meditation group. The wisdom that manifests in these groups can be very powerful. It is as if Christ Himself manifests in the group—not through any one member, but in the sum total of the parts. The Body of Christ of which St. Paul speaks[72] comes alive at this point, and serves as our personal teacher and guide. There are, of course, difficulties attendant to any group process. The collective wisdom of the group, however, can often perceive elements about your practice that you, by yourself, cannot. It is this function that is so valuable—the gift of seeing those elements of which you yourself are unconscious. None of us can see those parts of ourselves that we have so carefully hidden from ourselves. Others, however, often see them quite clearly. So learn, as you walk this path, to cultivate spiritual friendships for the specific purpose of gaining feedback and knowledge about yourself.

If you do not have access to a group, then you are forced to rely on the difficult procedure of self-diagnosis. The signs that you should look for, if you believe that you are ready to move on to another practice are several. First, what is the length of your attentional focus? After practicing the sensory meditations, you should be able, as a general rule, to maintain your focus *exclusively* on your chosen meditation subject for five minutes or more. This means that you can put your attention on your meditation subject and are able to concentrate there without the intrusion of gross thoughts. By gross thoughts, I mean those "large" thoughts that, when they occur, fully occupy your attention, if only for a moment. I do not mean the fleeting wisps of thought that will cross the back of your mind.

Second, how long are you able to sit in meditation? You should be able to sit for at least twenty minutes as a usual practice. On occasion, when your meditation spontaneously lengthens, you should be able to sit for two or three times this long. Further, during your period of meditation, you should be able to handle the dreaded itch, the painful muscles, and the ringing telephone without any voluntary movement. That is, you should be able to sit absolutely still.

Third, how rapidly do you enter into the meditative state after you have started your meditation period? You should be able to enter the meditative state quite rapidly, following the cessation of discursive intellectual activity. Thus, when the active part of your visualization ceases, or when your chanting stills, you should be immediately in a deep meditative state.

Fourth, you should find yourself exhibiting, in your outward life, some greater detachment. Without meditation or some other spiritual discipline, we are very attached to the outcome of our actions, and to how others perceive us. One of the fruits of spiritual practice is an increasing detachment. By detachment, I mean the gradual diminution of expecting that other people will treat you in a certain way.

The practice of meditation allows us to perceive ourselves more clearly. Through meditation, we become aware of our internal emotional programming and how that programming controls our behavior. As we develop this awareness, the power of that programming to control our behavior lessens, and we become more free. This is what I mean by detachment. We learn to act for the action itself, not for the reward that we hope will follow the act. If this is not increasingly visible in your outward behavior, if people do not allude to this when they talk with you, then you may not have mined the sensory meditations as deeply as you can.

Fifth, when you are ready to move on, you will find that the sensory meditations seem barren. Initially, after you gain a modicum of control over your attention, you will find that the sensory meditations are full of richness for you. There is a sense of spiritual consolation when you meditate; each time of meditation becomes a blessed encounter with the Divine. However, there will come a time when these consolations dry up. The sweetness will leave these practices for you and they will become barren. When this happens, it is time to move on to a deeper practice.

Of crucial importance in making this discernment is the distinction between a temporary dry period and the long period of barrenness which indicates that you need to move on. All of us will experience temporary periods of dryness at every level of the contemplative journey. Often these temporary dry spells result from our misapplication of the meditation technique.

Let me illustrate this. One day you are blessed with a wonderful meditation; a meditation in which you feel you have made a spiritual breakthrough. You hope that the next time you meditate you have a similar experience. In your next period, the seduction of this desire pulls you into a *remembrance* of the previous experience. You think you are meditating, but in actuality you are remembering. This remembrance is not quite as deep or as rich as the original experience, but it is only different by a little. You walk away happy, but without any awareness that you didn't meditate. In succeeding periods of meditation, your memory gradually fades, until your practice seems barren. In actual fact, you are remembering, not meditating. Your practice is not barren; rather, your memory is barren. Memory can never take you into an experience of the living God.

Distinguishing between these dead-ends and the living path is very difficult when you are by yourself. I hope that everyone who engages in contemplative practice works to gather a group of spiritual friends to walk with.[73] Your journey will be greatly eased by their company. Some time ago, I had reached a plateau in my spiritual practice. Nothing that I did seemed to get me moving again. To address this, I began to gather together a group of spiritual friends for the very selfish reason that I needed their help in my practice. We found the practice of meditation in a group to be so mutually supporting that the group has become a permanent fixture in our lives.

OneHeart now meets on a weekly basis. There is a depth to our group meditations that surpasses our individual efforts. We move more quickly and more deeply into the Mind of God when we move together. This seems to follow naturally from our Lord's work. He gathered, first a group of disciples, and then went on to larger groups. He even says to us, "When two or three are gathered together in my name, I will be in your midst."[74] Such a gathering will well repay your efforts.

The sensory meditations are powerful techniques which can take you deeply into the Presence of God. Over the years of my own practice, I have heard various teachers emphasize one or another of these techniques. These methods are all effective. They are based on the same principle—using the senses to focus awareness. They all have similar results.

You will find, however, that one or another of these methods are more engaging for you than the others. Just as people differ in which sensory modality they prefer to gather most of their information so, too, we differ in which sensory mode will be more effective

as a meditative tool. I hope that you will try each of the sensory
meditations over a period of a month or more. This is the best way
to determine what will work for you.

One last note, before we go on. I have occasionally heard people
say that the sensory meditations are all that the "ordinary person"
can dare to experience. I have known people who were told that
they could not engage in the deeper meditative practices, because
these practices were the province of a few special saints. This is
hogwash! Jesus offers His grace equally to all. Inhibiting someone
from these practices is like keeping an infant from the mother's
breast. The techniques described thus far are beginning practices.
If you stop here, you will attain a benefit, but only a limited benefit. For the sake of God's great love for you and for your own sake,
I hope you will continue.

Part IV

Divine Reading:
The Use of Lectio Divina

In previous chapters, we explored the sensory meditations. These practices help us focus our attention on God, creating a useful tool out of our undisciplined attention. These meditations also prepare us for the practice of Lectio Divina by introducing the technique of visualization.

Lectio Divina is an ancient practice, rooted in our Jewish heritage, and continuously practiced throughout the long history of Christendom. It is a method of meditation, based on holy scripture, that blends into an organic whole the practices of scripture reading, visualization, discursive prayer, and contemplative reflection. Thus, Lectio is an easy entry point into contemplative practice for those who have developed the discipline of regular scriptural study. For those who are less familiar with scripture, Lectio is a great avenue to learn how scripture is relevant to us today. The practice of Lectio opens up the word of God so that it lives for us. It puts us in the action, so that we can experience for ourselves the force of the biblical stories. Lectio is a powerful tool for inner development for all Christians.

The Roots of Lectio Divina

Lectio Divina has come down to us through the ages from those great centers of learning, the Benedictine monasteries. There is, however, considerable evidence of previous forms of Lectio Divina extending back into Jewish antiquity. In the Jewish tradition, believers have always been urged to enter into a living relationship with the Torah, the first five books of the Bible, which reveal the law of God. Of secondary importance are those biblical texts in which the lives of the prophets are described; and the wisdom literature, composed of Psalms, Proverbs, the Song of Songs, Ecclesiastes and the books of Wisdom and Sirach.

The Torah means literally, "the Teaching," and the devout Jew is directed to plunge into this teaching and to keep it always near. "Keep this book of the law on your lips. Recite it by day and by night, that you may observe carefully all that is written in it; then

155

you will successfully attain your goal."[75] Here the text indicates the way that the Torah is to be approached: it is to be constantly recited. This constant reading suggests the devotion with which the Torah is to be approached. This is not "reading" as we understand it today; it is not the reading that we do when we peruse the daily newspaper, or immerse ourselves in a novel. It is *holy* reading. As such, it presumes prayer and reflection. Reading, prayer, and reflection are the basic elements of Lectio Divina.

In the New Testament, while there are no direct commandments to read scripture, the practice of Lectio Divina is taken for granted. Throughout the gospels, Jesus' comments are so laced with references to the Old Testament that it is clear He had practiced Lectio extensively. Because Christians in our age are so unfamiliar with the Old and New Testaments, this assertion is difficult to demonstrate. But it will become clear, even to those unfamiliar with scripture, by looking at a cross-referenced Bible. In the New Testament, for instance, we see footnotes at the bottom of every page, indicating biblical books, with chapter and verse. These references refer to other passages of scripture which have been quoted or alluded to by the speaker or writer.

In the fourth gospel, Jesus gives a direct command to those who wonder about His Lordship. "Search the scriptures," He says, "in which you think you have eternal life—they testify on my behalf."[76] Jesus' understanding is that the divine word of God will reveal its meaning to those who read it with devotion, and that the centrality of the Son of God who comes to the Jews from the house of David will be revealed to the reader clearly.

There is even an example of Jesus doing Lectio Divina in the gospel of Luke during the Emmaus road story.[77] When the two followers of Christ recounted the events of the Passover weekend to Jesus, He replied, "What little sense you have! How slow you are to believe all that the prophets have announced!" And then the story continues, "beginning with Moses and all the prophets, He interpreted for them every passage of scripture which referred to Him." This passage alludes to the first two parts of Lectio Divina: reading the text and reflecting deeply upon it. Jesus' listeners later respond to this experience by saying, "Were not our hearts burning inside us as He talked to us on the road and explained the scriptures to us?" This is a testimony to the power of Lectio to touch and transform the heart.

With this strong basis in tradition in both our Jewish roots and in Jesus' teaching, Lectio Divina was taken for granted in the early church. Scripture formed the fundamental basis for the life of the Christian community. There are several differences, however, between the practices of the early church and what is done today with Lectio Divina. In the years of the early church, because copies of the scriptures were expensive and rare, they were memorized by the faithful. Thus, instead of the visualization that is done today, there was a slow repetition of the text in order to commit it to memory. This process was called *meditatio*, from which our word "meditation" developed. Meditatio was a slow rumination over the scriptures: first to memorize, and then to reflect on the meaning in order to develop a deeper understanding. Once the listeners had memorized the passage, they began to visualize the dynamic flow of scripture, entering into that flow personally.

The Transmission of Lectio

The process of Lectio Divina has been carried to us in modern times through the vehicle of monasticism. St. Benedict of Nursia, founder of the Benedictine order, enshrined the practice of Lectio in his rule, which has served as the constitution for Benedictines since A.D. 530. The Benedictine rule was the basis for most subsequent monastic rules in the West, so its effect has been substantial. Benedict directed that the monks spend three hours a day in Lectio Divina. Much of this time was given over to the process of the memorization of scripture. That way the monk could bring forth suitable passages during the hours of his work and reflect on them, so that work could take on a deeper spiritual dimension.

A further elaboration occurred with Guigo II, a monk of the Carthusian order in the twelfth century. Guigo made explicit the fourfold division of Lectio Divina into lectio, meditatio, oratio, and contemplatio. His summary of the process of Lectio Divina:

Reading is a directing of the mind to a careful looking at the Scriptures. Meditation is a studious activity of the mind, probing the knowledge of some hidden truth under the guidance of our own reason. Prayer is a devout turning of the heart to God to get ills removed or to obtain good things. Contemplation is a certain elevation above itself of the mind which is suspended in God, tasting the joys of eternal sweetness.[78]

The practice of Lectio, on the whole, has been a huge success. As a result of Benedict's rule and its widespread adoption, generations of monks have been steeped in holy scripture. When learning was close to being extinguished in the West after the fall of the Roman Empire, these monks kept learning alive. Their successors carried Christianity to the pagan people of Europe, and on missionary journeys abroad.

The process of Lectio has been kept alive not only in Roman Catholicism, but also within the Protestant traditions. With Martin Luther came a renewed emphasis on each Christian studying the scriptures. For the first time in the West, translations of the Bible into the common languages became available. Study of the Bible moved from the province of Latin-speaking clergy and into the realm of Everyman. While the fourfold form of Lectio Divina was often forgotten in this process, the spirit of Lectio remained. The Protestant emphasis on reading and memorizing scripture is strikingly similar to St. Benedict's much earlier emphasis on scriptural study. In this way, the fundamentals of Lectio have been carried forward to the present day.

Chapter 18

"People of the Book"

Christians are, above all things, a "people of the Book." Despite our many doctrinal and liturgical differences, we have in common the revelation of God that is found in the Old and New Testaments. The centrality of this book to our life in God is easily seen. The first book ever to be printed on a printing press was the Bible. The largest selling book in history is the Bible. Virtually every home in America has a Bible, even if it is never opened. It is a potent symbol of our ultimate unity as Christians, because we believe that it holds the revelation of God to Her sons and daughters on this earth.

In past times, the Bible has been more than a symbol. It has been the living reality that sparked the great movements of the church. Hearing the Bible prompted St. Anthony of the Desert to sell all that he had and to go into the desert to seek God. Much of the technology of Christian prayer developed from his action. The hearing of scripture galvanized Martin Luther into action, and began the great Protestant Reform. Not only has the Bible been crucial in these mass movements, but also in the personal conversions of many of the saints and ordinary people. So the power of scripture to spark change in every generation has always been an unspoken standard in Christendom, until our own day.

Unfortunately, the power of scripture for personal transformation has been systematically eroded over the last hundred years. The institutions that train the clergy have focused more and more on the modern tools of textual criticism in their efforts to understand scripture. On the positive side, textual criticism has helped us understand more profoundly the meaning of Jesus' message to those who first heard it. Unfortunately, it has had other, less desirable consequences.

Textual criticism of the Bible has contributed greatly to the ero-

159

sion of trust which we, as a people, have placed in this holy book. By means of this tool, we have discovered what Jesus Himself said, and what is merely attributed to Him by a gospel writer. So now we have two classes of information: that which is clearly authoritative, and that which may or may not be authoritative. As a result, the fundamental authority of the gospels has been thrown into question. What can we now believe with certainty? And how can our clergy teach or preach from the word of God, if their training suggests that it is not really the word of God?

In the past century, we, as a people, have turned away from regular Bible reading. Since the authority of scripture has been put into question, it is not clear what benefit is derived from Bible reading. If there is no clear benefit, then many have concluded that the scriptures are not "relevant" or important to their daily lives. Those who hold onto Bible reading are typically the conservatives of our culture.

We have experienced an increasing split between the biblical conservatives and the rest of the culture. The Bible has become a kind of totem for conservatives, which makes it even less likely that moderates or liberals will examine it. We have polarized into two camps: those who shout that the Bible is the unshakable word of God, and those who shout that it is an irrelevant icon of a hidebound past. Few examine scripture empirically, to see if it might be useful to them.

Thus, we have abandoned a cornerstone of our heritage. We have chopped off this deeptap root which fed us and nourished us as a people. Furthermore, we no longer have a systematic way of entering into scripture. We have lost that, too.

When we turn from those cultural wellsprings that have shaped us as a people we turn, not just from an outmoded heritage, but also from those forces which have shaped each individual to be a part of the larger whole. We turn away from that which has shaped each of us to be a unique individual within that culture. When a culture moves away from its underpinnings, its people and institutions lose shape and definition. We see the results of this now in our streets. Rampant drug use at all levels of the culture. A pervasive feeling of despair and meaninglessness. An empty, hollow feeling. We have turned away from that which has shaped us inwardly; we have turned from those forces which shaped our souls.

Lectio Divina offers us a way to return to that process of soul nurture. It gives us a method of entry; a means by which we can go into scripture for ourselves and see if there is nurture there. The older tradition of scriptural study, current in the nineteenth century and before, held that God speaks to us continually through Her revealed word. The way that people listened to that word was to go into the scriptures and rest there with it. Unlike textual criticism, which is an objective, highly rational process open only to a few experts, the older tradition is primarily subjective, and thus, open to everyone. The core of this older tradition is what happens in our hearts as we meet God. Through opening ourselves to God in this way, we learn through scripture what God wants for us. As one theologian puts it, "In textual criticism, the scriptures are placed under our scrutiny, while in Lectio, the Scriptures place us under their scrutiny."[79]

As we have been swept up by the revolution in the sciences, we have lost our appreciation for the subjective. Everything has to be objective and quantifiable these days. While the benefits of this worldview are undeniable, something has been lost as well. We have lost our appreciation for interior things. We have lost our character—those inner qualities by which we used to measure a person's real worth. Our measuring system now is money—net worth—and we attempt to evaluate those around us in these "objective" terms. Unfortunately, the money measuring stick only evaluates a person's business competence or success in being born into a wealthy family. It has little to do with the heart.

Lectio Divina, as with all of the practices we are exploring, focuses on our hearts. These practices work to change us from the inside out. Lectio Divina begins when we listen to the word of God: by taking a passage from scripture, usually a couple of verses long, and reading it slowly and thoroughly, until the passage is familiar. Then we visualize the passage. We put ourselves into the action and become part of it. In this way, we begin to appreciate scripture from the inside. We encounter God more directly than is suggested by our usual way of skimming over the surface.

After a period of visualization, we pray with words. We will find ourselves praying for those in the story, and for ourselves, as our own deeper needs have become clear from our engagement with the story. Finally, as discursive prayer comes to an end, we rest in God, letting ourselves go in order to penetrate more deeply into the Being of the Divine.

Chapter 19

The Process of Lectio Divina

Lectio Divina has four parts: lectio, meditatio, oratio, and contemplatio. While I am presenting the practice here in a formal manner for teaching purposes, there is a kind of informal rhythm to the practice that you will experience as you try it. In practice, these four divisions flow naturally into one another, and not always in the order which I will present here.

Lectio. You begin with reading from holy scripture. This is not ordinary reading, like reading a newspaper or a textbook. Rather, it is a quiet listening to God. If Jesus were right here in the room with you, preaching the sermon on the mount, you would be listening in a very special way. You are to listen in this special way during Lectio. You listen, not only with your mind, but also with your heart. Your whole being is bent to catch the meaning of the words. You enter into a special relationship with the One who speaks.

To enter into this relationship, put aside the distractions of the day. Let your mind and body settle into quietness. Take a moment and reflect on what you are about to do. You are about to go to Israel and listen to the Lord Jesus as He speaks to His people, as He speaks to you personally.

Sometimes you bite off too much of the text for real Lectio. In Lectio, start with a verse or two, and ponder that. It is better to take a verse or two and thoroughly listen, than to read a chapter or two and not hear much at all.

Recognize, too, that the first few times you read a text, you are listening with the outer ear, not with the inner. Slow yourself down. Think, for example, of how else God might have said this phrase. What other words could She have used? Be open and receptive to the One who speaks. What is She saying to you, today? Be quiet inside, and listen with your heart.

Meditatio. Meditatio is the process of reflecting on the word of God. Begin your meditatio by memorizing the passage you are reading. Read it over and over again, slowly. Take it inside of yourself so that it becomes a part of you. Meditatio is a kind of gentle rumination on the passage. You take the scripture within yourself, learn it fully, and then turn it over in your mind. First you view it from this perspective, then from another, until you come to a sense of its deepest meaning.

This is the stage in Lectio Divina where visualization and the other sensory meditations can be used. Once you have memorized the passage, close your eyes, and enter into the picture that you create in your mind. Let yourself be in the crowd as Jesus gives His sermon on the mount.[80] When Jesus speaks and says, "Blessed are *you*," hear His words and let yourself be the "you" to whom His words are directed. Use the text to enter into relationship with Him, and learn. Let His words teach you directly, now, in your heart.

Be the cripple who is lowered through the roof to receive Jesus' healing touch.[81] Enter fully into the scripture. What is the healing that you need from the Lord? Let yourself receive it. Be the prodigal son in the parable.[82] Be the woman who is saved from stoning.[83]

God gives Herself, in the person of Her Son, Jesus, to you. The Divine makes a free gift of Herself, to nurture you. She offers you the relationship that you have always longed for. Is there any reason why you should not enter into it?

Open yourself to the stirring that God will make in your heart. As we do Lectio, we are changed by it. Let yourself experience in your own heart the love which God pours out to you in scripture. Let your heart move in response to God's love. Let it flow where the Holy Spirit directs.

Oratio. Oratio is the spontaneous verbal prayer that comes as you meditate on the word of God. As you enter into the word by reading and rumination, as you experience the word in meditation by entering directly into the text, your heart will be touched. When there is understanding of what our Mother is doing in scripture, there is also an opening in your heart, as you respond to the love of God. When you are touched in this way, there will be a spontaneous simplification as your heart responds to the Divine. You will find yourself praying: sometimes in words, using discursive thought, and sometimes as an outpouring of feeling without words.

Because this part of Lectio Divina is a response of each person's heart, it is difficult to describe in a general way. Each person will be moved in his or her own style, and will pray as directed by the heart. For example, you listen to Jesus' sermon on the mount, you put yourself in the crowd—and depending on your needs of the moment, you will respond differently. One time you may feel deep gratitude just for being in the Son's Presence. Another time, the words about the "pure in heart" might move you. Still another time, some other part of the sermon will touch you.

Not only will you be touched by a different part of the scripture each time, but your response to the scripture may also be different. You may, for example, begin to think about how you have failed your God, and by this means continue in the process of repentance. Conversely, you may remember your successes in the Lord Jesus and think about how the Lord has acted in your life. You may be moved by overwhelming feeling, with little or no thought. Or you may be moved to give thanks in verbal prayer, or to pray for your own needs or the needs of others.

Over time, however, there are certain characteristics of oratio that emerge. You will find yourself spending less and less time in verbal prayer. Your words and thinking will simplify. Your emotional response will tend to increase. You will find your prayer coming less from your head and more from your heart. Furthermore, there will be a felt sense of "rightness" about these changes. You will know that this is what you are supposed to be doing.

As with other forms of meditation, you cannot rush this process. When you start Lectio Divina, your oratio is likely to be full of discursive prayer. Please, do not inhibit this discursive process or judge yourself harshly, saying that you are talking too much. Just stay with the process and develop an internal "openness" to it. The Lord will work His way with you, gently and over time. Only two things are required of you to make Lectio work. The first is the desire to draw closer to your God; and the second is the will to keep practicing.

Contemplatio. The final step in Lectio Divina is contemplatio, the contemplation of God. Here you will find your words drying up. This process happens to you; you do not control it. You cannot force it. There is a growing lack of interest in ideas about God and a growing conviction that your words are so inadequate that they would be better left unspoken. The feelings that you have had toward God will begin to dry up. You will be increasingly attracted to silence and simplification. When this occurs, simply flow with it.

Let yourself rest in God, without talking, without desiring. It is enough to keep Him company—to sit awhile without words.

This notion of not-doing is very hard for us to understand. All of our lives we have been told to "do." We are rewarded for what we do. The focus in our culture has moved away from being and the inward dimension, and rests almost exclusively now with the outer dimension of activity. As we move in meditation, however, this orientation toward activity changes. Our "doing" in prayer dries up, so that we may begin to explore our "being." It is our being that is the most important gift that God has given us. In our being, we are connected with our Creator, our Father/Mother in heaven. In our being, we are whole. Contemplatio will lead us to this understanding.

When you begin Lectio Divina, you will probably find that you spend much time in the first two steps, lectio and meditatio. This is your true need when you begin, and it is important to honor your true needs. As you gain experience, you will find that you want to spend more time in oratio and contemplatio. As these needs arise, honor them. When you find your process of oratio simplifying, using fewer and fewer words, let yourself flow with it. You cannot hurry the process along; you can only respond to God's gentle calling in your heart.

The Dynamic Rhythm of Lectio Divina. Psychologically, Lectio Divina embodies an important human quality, the quality of rhythm. Within each of us, there is a sense of balance that occurs in the midst of our daily rhythms. This balance is constantly changing, as we change emotionally, as our thinking shifts, as our bodies move. Lectio has a similar rhythm, when we practice it, that mirrors the dynamic flow inside of us. It moves from one phase to another, at its own speed, centering always around the heart.

For teaching purposes, I have presented Lectio Divina as a four-part system that moves from lectio to meditatio to oratio to contemplatio. In practice, however, this sequence is not as fixed as it appears. While it is useful to follow the format of Lectio Divina as described above, you will find that your own heart may lead you into a different sequence from time to time. When this occurs, you should follow your own heart's yearnings, and go where it leads you.

You may, for example, be so moved by a passage that you go immediately to oratio or contemplatio. Or, you may find that you move to meditatio and stay there without feeling the need to move into oratio. Once you have learned the form of Lectio Divina and have done it many times, allow yourself to move freely, as the Spirit of God directs you.

Lectio Divina affirms both our activity and our receptivity. Lectio is the most active pole, contemplatio is the most receptive. Our God has created us with both aspects in our nature, and She blesses them equally. There is a hidden message here. The true purpose of prayer is not to condemn the activity in our lives and forsake it for the receptive. Rather, the purpose of prayer is to bring both of these sides of our nature into balance, so that they complement and inform each other.

Lectio Divina is a way of allowing God to speak to us. The primary text for Lectio is scripture. Lectio is the practice of allowing the text to become a part of us, to touch our hearts. We take in the word of God, and we are changed by it. In this way, Lectio is like the eucharist. We take Jesus into our bodies and hearts, either by means of the bread and wine, or by taking the word into our hearts and meditating on it there. In both cases, we are made holy by His gifts.

But Lectio does not end with scripture. We can also make profitable use of the early church fathers, many of whom wrote in apothegms which are short, pithy statements that need Lectio to unlock their meaning. We can even do Lectio on our own life experiences. God writes in our souls every day. To discern this Presence more clearly in yourself, let your mind turn to a crucial turning point in your life, remember it, and practice Lectio with this focus. We will explore all of these applications of Lectio in the following chapters.

So let us continue...

Chapter 20

Lectio on Holy Scripture

The practice of Lectio allows us to enter into scripture and experience it from within, rather than standing on the outside like strangers. As such, Lectio is a practice that is very appropriate for our time. Most of us feel like strangers to scripture; we do not know how to approach the books of the Bible in a productive way. Lectio teaches us, in its own slow fashion, how to come inside the very heart of scripture and to meet our God there.

Of all of the stories that Jesus told, perhaps the most central to His message was the story of the prodigal son. This story speaks to us, because we have all left our spiritual home and wander around the world herding swine and other unclean animals of various sorts. We have an inherent sense that this is beneath us; that we were created for something different and far better. Thus, each of us knows the child in this story from our own personal experience.

SPIRITUAL EXERCISE 21
LECTIO DIVINA ON THE PRODIGAL SON

1. Position your body comfortably, spine erect, on a chair or cushions. Have your Bible within reach, opened to the story of the prodigal son, Luke 15:11–24.

2. Now take a moment to ground yourself in your physical sensations. Close your eyes and slowly become aware of the sensations of your physical body. Feel the sensations as they flow through you. The sensations in your head...in your neck and shoulders...your elbows...your wrists and the palms of your hands...the sensations in your knees...your ankles and the soles of your feet.

---

3. Place your attention in your heart. Let all of your attention gather there. Let the sphere of energy surrounding your head gradually become heavier and heavier, moving slowly down your spinal column, until it reaches your heart. Let your awareness anchor in your heart. Feel your body from this perspective.

4. Maintaining your awareness in the heart center, open your eyes and read the story of the prodigal son very slowly. Let yourself be the younger of the two children. If you are a woman, recast the story into that of the prodigal daughter. Read the story three or four times, until every detail is clear in your heart.

5. Now close your eyes again, and visualize the story. See the action as it happens to you, the son or daughter of this father. Let yourself feel fully your feelings when you get your inheritance, when you turn from your father and leave. The good times with your newfound friends. Experience your emotions when your friends leave you and you are destitute in a strange land. When you herd the pigs.

6. Visualize yourself when you make the decision to cast yourself on your father's mercy. The agony of making the decision, and the full measure of shame and guilt. Be aware of the selfishness of your decision. The shallowness of your perception. See yourself as you begin to walk home...and again notice your feelings as you draw near your home. What are you feeling when you think about approaching your father and saying your planned words of subjection?

7. What happens in your heart when he lifts you up in an embrace? Let yourself feel fully these experiences: hear the sound of your father's voice, see the look on his face, and feel how these touch your heart.

8. You are likely to find yourself wanting to talk with your Father in heaven, after you finish your visualization. So

open your heart in prayer...let your heart's desire flow toward the Lord, either in words or in feelings.

9. When your prayer is finished, let yourself rest in God. Still your heart and mind and rest in God's Presence. When you find your attention wandering, gently bring your attention back to the Lord.

(To close your meditation)

10. When you are ready, let yourself come back to this place. Let the feeling return to your feet...your hands...your face. Take a deep breath, and open your eyes. Take a moment and look around the room to reorient yourself.

The benefit of stories like the prodigal son is that they are concrete, full of vivid imagery and clear emotions. Many of Jesus' teaching stories are like this, and well repay our efforts to enter into them through Lectio. The Old Testament is also full of stories like this. Because of the clear nature of these stories, they are relatively easy to enter into, and easy to understand by means of Lectio.

There is another kind of teaching in scripture that is more difficult to understand. These teachings are more abstract, like the letters of Paul and the gospel of John. Lectio, however, can unlock this material for you, although you may find yourself ruminating over it for a longer period of time. To demonstrate this, let us focus on a passage from John that uses a concrete image to convey a very abstract truth.

SPIRITUAL EXERCISE 22
LECTIO DIVINA ON JOHN 15:5

1. Position your body comfortably, spine erect, on a chair or cushions.

2. Now take a moment to ground yourself in your physical sensations. Close your eyes and slowly become aware of the sensations of your physical body. Feel the sensations

as they flow through you. The sensations in your head...in
your neck and shoulders...your elbows...your wrists and
the palms of your hands...the sensations in your
knees...your ankles and the soles of your feet.

3. Place your attention in your heart. Let all of your attention gather there. Let the sphere of energy surrounding
your head gradually become heavier and heavier, moving
slowly down your spinal column, until it reaches your
heart. Let your awareness anchor in your heart. Feel your
body from this perspective.

4. Keeping your attention focused in your heart, slowly read
John 15:5:

> I am the vine, you are the branches. He who lives in me
> and I in him, will produce abundantly, for apart from
> me you can do nothing.

Read this passage several times, until you have memorized
it.

5. Now close your eyes again, and visualize the first part of
this passage: "I am the vine, you are the branches." See
Christ as a vine, and notice all of the branches that come
from the vine. Feel yourself as one of these branches. Feel
what it is like to be connected to Christ in this intimate
fashion.

The life force which flows through the vine flows also
through you. Feel fully the power of that life force. Look at
the juncture of vine and branch. Where does Christ stop
and where do you begin? In an earlier statement, Jesus
says, "The Father and I are one."[84] Where does the Father
stop and where do you begin?

6. Visualize the second part of the passage: "He who lives in
me and I in him, will produce abundantly, for apart from
me you can do nothing." See how you live in Christ. See
how you cut yourself off from Christ. Experience deeply
how each of these states feels.

7. You are likely to find yourself wanting to pray after you finish your visualization. So open your heart in prayer…let your heart's desire flow toward the Lord, either in words or in feelings.

8. When your prayer is finished, let yourself rest in God. Still your heart and mind and rest in God's Presence. When you find your attention wandering, gently bring your attention back to the Lord.

(To close your meditation)

9. When you are ready, let yourself come back to this place. Let the feeling return to your feet…your hands…your face. Take a deep breath, and open your eyes. Take a moment and look around the room to reorient yourself.

Notice that a single verse was used here. One of the hallmarks of Lectio is that we begin to use shorter and shorter passages from scripture, and we go over them more and more intently. This is backwards from our usual way of doing things. In the world, we value things that are done quickly. The Spirit, however, does not give up its mysteries so easily. As we learn and develop the practice of Lectio, we will find ourselves going more and more slowly. This is natural and should not be resisted.

What should be resisted is our schedule. The notion of doing Lectio on a chapter a day is not appropriate. That is far too much. Even the idea of working through a particular book or even a chapter in a week or a month is inappropriate. The Spirit will move us through the scripture at a speed that will allow us to learn what we need. So let yourself go and flow with the Spirit's gentle guidance.

Chapter 21

Lectio on the Church Fathers

Lectio is an appropriate tool for other kinds of spiritual reading besides the Bible. In fact, many of the early fathers of the church wrote in short pithy sayings called apothegms that were designed for the meditation of Lectio. These apothegms simply will not reveal their meaning in a cursory reading.

One of the most influential compilations of the wisdom of the early church fathers is *The Philokalia*,[85] a book composed of the edited writings of the early fathers, and meant to help sincere Christians learn to pray effectively. *The Philokalia* became the literary backbone of the Hesychast renaissance in Greece in the seventeenth century, and in Russia in the nineteenth.

Prominent in *The Philokalia* are the writings of Evagrios the Solitary.[86] Evagrios was a deacon in Constantinople, born in 345, who had to leave the city because of an illicit love affair. He fled to the desert in Egypt, became a monk, and in time gave the world some of the most penetrating psychological insights about the spiritual life that have ever been written. His understanding of the passions that drive human beings, and the remedies that can harness these passions for life in the Spirit is without parallel.

SPIRITUAL EXERCISE 23
LECTIO ON EVAGRIOS

1. Position your body comfortably, spine erect, on a chair or cushions.

2. Become aware of the physical sensations which flow through you. Close your eyes and experience the stream of sensations that course through your physical body. No

---

need to change them. No need to judge them. Simply let yourself feel deeply the multitude of sensations that cascade through your body. Gently focus on the sensations in your head...in your neck and shoulders...your elbows... your wrists and the palms of your hands...the sensations in your knees...your ankles and the soles of your feet.

3. Be aware of the sensations around your head. Let all of your attention gather there. Let the sphere of energy that surrounds your head gradually become heavier and heavier, moving slowly down your spinal column, until it reaches your heart. Let the energy of your awareness anchor in your heart. Feel your body from this heart center.

4. Keeping your attention focused in your heart, open your eyes and slowly read this passage from Evagrios of Ponticus:[87]

> Of the demons opposing us in the practice of the [spiritual] life, there are three groups who fight on the front line: those entrusted with the appetites of gluttony, those who suggest avaricious thoughts, and those who incite us to seek the esteem of men. All other demons follow behind and in their turn attack those already wounded by the first three groups.

Read this passage several times, until you have memorized the essence of it.

5. Now close your eyes again, and visualize each of the major parts of this passage. Let yourself see the demons of gluttony. What do these demons look like? Put a face on them. How do they push you toward consumption? Take a moment and reflect on how your needs to consume drive your behavior.

6. Be aware of the demons that incite all of your grasping, your drive toward getting more and more of everything. What do these demons look like? Put a face on them. How do they push you into feeling needy, into wanting more

and more? Reflect on how your need to have more drives your everyday behavior.

7. Be aware of the demons that drive you to want to be liked by others. What do these demons look like? Put a face on them. How do they influence you? Do they suggest that certain actions will make someone dislike you? Do they push you to be more outgoing than you really are, or to hide more than is really comfortable for you? Look carefully at how these demons drive your behavior.

8. Consider how much of your day-to-day behavior is driven by these demonic needs, identified by a writer in the fourth century. Look over the course of this day, or yesterday. This past week. How have these forces tugged and pulled at you? What have been the consequences when you assent to these forces?

9. You are likely to find yourself wanting to pray after you finish your visualization. So open your heart in prayer... let your heart's desire flow toward the Lord, either in words or in feelings.

10. When your prayer is finished, let yourself rest in God. Still your heart and mind and rest in God's Presence. When you find your attention wandering, gently bring your attention back to the Lord.

(To close your meditation)

11. When you are ready, let yourself come back to this place. Let the feeling return to your feet...your hands...your face. Take a deep breath, and open your eyes. Take a moment and look around the room to reorient yourself.

Evagrios speaks about three of the seven deadly sins. He has an intriguing and very different perception about where our enemy is located. Evagrios says that the demonic forces are located within us. Certainly since the movie, *The Exorcist*, our popular culture has understood demonic forces as existing outside of us. Typically we have understood the demonic as something which will reach out and "possess" us; something that will take control of our minds. While this is quite spectacular and makes very exciting movies and fiction, it is most unlikely.

Instead, the early church understood that the demonic comes from within us. It is part of our fallen, imperfect human nature: our pride, our greed, our lust for good things. These are what typically corrupt us, and turn us from the love of God. Evagrios, by his clear understanding of the location of these demonic forces, allows us to do combat, successfully. If you don't know where your enemy is camped, you will always be taken by surprise. And surprise is half the battle.

There are other, equally useful sources throughout the early writings of the church. Especially important among these early sources are the wisdom sayings of the desert fathers.[88] Shortly after Constantine recognized the Christian church and established it as the state religion in the early fourth century, great hordes of pagans flocked to the church. There were so many in such a short time that they overwhelmed the congregations, and Christianity was much watered down. In reaction to this, some of the faithful left the cities and the enormous congregations there, and went off into the desert, following our Lord's example. These few hardy souls became known as the desert fathers,[89] for they congregated in the deserts of Egypt, Palestine, and Syria.

Not much of their work has survived to our time. There are a few short stories, and some of the lives of the more prominent ascetics. These stories were designed to be processed using Lectio. When we practice Lectio with these apothegms, we will find a deep reservoir of spiritual wisdom, gathered by these wise old men ages ago.

For economy of space, we will not go into these apothegms here. In exercise 20 above, we explored an apothegm from the desert fathers about Abba Joseph. You may wish to explore other apothegms in your practice using this as a model.

The desert fathers seem far distant from us. This is an illusion. The concerns with which they wrestled are similar to our concerns today. They wanted to know how to draw close to God, how to manifest fully the love of God. They, too, lived in a chaotic, secularized world with few sources of authentic wisdom available. They, too, had to blaze new trails in the wilderness, looking for God. Are these not also the concerns and trials of you who read this book?

As we practice, it is helpful to process the stories of those who have gone this way before us; to read their stories and ponder them. Not only to read, but to enter fully into the story, that we might begin to stretch ourselves and see the full glory that God has prepared for us. Why not, indeed, become totally fire!

Chapter 22

Lectio on Your Personal Experience

One of the errors of our time is the belief that God stopped writing scripture on the last page of the book of Revelation. This is simply untrue. At its root, scripture is simply a record of people's experience of God. Because we are still experiencing the Divine, scripture is not yet finished.

What this means is that God is writing His scripture in our hearts right now. He makes Himself manifest to us in many ways, some of which we realize, and many that we cannot comprehend or even sense yet. But, just as we can do Lectio on written scripture to unlock its meaning, so also we can do Lectio on God's action in our life for the same purpose.

Often people have trouble thinking of their own lives as a place where God is acting. God is usually talked about as something "out there" who acted on people only in the past. To overcome this modern tendency, it is often helpful to do a brief exercise. Take a few minutes and jot down the ten most important spiritual turning points in your life. These may include a marriage, a divorce, some personal change of heart, or a peak experience. Then do Lectio on one of these ten.

Lectio can be done on any experience; it is not limited to your ten most powerful turning points. For those who are beginning to practice Lectio on their own life experiences, however, these ten turning points are often a good place to begin, since they usually hold much material that is not fully understood or integrated yet.

SPIRITUAL EXERCISE 24
IDENTIFYING YOUR SPIRITUAL MILESTONES

1. Unlike the other exercises in this book, this is not so much a meditation as a time of thought and reflection. Begin by

---

setting aside a period of time for this exercise, perhaps a half hour to an hour. Arrange to minimize distractions such as the telephone or other interruptions. Turn off the radio or television.

2. Reflect on those turning points in your life where you have moved in a new direction spiritually. Some people feel the hand of God while they are in the midst of these turning points. More commonly, it is only through reflecting on past experiences that people see God's hand in their lives.

3. Often people feel that God has not been present to them, or acted in their lives. If you are one of these, list only two or three of these spiritual turning points—major milestones like your birth, your marriage, and so forth. I suspect, however, that God has been busy in your life, just as She has in the lives of everyone else. So try to push yourself to identify ten or twelve turning points.

4. If you are one of those who has written more than fifteen such turning points, you are likely to lose sight of the whole scope of your journey due to your intense involvement in the details. Limit yourself to ten or twelve. Focus on the real *milestones* of your spiritual life.

5. List these experiences; actually write them down. Write a descriptive paragraph or two about these direction changes. What did they feel like at the time? Did your inner world feel chaotic, calm, afraid, joyous? How did people respond to your changes? How did you respond? What happened in your life and the lives of others as a result of these changes?

If you haven't done so already, copy the results of this exercise into a journal.[90] Keeping a journal of your spiritual experiences is extremely valuable. It gives you a place to record, think about, and understand your experiences. Later, after you have kept your journal for some time, it can serve as a valuable tool for getting perspective on your spiritual journey. Now let us go forward and work on these milestones. These can be the bases for beginning Lectio

on our personal experiences. The following exercise will show you
how to do this.

SPIRITUAL EXERCISE 25
LECTIO ON PERSONAL EXPERIENCE

1. Position your body comfortably, spine erect, on a chair or
   cushions.

2. Choose a life experience, and we will explore it to find the
   word that God has written in your heart. You may wish to
   choose one of your spiritual milestones from the previous
   exercise.

3. Now take a moment to ground yourself in your physical
   sensations. Close your eyes and slowly become aware of the
   sensations of your physical body. Feel the sensations as
   they flow through you. The sensations in your head...in
   your neck and shoulders...your elbows...your wrists and
   the palms of your hands...the sensations in your knees...
   your ankles and the soles of your feet.

4. Place your attention in your heart. Let all of your attention
   gather there. Let the sphere of energy surrounding your
   head gradually become heavier and heavier, moving slowly
   down your spinal column, until it reaches your heart.
   Anchor your awareness in your heart. Feel your body from
   this perspective.

5. Bring to mind the life experience that you have selected.
   Take several minutes to go back to the beginning of the
   experience and remember it fully and completely. Now see
   yourself in the action. Feel what it felt like. Hear the
   sounds as they took place around you. Relive it fully. What
   were the consequences of this event? How did it shape your
   life? How was God moving in your life then?

6. When you finish with your visualization, open your heart
   in prayer...let your heart's desires over these things flow
   toward the Lord, in words or in feelings.

---

7. When your prayer is finished, let yourself rest in God. Still
   your heart and mind and rest in God Presence. When you
   find your attention wandering, gently bring your attention
   back to the Lord.

   (To close your meditation)

8. When you are ready, let yourself come back to this place.
   Let the feeling return to your feet...your hands...your face.
   Take a deep breath, and open your eyes. Take a moment
   and look around the room to reorient yourself.

When we do Lectio on our own experience, several things become apparent. First, we cannot go quickly and have any hope of being productive. Lectio is a slow process of intense reflection. We cannot rush it. Second, not everything in our lives will be immediately understandable, even through Lectio. When tragedy strikes, for example, it can be very hard to accept and make sense of the experience. Tragedy seems to be a random event, and evidence either that God does not exist, or that He tolerates and perhaps condones evil.

One of the great Russian saints of our day, Father Michael, the Recluse of Uusi Valamo, a man who suffered the horror of the Soviet suppression of the church in Russia, wrote of a conversation he had with our Lord. In this vision, the Lord Jesus said:

Happiness and misfortune, rise and fall, health and sickness, glory and dishonor, wealth and poverty—everything, comes from Me and must be accepted as such. Those who entrust themselves to Me and accept all the trials which I send to them will not be ashamed in the Day of Judgment. They will realize even here in this world why their life took this course and not another. I send to everyone that which is best for him.[91]

This statement is strikingly similar to St. Paul, when he writes from prison in Rome, saying: "I am certain that neither death nor life, neither angels nor principalities, neither the present nor the future, nor powers, neither height nor depth nor any other creature will be able to separate us from the love of God that comes to us in Christ Jesus."[92]

What does become clear through Lectio on personal life experiences is how the hand of God moves in our lives. We begin to discern the outline of a pattern. We start to see how our pride, our greed, our lust, our tendency to sin and be separate, is addressed by our Father. As we reflect, it will seem as if our Father has placed in front of us certain lessons which must be learned. If we do not learn them at first, He will repeat them for us, again and again through different life circumstances, until we grasp what is necessary. Then we will go on to the next lesson. It is helpful, however, to have the assurances of St. Paul and Father Michael when we find ourselves in the midst of a painful lesson.

What Can We Conclude from Lectio? Often people who do not know the long tradition of Christian meditation and contemplative prayer wonder where it came from. They ask, "Is this not just a set of practices stolen from the Eastern religions, and dressed up in a Christian window–dressing?"

One of the great calamities in Christendom is that ordinary people are unaware of their spiritual birthright. We are God's children, but we do not know that or experience our lives in this way. The practices of meditation and contemplative prayer are nothing less than the means for realizing our spiritual birthright. For a variety of historical reasons, this patrimony has been concealed from those whose inheritance it rightfully is. This means that God's people starve in the midst of plenty, because they do not know how to access their own spiritual wealth. This is a tragedy of epic proportions.

The Christian practices of meditation and contemplative prayer are not the warmed-over practices of another religion, quickly thrown together for the modern reader to stem the tide of those leaving the church. These practices are rooted in a long history that goes back to our Jewish roots. Historically, we can trace the different spiritual lineages from teacher to student from the third century onward, when the Roman persecutions stopped and the Christian literature started to have some survivability. With some practices, like Lectio Divina, we can see clear evidence extending from its Jewish roots, through the life and teachings of Jesus, and into the early church. These are not warmed-over techniques from somewhere else. They are woven into the fabric of our faith, and are inextricable from it.

Lectio Divina was one of the tools used by our Lord to more fully understand the scriptures, and to expound the truths of scripture to those who followed Him. Over the centuries, the format of Lectio has been adapted and revised, in order to open the student to the living truth that is God more effectively. That Lectio has survived over 2000 years, influencing millions, perhaps hundreds of millions, in the process, is the *best* testimony to its effectiveness that can be offered.[93]

Part V
Monologistic Prayer

With Lectio, we began the critical movement from meditation to contemplative prayer: from the discursive, image–making part of the intellect, into the non–discursive intellect. This is a step that has great significance for our spiritual growth. In our culture, we have tied ourselves to the discursive intellect. As a result, we focus outwardly, toward the world. We understand sensory things to be "real," while things of the mind are typically seen as "unreal" or insubstantial, something of lesser or no importance.

The discursive mind is active. It searches after answers; it pursues knowledge. The non-discursive mind, however, is not concerned with activity. Its realm is that of "being." When we enter the non-discursive sphere, we move into ways of being. Since Descartes, our culture has systematically abandoned the non-discursive ways of examining ourselves and the world. We have, in effect, abandoned any concern with being or meaning. As such, spiritual endeavors are not seen as important by the majority of people. Lip service is given to religion and spirituality, but the vast majority are simply not concerned with their own spiritual growth.

The meaninglessness of contemporary philosophical and artistic endeavors, such as French existentialism and the schools of nihilism and post-modern deconstructionism, are the intellectual fruits of this abandonment. The practical consequences are found in the pervasive drug use, violence, and other thrill-seeking behaviors in our culture. By abandoning our inner being, we have left behind all meaning and purpose. Only emptiness remains. We have effectively cut God out of our lives.

Using Lectio in the preceding section, you began to move away from the discursive intellect, which thinks actively about a scripture passage. You were introduced to another way of using the intellect: to simply hold a focus in your attention, without doing anything, without pursuing anything. To "contemplate" the passage. As we continue, you will develop this capacity further by learning monologistic prayer. The word "monologistic" comes from the Greek root *mono*, meaning one, and *logos*, meaning word. This type of prayer revolves around the use of a short phrase, as short as one word at times, which is employed in a repetitive manner to focus the mind on God. This process has the effect of stilling the discursive intellect, so that we gradually become aware of that vast storehouse of treasure which lies hidden underneath its busyness.

Some modern writers have confused the monologistic prayers of the Christian church with the mantras used in Hinduism and Buddhism. There are, however, significant differences. As I understand it, a mantra is a phrase that is repeated over and over in a mechanical way. Monologistic prayer has in common with mantras this aspect of repetition. Monologistic prayer differs, however, in that it involves developing an awareness of God's Presence. Furthermore, the purpose of this prayer is to lead the discursive intellect into stillness. When the intellect is still, the practitioner does not continue the repetition, but simply rests in that stillness. The function of monologistic prayer is to lead us into participation in the Mind of God—into that vast still space that lies within each one of us.

This section on monologistic prayer is meant to introduce these methods in a comprehensive way. My intent is to survey the major developments in monologistic prayer that have developed in both the Eastern and Western Christianity, and to give practical examples of how to use these methods. We will begin by exploring the history of monologistic prayer in the church, to provide a context in which to understand this development. Then we will examine the Jesus Prayer, which was the first great development of monologistic prayer. The Jesus Prayer is still the primary monologistic tool of the Eastern churches.

We will go on to survey the development of monologistic tools in the West. This will include an examination of the rosary, which involves using monologistic prayer to explore the feminine mysteries of God. We will proceed to examine the Cloud of Unknowing and centering prayer, which is a modern adaptation of the Cloud. We will conclude this section by exploring some of the benefits of this form of prayer.

Chapter 23

Calling on God

The roots of monologistic prayer extend widely throughout Christendom, and deeply into our Jewish heritage. It is only in modern times that this powerful form of prayer has been neglected. As with Lectio, the roots of monologistic prayer go back to the roots of Judaism. In the Jewish tradition, worshipers were instructed to keep the word of God, the word of the law, always upon their hearts and their lips. The great model for this is the Shema:

> Hear, O Israel! the Lord is our God, the Lord alone! Therefore you shall love the Lord, your God, with all your heart, and with all your soul, and with all your strength.[94]

As we read the book of Deuteronomy, we find an intriguing connection between the word "heart" and the idea embodied in the Shema, that God is one God. The author of Deuteronomy ties the two together, as if the place to recite the Shema is in the heart. "Fix in your heart that the Lord is God."[95] "Take these words of mine [the Shema] into your heart and soul. Bind them at your wrist as a sign, and let them be a pendant on your forehead. Teach them to your children, speaking of them at home or abroad, whether you are busy or at rest."[96] There is an understanding that the Shema is to be recited in the heart, and to be recited constantly.

This is not an ordinary thing, to speak words in the heart. We don't think of our hearts with little mouths, speaking words. Furthermore, the words we are asked to recite there, "The Lord is our God, the Lord alone!" are not ordinary words. This unusual combination of words and the place of speaking them indicates that something special is occurring. This special something is meditation, specifically monologistic prayer. There is an invocation of God's Presence, and the repetition of a short phrase. The action is

focused not in the intellect, but in the heart. These are the key elements which thread through all monologistic prayer.

Our Christian Heritage

Although we can trace the heritage of monologistic prayer to
Judaism, there is very little historically verifiable material that
survived the three centuries of persecution that the church
endured from the time of Jesus' death to the time of Constantine,
around A.D. 300. Thus, it is not possible to trace the movement of
monologistic prayer from Judaism directly into the Christian tradition. We come across monologistic prayer again in the writings of
the desert fathers.

The desert fathers were Christians who took the call of Jesus
with utmost seriousness. They left the churches in Egypt, Palestine,
and Syria, with all of the usual distractions of urban life, to withdraw into the deserts where they could pursue their goal of drawing
closer to God. Their lives were based on *ascesis*, a Latin word meaning discipline. The central thrust of their living was to engage in disciplined activities which would move them away from the
omnipotent "I" as the center of the world, so that they could know
God as their center.

The word "ascetic" has a bad flavor today. In the popular culture, an ascetic is seen as someone who has renounced real life for
some deliberately miserable travesty of life. Thus, the popular culture believes that the ascetic is usually found living alone in a barren cell, wearing poor clothing, and subsisting on bread and water,
or some other poor fare. An ascetic is someone to feel sorry for.

Unfortunately, this popular image of asceticism completely misses the point, and shows no understanding of the goals of the ascetic
life. Most people would firmly agree that some sort of discipline is
necessary to achieve whatever goals we might have. Whether our
goals are to learn a profession, how to run a business, or how to play
a game, we use some form of discipline, putting off today's pleasure
for the pain and difficulty inherent in the learning process.
Asceticism is simply the discipline necessary for spiritual learning;
the discipline necessary to learn how to come into the Presence of
the Divine and to see the face of God. When you think about the
alternatives, what could be so bad about asceticism?

On the one hand, there is this crazy world of competing desires and impulses, where each individual puts himself at the center. As a result, we have no real center in our lives: we are blown here and there by every passing fad and fashion. We run from one thing to the next, seeking some ill–defined satisfaction. We know we are missing something, but we don't know what it is. Advertisers keep promising that they have *the answer* to our needs. But their solutions are never satisfactory for more than a little while. We keep looking for satisfaction, but we only find emptiness. And we keep finding the same old emptiness over and over again. Our lives are meaningless.

On the other hand, with a disciplined Christian life, we are grounded in the Lord Jesus. We come to know Him intimately, and daily are filled up with His loving–kindness. With the considerable effort and work that a spiritual discipline entails, we find the answer that we all so desperately seek. We fill our burning emptiness.

It comes down to this: What is it that we truly want? Do we want to spend ourselves investigating every passing fad, hoping to fill that empty void inside? Or do we want to spend ourselves exploring a spiritual path whose every stone is marked, and whose result is known and testified to by many?

This is the same choice that our forebears faced. The desert fathers made a clear and firm commitment to leave the "self–center" and to move toward God as their center. Thus, the time of the desert fathers was a time of extraordinary fertility for spiritual practice. The desert fathers were far enough away from the historical Jesus that they did not know anyone who had actually walked with the Lord or heard Him speak. Their world was much like our own: a world cut off from any meaningful spiritual roots. It was a smaller version of our global village, with Greek instead of English as the *lingua franca* around the Mediterranean, and ready trade and movement between cultures. In their world, as in ours, there was a striking emphasis on the sensual, on the pleasures of "right now!" The rights of people meant nothing, with a sharp division between the haves and have-nots.

The desert fathers were confronted with many of the same choices that we face today. Should I live as the society demands? Should I get a good education, get married, get a job, and pursue sensual pleasure and the accumulation of goods for the rest of my life? Or should I live for something more than myself and my own gratification? Should I live for the Lord? Should I leave this little

"I" that stands in the center of my subjective experience, and try to find a larger, more enduring "I Am,"[97] of which I can be a part?

St. Anthony of the Desert. Perhaps the clearest example of a soul confronted by these choices is that of St. Anthony of the Desert.[98] Anthony was an Egyptian, born to wealthy and prosperous Christian parents. When he was around eighteen years old, his parents died, leaving him as sole heir and responsible for the care of a much younger sister. He evidently was a thoughtful young man, and was not clear about what he should do with his life. One day, after pondering the deep questions posed by our Lord about how to live, he went into a church to pray. The liturgy was being celebrated, and Anthony heard the words of the gospel as if Christ Himself were speaking: "If you would be perfect, go, sell what you possess and give to the poor, and you will have treasure in heaven."[99]

Transfixed by these words, Anthony immediately went home and began to distribute his possessions to the poor. He kept enough aside to support his sister, and left her in the care of a convent to finish her upbringing. He then left his village around 269 A.D. and sought out the company of an old man who lived a disciplined Christian life in isolation, not far from his village.

In the desert, Anthony developed a new kind of interior discipline. Daily he renounced his own desires in order to draw closer to God. He saw this as a way to continually lay down his life for Christ. Considering that he had renounced considerable wealth, the early stages of his discipline must have been very distressing for him. He was tempted, over and over again, by the memory of his property and his easy life of prosperity. Living a solitary life, he was also tempted by the memories of his now-sacrificed intimacy with family and friends.

As Anthony stayed true to Christ, constantly sacrificing his memories and desires, there arose in him an awareness of the deeper longings. When you are alone in the desert, the deep passions of greed, pride, and lust come to the surface, and for Anthony this is what occurred. For a time, he became obsessed with greed for money, and then came to recognize this as a temptation from the devil. Then he was tempted with the lust for power and the desire for fame. All these dark desires he laid out before the Lord, sacrificing them to God.

Anthony is a marvelous example of someone purifying his heart in order to see God more clearly. As Anthony kept to stillness and

solitude, all of the desires which also obscure the Christ dwelling
in our hearts came into his awareness. Instead of acting on these
desires, Anthony offered them up to God.

This is a central point that should not be missed! Offering our
dark desires is a poor offering to give to God. But it is the offering
that God asks of us. The only thing that is wholly ours are these
dark desires. Our bodies, souls, minds...all these are gifts from
God to us. The darkness of our desires, however, is ours; our own
creation. It is this darkness that Anthony gave to God, just as we
are called in our own time to offer our darkness to God. "A broken
and contrite heart, O God, you will not despise."[100]

Anthony's part was to engage in the disciplined offering of himself and his darkest desires, over and over again. His part was to
offer himself in prayer to the Lord. Christ then, acting in Anthony's
heart, purified his conscience over a period of many years. Finally,
Anthony entered into a transforming union with Christ; and
through Christ, into union with all reality. Anthony's life serves as
a model and guide for all those who would draw closer to God
through prayer and discipline.

Anthony was one of the first of the desert fathers who left the
cities of Egypt and sought solitude in the desert. He was followed
by hundreds, perhaps thousands of other seekers: men and women
who were looking for something more than what they found in the
city. It was a time of great experimentation with spiritual methods. Many different kinds of discipline were tried, some of which
are too harsh or extreme for people today. Many different methods
of prayer were created and explored by them. This work done by
our forebears in the deserts of Egypt, Palestine, and Syria provides
the foundation for much of the prayer which followed.

Monologistic Prayer in the East. Coming out of this fertile period of the desert fathers are the two characteristic forms of monologistic prayer which have sustained the Eastern and Western
churches. In the East, the Jesus Prayer was developed in the fourth
century in Egypt. By means of experimentation and continual trial
and error, the desert fathers laid the conceptual and practical foun-
dations for this prayer.

By the fourth century, the four main components of the Jesus
Prayer took recognizable shape:

1. Devotion to the name of Jesus, "which is felt to act in a semi-
   sacramental way as a source of power and grace.

2. "The appeal for divine mercy, accompanied by a keen sense of compunction and inward grief (*penthos*).

3. "The discipline of frequent repetition.

4. "The quest for inner silence or stillness (*hesychia*), that is to say, for imageless, non-discursive prayer."[101]

These elements comprise the heart of the Jesus Prayer, and have been fashioned into the characteristic monologistic prayer of the Eastern churches.

Monologistic Prayer in the West. In the West, John Cassian, who visited the desert fathers in the late fourth century, took to the West the "arrow prayer,"[102] which he learned during his stay in the desert.[103] Echoes of Cassian can still be heard in monasteries today, as the eucharistic liturgy opens with the responsorial chanted prayer that he brought back from the East:

> O God, come to my assistance.
> O Lord, make haste to help me.

These are the very words which he brought back, repeated by countless generations of monks and lay people, down to our own times.

When Cassian was given charge of a monastery, he enjoined his monks to repeat this refrain constantly, during all their waking hours. For Cassian, the purpose of a monk is to engage in continual prayer. From this beginning in his own monastery, Cassian wrote for other monks in his *Conferences* and *Institutes*. By these means, the prayer spread throughout the monasteries of the Western church.

In the West, many different arrow prayers have been used, most of them being short sayings from scripture. In all cases, though, the purpose of the arrow prayer is to go beyond the discursive intellect into the stillness and quiet of being in God. All of the later arrow prayers of the West rest on Cassian's foundation. This includes the prayer of the *Cloud of Unknowing*, centering prayer, and the rosary.

These prayers of the Eastern and Western churches are ways that we call upon God. With these prayers, we don't call upon God to petition or beg; we don't call to intercede for others. Instead, we call upon God to offer up all those thoughts and desires which pull us away from the love of our Father. We call upon God in order to quiet our restless passions; if you will, to bore our discursive intellect into moments of quietude and stillness. We call upon God in order to uncover that deeper center which lies in our hearts, where Christ dwells with us.

Chapter 24

The Jesus Prayer

The Jesus Prayer, in its several variations, holds the distinction of being the oldest continually-used monologistic prayer in Christendom. Furthermore, it has probably been used by more people, and in more varied circumstances than any other. It is one of the great treasures of the church.

The Jesus Prayer has three parts which are practiced simultaneously. First, the practitioner opens to God's Presence, using one of the practices of recollection. Second, the practitioner places his attention in the heart region. And third, he begins to repeat the words from the heart, "Lord Jesus Christ, have mercy on me."

Unfortunately, the Jesus Prayer was introduced to the popular culture in America in a severely truncated manner, in a rendition that, literally, tore the heart out of it. In 1961, J.D. Salinger gave the Jesus Prayer a central role in his novel of modern emptiness and ennui, *Franny and Zooey*.[104] In his novel, the Jesus Prayer was taken out of context, and understood as merely the words, "Lord Jesus Christ, have mercy on me." The other, more crucial operations of the prayer were evidently not known to the author.

Despite the truncated nature of this rendition, the benefit of Salinger's mention of this prayer, and the prominent place that it takes in the protagonists' struggle to find meaning in life, has done enormous good. From this introduction, many readers have tried his abbreviated form of the prayer and found some relief. Others have investigated Salinger's primary source, the work by an anonymous Russian, entitled *The Way of a Pilgrim*.[105] Thus, the Jesus Prayer was introduced into the mainstream of our culture.

The Development of the Jesus Prayer

The roots of this prayer extend back to the time of Christ Jesus. From the earliest times, devotion to the name of Jesus has been a

194

part of the church. This devotion is embodied in two central references in the New Testament. The first, from St. Paul, says,
"God...bestowed on Him the name above every other name, so that
at Jesus' name, every knee must bend in the heavens, and on the
earth, and under the earth."[106] The second reference is in St. John's
gospel: "Whatever you ask the Father, he will give you in my
name."[107] These texts form a powerful rationale for praying using
the name of Jesus. As a result, in the liturgical churches most
prayers close with the petition, "in Jesus' name we ask." The Jesus
Prayer refines this. It focuses directly and exclusively on the name
of Jesus. In this way, the prayer functions as a tool through which
divine grace is channeled into the heart of the believer.

The second element of the Jesus Prayer, embodied in the
words, "have mercy on me," appeals for God's mercy and forgiveness. Here the one who prays implicitly focuses on the relationship to God, and asks for grace. In practice, as the practitioner
prays in this way, there frequently arises a deep sense of grief
and an outpouring of tears. These tears seem to cleanse the soul
from the passions which separate one from God.

The third element, the frequent repetition of the prayer, is an
attempt to follow St. Paul's injunction to "pray without ceasing."[108]
We hear mention of this practice of constant repetition throughout the surviving writings of the desert fathers. By this means,
those early monks strove constantly to remember God, and to live
and move in the awareness of God's Presence.

The fourth element, the quest for inner stillness, is the hallmark
of non-discursive prayer, and the beginning of contemplation.
Evagrios of Ponticus, who lived with the desert fathers, states that
"prayer means the shedding of thoughts."[109] Another translation
renders the passage, "Prayer is the rejection of concepts."[110]
Evagrios' concern was to still the restless wanderings of the intellect so that the essential unity of the soul can stand revealed. In
most people, their mental turmoil obscures the Presence of God.
Only through focusing our attention can we go beyond conceptual
thinking into those unitive states where we dwell with God.

The History of the Jesus Prayer. While the four elements of
the Jesus Prayer were developed by the fourth century and used in
various combinations by monks and nuns, it was not until Bishop
Diadochus of the fifth century that these elements were crystal-
lized into one recognizable prayer. Diadochus was the first to bring
these elements together for the purpose of entering into the state

of non-discursive, imageless prayer. He states that the intellect is inherently "restless," and needs some activity to satisfy its needs. He engages the intellect with the ceaseless repetition of the name of Jesus, which ultimately leads to the quieting of the discursive mind. Of importance is Diadochus' instruction to "give [the mind] nothing but the prayer, 'Lord Jesus.' "[111] This unvarying repetition brings the restless intellect into stillness, "reaching out beyond language into silence, beyond discursive thinking into intuitive awareness."[112]

From this essential catalyst, the Jesus Prayer appears again in clear form in the deserts of Egypt, Sinai, and Palestine. St. John Climacus, who lived in the Sinai and wrote the core work, *The Ladder of Divine Ascent*,[113] recommends the prayer. Due to the widespread influence of his writings, the Jesus Prayer spread throughout the Orthodox churches. St. John's followers, St. Hesychius[114] and St. Philotheos,[115] are even more explicit in extolling the virtues of the Jesus Prayer.

Thus, between the fifth and eighth centuries, the Jesus Prayer emerges as a recognized spiritual way, sanctioned by the church hierarchy and widely practiced by both monastics and the laity. In later centuries, as the Eastern churches in general declined in spiritual vigor, the practice of the Jesus Prayer fell into disuse. In each of the several revivals which have swept through the Eastern churches, the Jesus Prayer has played a significant role. In Greece in the fourteenth century, and then again in the eighteenth century when the *Philokalia* was compiled, the Jesus Prayer was the central practice which fueled and sustained the revival. Again, in Russia during the late eighteenth and nineteenth centuries, the Jesus Prayer plays a now-familiar and significant role in revitalizing the faith of an entire people.

The Russian Pilgrim. We in the West are familiar with this last revival through the works of the anonymous Russian author of *The Way of a Pilgrim*.[116] This anonymous author tells a fascinating story of his adventures during the decades before the freeing of the serfs in 1861. An orphaned peasant from the province of Orel, he was raised by a grandfather, along with his older brother. This brother was a drunkard and injured him repeatedly, first crippling his hand, and then burning his house down. Crippled and widowed, with no ties to keep him, the younger brother began his wanderings.

Like St. Anthony, the pilgrim's spiritual journey started in a church, as he heard the words of St. Paul, "pray without ceasing."[117]

He began to wonder how this was possible, and asked every learned clergyman that he encountered. No one gave him a satisfactory answer. He kept looking for a method, but all he received were pious platitudes that begged the question. Finally the pilgrim found a *staretz*, a wise old spiritual guide, who taught him the following:

> The continuous interior Prayer of Jesus is a constant uninterrupted calling upon the divine Name of Jesus with the lips, in the spirit, in the heart; while forming a mental picture of His constant presence, and imploring His grace, during every occupation, at all times, in all places, even during sleep. The appeal is couched in these terms, "Lord Jesus Christ, have mercy on me." One who accustoms himself to this appeal experiences as a result so deep a consolation and so great a need to offer the prayer always, that he can no longer live without it, and it will continue to voice itself within him of its own accord.[118]

In addition, the *staretz* read to the pilgrim from the *Philokalia*, a compendium of writings from the early fathers which describes the "detailed science of constant interior prayer."[119] Various postures and other details about the Jesus Prayer were explained by reference to this work, introducing him to the writings of the early church fathers. As the pilgrim began to progress in the prayer, his psychology started to change. After a summer of practice, he reports:

> I felt an absolute peace in my soul. During sleep I often dreamed that I was saying the Prayer. And during the day if I happened to meet anyone, all men without exception were as dear to me as if they have been my nearest relations....All my ideas were quite calmed of their own accord. I thought of nothing whatever but my Prayer, my mind tended to listen to it, and my heart began of itself to feel at times a certain warmth and pleasure...My lonely hut seemed like a splendid palace, and I knew not how to thank God for having sent to me, a lost sinner, so wholesome a guide and master.[120]

The Three Operations of the Jesus Prayer

The Jesus Prayer, as it was taught in Greece and Russia, has three mental parts or operations, and all of these need to be present for the prayer to be effective.[121] First, there is the recollection of God's presence. We must engage in the practice of the Presence of God, which is to be aware that our God, whose name is Emmanuel, "God with us," is right here with us now. This is the first and most important part of the Jesus Prayer.

The second operation of the prayer is to put the "head in the heart," which means to move our attention from our head, where it usually resides, into our heart center, and to pray from the heart. In the words of St. Theophan the Recluse, a major figure in Russian mysticism in the nineteenth century:

> In order to keep the mind on one thing by the use of a short prayer, it is necessary to preserve attention and so lead it into the heart: for so long as the mind remains in the head, where thoughts jostle one another, it has no time to concentrate on one thing. But when attention descends into the heart, it attracts all the powers of the soul and body into one point there. This concentration of all human life in one place is immediately reflected in the heart by a special sensation that is the beginning of future warmth....This warmth then holds the attention without special effort....From this there follows a rule of spiritual life: if you keep the heart alive towards God, you will always be in remembrance of God.[122]

This means that if we keep our attention focused in our hearts, our hearts will always be oriented toward God. This mental operation of putting the attention into the heart is quite unusual for Westerners. We tend to think of attention as something fixed in the head. Our reasoning goes like this: "the brain is the organ of thought, so our attention must be physically rooted in the head." Actually, we can place our attention anywhere in the body that we choose. Placing our attention in the heart feels strange at first, and many wonder whether they get it right. But we will become more comfortable here as the practice becomes familiar.

The third, and least important of the three operations of the Jesus Prayer is the repetition of the words: "Lord Jesus Christ, have mercy on me," over and over. If our minds are particularly unsettled in our meditation, we may need to repeat this phrase quickly, to drive out the distractions. If our attention is collected and focused, we may adopt a more receptive attitude, and say the words slowly, with pauses in between the phrases.

Putting the three operations together looks like this. First, open yourself to feel God's Presence with you. Be aware of that special "feel" or "Presence" that is God. Then feel the sphere of energy that surrounds your head. This is your attention. Move that sphere of energy slowly down into your heart. From your heart, not from your head, repeat the words of the prayer, "Lord Jesus Christ, have mercy on me." "The essence of the whole thing is *to be established in the remembrance of God, and to walk in His Presence.*"[123]

The Jesus Prayer is not a visual meditation. You should not make pictures of the Lord or of yourself in this practice. Simply engage in these three operations. When your attention wanders from them, gently bring yourself back, and reestablish each of the three operations. If you notice, during the course of your practice of the Jesus Prayer, that you are no longer doing one of these operations, gently reestablish that part of the prayer and then continue.

Images are rather complex ways to mediate the Presence of God to ourselves. The words of the prayer are less complex ways of mediation, so that we can approach more closely. "The main thing is to stand before the Lord with the mind in the heart."[124] Eventually, even the words will disappear, as we begin to approach contemplative prayer. This is the experience of *hesychia*, or inner stillness. When the words and thoughts of the Jesus Prayer disappear of their own accord, the one who prays has entered into the stillness of the Mind of God. This experience is one of sublime peace and tranquility. When this occurs, do not force yourself to continue repeating the Jesus Prayer. Let yourself dwell in stillness.

The purpose of the Jesus Prayer is to collect and order the attention, and to focus this attention on God in such a way that we gradually are drawn into the deepest awareness of the Divine Presence in all things and manners of life.

SPIRITUAL EXERCISE 26
THE JESUS PRAYER

1. Position your body comfortably, spine erect, on a chair or cushions.

2. Ground yourself in your physical sensations. Close your eyes and slowly become aware of the sensations of your physical body. Feel the sensations as they flow through

you. The sensations in your head...in your neck and shoulders...your elbows...your wrists and the palms of your hands...the sensations in your knees...your ankles and the soles of your feet.

3. Now open your awareness to feel God's Presence right here with you. Feel that Presence all around you...within you. Breathe in the Divine with every breath. Breathe God out. Let yourself rest in this Presence.

4. Be aware of the sensations in and around your head. You probably are aware of a sphere of energy around your head. This is where most of us live. Let this sphere of energy begin to get heavy and drift downward toward your heart center. When you begin this, it may be a little difficult. We are so accustomed to having this energy in our heads that we don't know what it would feel like somewhere else. But let that sphere of energy gradually grow heavier and heavier. Let it sink down into your heart. If you have trouble with this, imagine that with each inhalation this sphere of energy is pushed down about an inch or so. With every breath, your head energy is moved downward, until your head rests in your heart. Anchor yourself here, so that you are able to perceive through your heart.

5. Now, in your heart and from your heart, slowly say the words, "Lord Jesus Christ, have mercy on me....Lord Jesus Christ, have mercy on me." Let your heart repeat these words over and over again, feeling God's Presence right here with you.

6. When your attention wanders, be patient with yourself. Gently bring your attention back to the three operations of this meditation: feel God's Presence; put your head in your heart; and say the words, "Lord Jesus Christ, have mercy on me."

(To close your meditation)

7. When you are ready, let yourself come back to this place. Let the feeling return to your feet, your hands, and your face. Take a deep breath, and open your eyes.

The Interior Movement of the Jesus Prayer

The practice of the Jesus Prayer will take us on a predictable interior journey. At first, we are likely to have difficulty engaging in the three operations of the prayer simultaneously. While each of these operations is relatively simple, the first two are unusual for us in this culture. We seldom try to experience the Presence of God in a deliberate way. And we never strive to put our attention into our heart! So there will be a period of some frustration, as we try to keep each of these three things going at once. It feels something like juggling, trying to keep three things going at the same time. Once you get the hang of it, though, the experience seems quite natural and enjoyable.

During the initial time of frustration, you will find yourself distracted, as with the previous practices. Your attention, while strengthened, is still not a focused tool. As you become aware of your distractions, the initial impulse will be to punish yourself: to engage in the punitive internal dialogue which emphasizes how inadequate you are to accomplish even the simple tasks of this prayer. This inner dialogue is only a furthering of the distraction. You obtain no benefit from it. Simply withdraw your attention from these distractions, and engage or re-engage in the three operations of the prayer.

The complexity of the Jesus Prayer, with its three specific and simultaneous operations, is actually a substantial aid toward the development of a stable attention. These three operations place such a load on conscious awareness, that it rather quickly moves beyond distraction. You notice I said "rather quickly." I mean this in relationship to other meditations which do not have this loading effect. Your progress may still seem slow to you. After continual practice, two things begin to emerge. First, you are more and more able to do all three operations of the prayer simultaneously. Second, the number and intensity of distracting thoughts and feelings seem to diminish. There is a gradual quieting of the mind, as if the intellect becomes content with the activity of the prayer.

The Arising of Spiritual Phenomena. As your practice continues, several phenomena may arise that are important to understand. While there is no specific order to their occurrence, in my experience, they tend to follow the order described here.

First, there is the arising of great internal heat. You will be sitting in meditation and you will become aware that your body is very warm, even hot. You may begin to perspire profusely. This is one of the spiritual fruits of the deepening of your interior prayer. It is the action of God within us, burning away the subtle and gross sins which keep God veiled from our awareness. You may find this burning to be so intense that you become frightened of it, thinking that something is wrong. Do not worry. You are simply tasting the first fruits of the interior life. As this experience comes, you may need to loosen your clothing before you meditate, or even wear lighter clothing, so that you are not too distracted by the heat.

The second phenomenon which frequently occurs is known as the gift of tears. This is the experience of inner grief and compunction, which seems to arise spontaneously as you explore your interior depths. This experience is cause for rejoicing, because it signifies a deepening of the interior cleansing which usually begins with the experience of interior heat.

The gift of tears may begin with a feeling of grief or sadness, centered in the heart or the throat. You will find tears beginning to trickle out of your eyes. On occasion, there is full-blown weeping, but more often just a sweet-sad grief which causes tears. When this occurs, do not be surprised if your tears continue, even beyond the period of your meditation. You may find your eyes "gently leaking," producing very small amounts of moisture throughout the day. Usually no one will notice this but you.[125]

A third phenomenon, which is more rare than the first two, and which typically follows after a long period of practice, is the experience of interior light. There arises within your heart an interior light that carries with it such tender sweetness that you will marvel at its intensity. This is your first clear sight of that great light that is Christ the Lord. Words do not suffice to describe it, nor the interior feelings which accompany it.

These three phenomena cannot be sought after. This is very important for you to understand. These phenomena accompany the deepening of practice in a natural way. So do not strive after the phenomena. Your striving after these "markers" of experience will only serve to keep you from them. Instead, strive to be present to God at all times. As our Lord says, "Do this, and all else shall be added to you."[126] As you continue your practice, you will find that your mind begins to quiet down. There is a gradual dawning of interior stillness. This occurs both within the practice of the Jesus Prayer and between the formal periods of practice.

Within the practice, your recitation of the words will be broken, from time to time, by a vast stillness. It is as if you have been traveling along a heavily wooded road in the mountains, where you cannot see anything because of the thick forest. Then the road suddenly turns out to a cliff, and a stunning vista opens before you. You stand, dumbstruck with awe, held suspended in the vastness of all that you survey.

This is what interior silence is like. Your recitation of the words of the prayer will, at times, spontaneously cease, and you will stand in the Presence of God in awe. There are simply no words, only stillness. This deep experience cannot be achieved by wishing it, by imagining it, by striving for it, or by promoting yourself beyond the reach of your own experience. It lies within you, awaiting your discovery. You can do nothing to hurry it. You can only open your heart to God, and fix your attention there. God will give you His grace in His own time, not in yours.

With the arising of this deep inner stillness, you begin to approach contemplation. The contemplative process is different in character than all the spiritual exercises that go before it to prepare your soul. We will explore the contemplative process at a later time.

Enhancing the Jesus Prayer

As wondrous and powerful as the Jesus Prayer is, there is a way to increase its efficacy still further. To do this, you connect the power of your emotions to the intent of the prayer. Instead of simply reciting the words over and over, you emotionally charge the words, imbuing them with your own longing.

This is not a practice for those who are just starting to learn the Jesus Prayer. It is enough, for those who are just learning, to develop a focused attentiveness to the Lord. After six months or so of continuous practice with this prayer, and after the attainment of some interior stability, you may wish to enhance the power of the prayer by connecting your emotions to the words, enlivening the words with your emotional power.

SPIRITUAL EXERCISE 27
ENHANCING THE JESUS PRAYER

1. Position your body comfortably, spine erect, on a chair or cushions.

2. Become aware of the physical sensations which flow through you. Close your eyes and experience the stream of sensations that course through your physical body. No need to change them. No need to judge them. Simply let yourself feel deeply the multitude of sensations that cascade through your body. Gently focus on the sensations in your head...in your neck and shoulders...your elbows...your wrists and the palms of your hands...the sensations in your knees...your ankles and the soles of your feet.

3. Now open your awareness to feel God's Presence right here with you. Feel that Presence all around you...within you. Let yourself rest in this Presence.

4. Be aware of the sphere of energy around your head. Let this sphere of energy begin to get heavy and drift downward toward your heart center, until your head rests in your heart.

5. In your heart and from your heart, slowly say the words, "Lord Jesus Christ, have mercy on me....Lord Jesus Christ, have mercy on me." Let your heart repeat these words over and over again, feeling God's Presence right here with you.

6. After the words have stabilized, begin to *feel* the words. Instead of saying the words, *feel* the meaning of them. *Feel the Lord Jesus Christ. Feel* your own need as you ask, *"have mercy on me."* Repeat the words from this feeling level, letting yourself explore the depths of your feeling. Your emotion is like the locomotive on a train: it can power your prayer. Create this inner train, and power it fully.

(To close your meditation)

7. When you are ready, let yourself come back to this place. Let the feeling return to your feet, your hands, and your face. Take a deep breath, and open your eyes.

This connection of the emotions to prayer is one of the great contributions that Christian contemplatives have made to the development of prayer. Our Christian heritage is full of emotion: from Christ, the Messiah, being born in a stable, to the bloody crucifixion and then the sweetness of Jesus' resurrection. It is natural for us to use the strong feelings that are aroused in us as we read the narratives of our Savior's work, and to apply these feelings to our prayer.

To state the obvious, our emotions *move* us. There is a moving force in our emotions that has the power to take us to different places. So, too, it is in prayer. When we find ways to connect our emotions to our prayer, ways to power our prayer with our emotion, then that power to move us is unleashed and channeled into spiritual pursuits. In this way, our emotions can become a great force for good in our inner development.

The Jesus Prayer is one of the great spiritual tools that the church has developed to aid us in our walk with the Lord. It has been developed and refined over virtually the entire scope of Christian history, a period of some 2000 years. It has been used by many different peoples, from many different walks of life. It has been used both by monastics and the laity to effect the deepest sort of spiritual change.

Over this period of time, those elements of the prayer which were not efficacious in producing spiritual transformation for everyone have been pruned away. What is left is the pure essence. The prayer is like a powerful vehicle, waiting only for us to use it. Because of its power, it should not be used lightly. This is not a child's toy to be played with. It has the capacity to provoke the most profound kinds of spiritual changes in our hearts. So we should not use this prayer until we are quite ready, in our own minds, to move into the depths of God.

The prayer will lead us, as directly as possible, into direct encounter with the Divine. The benefits which accrue from this encounter are impossible to enumerate. There is such a sweetness, such a joy that arises from this direct encounter, that language is simply too gross a vehicle to adequately describe the experience. This, of course, has not stopped people from trying to describe what has happened to them. So let us close this chapter with a description of the effects of this prayer, as described by the anonymous Russian pilgrim in the last century.

The Prayer of my heart gave me such consolation that I felt there was no happier person on earth than I, and I doubted if there could be greater and fuller happiness in the kingdom of Heaven. Not only did I feel this in my own soul, but the whole outside world also seemed to me full of charm and delight. Everything drew me to love and thank God; people, trees, plants, animals. I saw them all as my kinsfolk, I found on all of them the magic of the Name of Jesus. Sometimes I felt as light as though I had no body and was floating happily through the air instead of walking. Sometimes when I withdrew into myself I saw clearly all my internal organs, and was filled with wonder at the wisdom with which the human body is made. Sometimes I felt as joyful as if I had been made Tsar. And at all such times of happiness, I wished that God would let death come to me quickly, and let me pour out my heart in thankfulness at His feet.[127]

Chapter 25

Praying the Rosary

The rosary is quite different from the Jesus Prayer and other monologistic prayers. The rosary focuses on Mary, the mother of God. This focus is extremely important for our spiritual growth.

Protestant Christians often misunderstand the importance of Mary. They see devotion to Mary as a mistake: Mary is not God, so why pray to her? This misses several crucial points. First, and most importantly, Mary illustrates submission to God's will. Mary demonstrates, by her acceptance of the angel's message, how the true self can respond directly to the Divine. She illustrates, through her quiet obedience, how to turn from the false self that is concerned with what everyone thinks. She shows us how to live for God. There is not one of us who cannot learn from her example.

Second, Mary is the Theotokos, the God-Bearer. She is the one who carries Christ and brings Him into the world. In this capacity, she serves as a model for every human being, for each of us who also carry Christ in our hearts. She shows the proper relationship that we have with the Divine. She illustrates the responsibilities. And in her life, the fruits of carrying the Christ are amply demonstrated. She is the quintessence of generous loving-kindness: protecting and nurturing and living as each of us is called to live.

For these two reasons, we have much to learn from Mary. She teaches us the feminine virtues. For men, especially, these are important. We men need to integrate these virtues into our daily living, for without them, we cannot know God. Without full submission, which can be very hard for a man, we cannot draw close to the Source of all things.

The History of the Rosary

The rosary began as a Marian devotion. It is the only popular monologistic prayer that focuses on the feminine aspects of the

Divine. This focus on the feminine is, by itself, enough to set the
rosary apart from other forms of monologistic prayer, which are
more typically focused on some aspect of the Trinity. A second
major difference is the origin of the rosary. This prayer sprang
from the popular culture of the High Middle Ages. Virtually all of
the more advanced prayers have had their origin in monastic practice. The rosary is the only prayer which has its origin from the
people. Furthermore, the laity have continued through the centuries as the driving force which has kept the rosary alive. It is,
above all, a prayer of the people and for the people.

During the High Middle Ages there were not many books
because of the huge expense to copy them by hand. As a result,
most of the population was illiterate. This posed a considerable
problem for monastics of the time, who recited the 150 psalms in
the daily Offices every week. To get around the massive memorization necessary to recite the psalms, the practice arose of having
the illiterate monks and nuns recite the Lord's Prayer. Thus,
instead of reciting the 150 psalms during the daily Offices, they
would recite 150 Our Father's, which they counted off on a ring of
beads. This became known as "The Psalter of the Father."[128]

At about the time that the Psalter of the Father was taking
hold, devotion to Mary was increasing dramatically in Western
Europe. The prayer known as the Hail Mary began its life as a
liturgical antiphon for the fourth Sunday of Advent. It was used in
the mass on this one Sunday each year. This prayer was picked up
by the illiterate populace. Among the unlettered, the Hail Mary
began to be used as a short, arrow prayer said throughout the day.
Within a short while, the Hail Mary was being said repetitively,
using the ring of beads from the Psalter of the Father. Shortly
afterwards, this practice was formalized as "The Psalter of the
Blessed Virgin," and its popularity quickly surpassed that of the
Psalter of the Father.

Thus, the rosary came into being. Although it has been modified
extensively since its origin in the Middle Ages, its essential character as a Marian devotion remains intact. This is especially
important, I think, for a religion as patriarchal as Christianity. It
is as if the masses sensed the essential imbalance in our faith, and
moved intuitively to restore some sense of the feminine presence
which is so important for true spiritual growth.

There have been several modifications to the Psalter of the
Blessed Virgin that have given the rosary its present form. In the
fourteenth century, Henry Kalar divided the 150 Hail Mary's into

fifteen groups of ten, called decades. These decades were marked out by the recitation of an Our Father. One of Kalar's colleagues, Dominic of Prussia, added material that turned the Rosary into a kind of Lectio Divina. He added a phrase to the end of each recitation of the Hail Mary which focused on one of the events in the life of Christ. The first mystery attended to in the first decade of the rosary is the Annunciation of Jesus to the Blessed Virgin. After each Hail Mary, the following phrases were added to focus the meditation on aspects of that mystery:

1. ...who has freed us from the sin of Adam.

2. ...for whom the patriarchs and the prophets sighed.

3. ...for whom you and Joseph waited in an attitude of prayer. Etc.

These phrases were further clustered into three main groups, the joyful, the sorrowful, and the glorious mysteries. This began the threefold division of the mysteries of the rosary. Since this initial meditative structure, there have been many other meditations which have been grafted onto what is, in its essence, a monologistic prayer.

The rosary is a very complex form of monologistic prayer, the most complex that I have seen. Although it began as a simple devotion to Mary, over the years various layers have been added to this simple form, until it has reached its present-day complexity. There are even more complex versions of the rosary than the ones presented here. For our purposes, however, it is enough to focus on the monologistic aspects of the rosary. For this reason, we will not elaborate on the meditations on the mysteries of Christ, nor on the more elaborate forms of the rosary.

The Shape of the Rosary

There is a fundamental core which threads through the multitude of different forms that the rosary has taken. This core is composed of two prayers and a doxology: the Hail Mary, the Our Father, and the Glory Be. Typically, these units take the form of fifteen decades of Hail Mary's, each separated by an Our Father and a Glory Be. That is, the Hail Mary is recited ten times, followed by the Our Father, and a Glory Be. This sequence is repeated fifteen times. This is the fundamental shape of the rosary today.

In addition to this fundamental structure, there are more elaborate and less elaborate introductions and endings to the rosary. But the heart of this monologistic prayer is the fifteen decades of Hail Mary's, each separated by an Our Father and a Glory Be. Because the rosary is a prayer of the people, it is constantly being changed. While the core remains, the structure of the rosary is constantly added to, in ways that reflect the needs of a particular people.

In addition to the many different shapes that the rosary can take, there are also many different levels through which it can be approached. This prayer can be a simple recitation, used as a monologistic prayer during the course of the day. It can be a structured meditation, used to explore the great mysteries of the life of Christ. Or it can be used as a springboard to contemplation. In its complexity, the rosary is more like Lectio Divina than the more typical monologistic prayers with their repetition of a short phrase.

The Practice of the Primitive Rosary. Two versions of the rosary are presented in this chapter. The first is the original rosary, the Psalter of the Blessed Virgin, and it consists of the repetition of 150 Hail Mary's. This is presented for those who are not familiar with the rosary, and need to memorize the prayer. Even those who are quite familiar with the rosary may find this more primitive version helpful. Some practitioners of the rosary report that the saying of an Our Father at the end of every ten Hail Mary's is intrusive. Going back to the primitive rosary, you are able to move more directly into the monologistic aspects of this great prayer.

Prior to practicing the rosary, you will find it necessary to purchase the rosary beads. This string of beads is divided in such a way that you do not have to keep count by means of the intellect. The tactile touch of the beads will show you where you are. This way, you can give yourself over to your praying more fully. For those who have never prayed the rosary before, this should be considered a "must buy." Too much mentation will pull you away from your intended practice. In addition, you may wish to practice in front of a statue or other image of Mary. While the rosary is not a visualization, it can be helpful to have a visual image in front of you, to load and steady your concentration.

SPIRITUAL EXERCISE 28
PRAYING THE PRIMITIVE ROSARY
THE PSALTER OF THE BLESSED VIRGIN

1. Position your body comfortably, spine erect, on a chair or cushions.

2. Ground yourself in your physical sensations. Close your eyes and slowly become aware of the sensations of your physical body. Feel the sensations as they flow through you. The sensations in your head...in your neck and shoulders...your elbows...your wrists and the palms of your hands...the sensations in your knees...your ankles and the soles of your feet.

3. With your rosary beads in hand, begin to pray the Hail Mary.

   Hail Mary, full of grace, the Lord is with you. Blessed are you among women, and blessed is the fruit of your womb, Jesus. Holy Mary, Mother of God, pray for us sinners now and at the hour of our death. Amen.

   Repeat the prayer at a pace that seems natural to you. When you come to the separated single bead, simply acknowledge to yourself that you have completed ten Hail Mary's, and go on to the next decade. Devote yourself to this for the period of your meditation, praying around the ring of beads.

4. When you find your attention wandering, don't scold yourself. Simply bring your attention back to your prayer, and pray with your whole heart.

(To close your meditation)

5. When you are ready, let yourself come back to this place. Let the feeling return to your feet, your hands, and your face. Take a deep breath, and open your eyes.

This is the primitive rosary; the rosary as it first originated, and in its simplest form. In this form, it is a pure and unadulterated devotion to the Blessed Virgin. Many Protestants, who have lost any sense of veneration for Mary, may find this practice strange or difficult because it does not fit well with the values they have been taught. If you are uncomfortable here, feel free to leave the rosary and focus your practice with other monologistic prayers. Or, conversely, you may wish to stay with the rosary to explore the feminine side of the Divine. There are no prescriptions in this matter. Simply follow your heart, and do what the Holy Spirit lays out before you.

For all Christians, Mary exemplifies qualities that are crucial for the spiritual journey. Mary embodies the rich qualities of receptiveness—that ability to wait upon God with an open heart and an open mind. The ability to wait without understanding and without judgment. The ability to rest in her own being and to rest in the Divine.

For those who are devoted to Mary, she is seen as the epitome of generous loving-kindness, of rich compassion. She is the eternal mother who holds us and caresses us, never getting angry. She protects us from harm. She tames our unruly spirits, helping us focus on her Son, so that we can move more quickly into the Divine.

Without these qualities, none of us will move far along the path our Lord has marked out for us. We do not know the end. We do not know the way. We are utterly dependent on God's grace to move us. Thus, our movement is dependent wholly on being receptive to that grace. We can have no better model for this than His mother, Mary, who says to the angel, "I am the servant of the Lord. Let it be done to me as you say."[129]

The Practice of the Contemporary Rosary. Now we come to the rosary in the form we have received it today. There are a multitude of variations on the contemporary rosary. These variations have grown up in different places, often without any awareness that the usage is variant. This phenomenon naturally occurs in a prayer that has such popular following.

The form of the rosary presented here consists of the fifteen decades of Hail Mary's, each separated by an Our Father and a Glory Be. In addition, a more elaborate introduction and the Salve Regina at the end are added. This is the rosary in common use today, and gives the practitioner the full flavor of its contemporary practice. I have not included the meditations on the life of Christ: the five joyful, the five sorrowful, and the five glorious mysteries.[130] The addition of these meditations pushes the practice of the rosary toward Lectio Divina. In this section, we are practicing monologistic prayer. For heuristic purposes, it does not seem appropriate to utilize this aspect of the rosary here.

**SPIRITUAL EXERCISE 29
PRAYING THE ROSARY**

1. Position your body comfortably, spine erect, on a chair or cushions.

2. Ground yourself in your physical sensations. Close your eyes and slowly become aware of the sensations of your physical body. Feel the sensations as they flow through you. The sensations in your head...in your neck and shoulders...your elbows...your wrists and the palms of your hands...the sensations in your knees...your ankles and the soles of your feet.

3. To begin the rosary, make the sign of the cross on yourself,[131] and pray the following petitions:

   O God, come to my assistance.
   O Lord, make haste to help me.

   Glory be to the Father, and to the Son, and to the Holy Spirit, as it was in the beginning, is now and ever shall be, world without end. Amen.

   O my Jesus, forgive us our sins, save us from the fires of hell. Lead all souls to heaven, especially those who have most need of your mercy.

4. Then take the rosary beads in your hands, holding on to the crucifix. The Apostles' Creed is recited:

   I believe in God, the Father Almighty,
   creator of heaven and earth;

   I believe in Jesus Christ, His only Son, our Lord;
   He was conceived by the power of the Holy Spirit
   and born of the Virgin Mary.
   He suffered under Pontius Pilate,

was crucified, died, and was buried.
He descended to the dead.
On the third day, He rose again.
He ascended into heaven
and is seated on the right hand of the Father.
He will come again to judge the living and the dead.

I believe in the Holy Spirit,
The holy catholic Church;
the communion of saints;
the forgiveness of sins;
the resurrection of the body;
and the life everlasting. Amen.

5. With the five beads that lead from the crucifix to the ring of beads, pray the following:

With the first bead, an Our Father.[132]

With the next three beads, three Hail Mary's, to obtain the three gifts of faith, hope, and charity.

With the fifth bead, a Glory Be:

Glory be to the Father, and to the Son, and to the Holy Spirit, as it was in the beginning, is now and ever shall be, world without end. Amen.

6. With the ring of beads in the body of the rosary, pray the following:

Ten Hail Mary's for the ten beads that are found grouped together.

One Our Father for the single bead that divides each decade.

7. When you find your attention wandering, don't scold yourself. Simply refocus your attention back to your beads, and find your place in the prayer. Then engage in mentally reciting the appropriate prayer, a Hail Mary or an Our Father.

8. Go around the ring of beads three times. You will find that it is easy to find your place because the crucifix marks each circumnabulation.

9. To close, at the end of your third time around the ring of beads, pray the Salve Regina:

Hail, holy Queen, Mother of mercy,
Our life, our sweetness and our hope,
To you do we cry, poor banished children of Eve;
To you do we sigh, mourning and weeping in this valley
    of tears.
Turn, then, most gracious advocate,
Your eyes of mercy toward us,
And after this, our exile,
Show unto us the blessed fruit of your womb, Jesus.
O clement, O loving, O sweet virgin Mary.

10. Conclude the rosary with the following:

Pray for us, O holy Mother of God.
That we may be made worthy of the promises of Christ.

Pour forth, we beseech you, O Lord, your grace into our hearts, that we—to whom the Incarnation of Christ, your Son, was made known by the message of an angel—may, by His passion and cross, be brought to the glory of His resurrection, through the same Christ, our Lord. Amen.

11. When you are ready, let yourself come back to this place. Let the feeling return to your feet, your hands, and your face. Take a deep breath, and open your eyes.

Interior Movement during the Rosary. Much like the Jesus Prayer, the rosary pushes the practitioner into developing a receptive attitude. Consider the primary words of the *Hail Mary*: "Hail Mary, full of grace, the Lord is with you." These words have no action component; they do not push you to act in any way. Rather, they invite you to salute Mary, who is herself the primary model of receptivity for the Christian churches. The prayer is a vehicle for teaching us to be receptive and open to God.

Of course, when we try to graft this prayer in our hearts, there is immediate conflict. Our whole lives have been spent in *doing*. We are not comfortable letting go of our doing and moving to that more primary mode, which is *being*. So our false self, our intellect, throws up distractions of all kinds. Just as with every other spiritual practice described in this book, the practice of the rosary results in the emergence of immediate distractions. Our task is to persevere with our prayer. Gently disengage from any distracting thoughts or emotions and return attention to the prayer.

The rosary is designed to keep our attention loaded with a variety of activities—the different prayers in the rosary—and thus, to keep the attention stabilized by activity. It is a useful practice for those who find themselves easily distracted. As we practice with the rosary, we will develop a much deeper appreciation for the qualities which Mary embodies. There is a sense of comfort which arises, a sense of her deeply feminine presence, which holds us like a child. A mother who is never angry, never critical, but who points us in a clear consistent direction, nevertheless. As we practice here, we will, by contact with Mary, begin to increase in those receptive qualities which will help us move spiritually.

The rosary is a complex monologistic prayer, designed to load awareness in such a way as to bring the practitioner into the felt presence of the Divine. Specifically, the rosary is designed to develop the qualities of receptivity in the practitioner. These qualities are essential for spiritual growth. The deeper we go in our practice, the more we discover that we can do very little to move ourselves forward spiritually. What we *can* do is open ourselves more fully to God, being more receptive to His action in our hearts and lives.

That is not to say that there is nothing we can do. It is our task to prepare the ground for the Lord. We prepare by ordering our lives so that we have time for prayer, both individually and in community. We prepare by changing our behavior so that we conform to God's will for us. We prepare by reading scripture and other good books which help us recognize those holy qualities that already exist within ourselves. We prepare by quieting ourselves and focusing attention on the Divine. But after these preparations, it is God who does the real work.

By focusing our attention on Mary in prayer, we open ourselves to follow in her footsteps. She did not try to actively do God's work.

Rather, she was receptive to God working within her. It is for the cultivation of this receptivity that the rosary can be so important.[133]

God is the One who moves in our hearts and changes us. It is the love of God that warms us and brings us closer. We cannot bargain with God for this, nor can we force this closeness from God. We must learn to be open and receptive to His actions. We must learn to recognize them, so that we can facilitate His good work in us. Just like a farmer, we prepare the ground and plant the seed. Whether it grows or not depends on the action of those things that are out of our control. The rains, the winds, the warmth of the sun; these things are beyond us. Our task, then, is to prepare our ground well. Our task is to wait in prayer, doing those things which help us grow quiet.

The saints assure us that Christ is speaking in our hearts, constantly. He murmurs direction and advice, words of encouragement and love. Our inability to hear does not signify that the Lord has abandoned us. It only signifies that we do not know how to listen well. So we must learn to quiet our interior noises so that we can better receive the Lord.

Chapter 26

The Cloud of Unknowing

With so many translations and editions of *The Cloud of Unknowing* available to the contemporary reader, it almost passes credulity to realize that this text was inaccessible to all but the most arcane scholars through the first third of the twentieth century. Only then was the text translated into modern English.

The Cloud of Unknowing[134] was written by an anonymous author in fourteenth-century England. The author was certainly writing for a solitary hermit, and may have been one himself. He was so successful in concealing any personal references to himself, however, that attempts to identify him in both medieval and modern times have failed.

Just as the Jesus Prayer typifies the monologistic prayer of the Christian East, so also does the prayer described in *The Cloud* stand as a typical representative of Western contemplative teaching. Our anonymous author's teaching about the clouds of unknowing and forgetting is taken directly from that great mystic, Richard of St. Victor,[135] who died A.D. 1173. The author of *The Cloud*, in turn, prefigures the "dark night" described so vividly by St. John of the Cross,[136] who lived and wrote during the last half of the sixteenth century. Thus, we can place our anonymous writer squarely in the apophatic tradition in the mainstream of Western contemplative understanding during the medieval period, which stretched roughly from 1100 to 1600 A.D.

The Apophatic and Cataphatic Ways

Very early among those Christians who engaged in the practices of deep prayer, there developed an understanding that there are two ways of "knowing" God. These came to be known as the apophatic and cataphatic theologies. The cataphatic way is distinguished by the use of sense data; it focuses on the revelation of God to humankind by means of the sensory tools of vision, hearing and feeling. Cataphatic theology involves the use of concept, symbol, and story, and we have explored its manifestations in the sensory meditations and Lectio Divina.

Apophatic theology, on the other hand, rests on the premise that no human concept is adequate to contain God, or to understand God. God is, therefore, essentially unknowable, except as She deigns to grace us with revelation. As a result, any attempt to approach God through the senses, using devices such as the sensory meditations, will have only a partial success. These forms of prayer allow us to draw close to God, but we are unable to penetrate deeply with them. God simply cannot be known in this way.

The apophatic way is the way of negation. The one who prays opens to a passive, receptive state of mind, and deliberately enters the darkness of unknowing: coming to God in an open, receptive state, with no predetermined concepts about God that would limit God's action in the soul. Here, according to writers in the apophatic tradition, between the cloud of unknowing above us, and the cloud of forgetting beneath us, God manifests to us in the dark recesses of our souls.

The apophatic way is outside the experience of most Americans. We come from a pragmatic, sensory-based culture, that values—perhaps overmuch—the life of the senses. Because the apophatic approach to God is so different from what we are accustomed to, we may tend to ignore or discount this tradition. We do this, however, to our own detriment.

The apophatic tradition has deep roots in the church, extending back to our Jewish heritage. For Jews, God is the One who is utterly transcendent. His name is so precious that it cannot be said. He deigns to dwell in the temple in Jerusalem, but is only approached by a special priest once every year. This apophatic way of approaching God carried into Christianity. It surfaces in writings of the desert fathers and the Cappadocians in the fourth and fifth centuries, in Denys the Pseudo-Areopagite[137] in the fifth and sixth centuries, and through Denys into the wider church. Due to the great influence of Denys, there developed a substantial apophatic tradition in both the Eastern and Western churches which has endured through the centuries. Unfortunately, because of our cultural emphasis on the sensory, it has remained mostly unknown to us today.

The apophatic way complements the sensory approach, and rests on the substantial base developed by cataphatic means. It rests squarely on the stories of our Lord, and on the understanding of these stories that has been developed by theologians. But these intellectual understandings, by themselves, are not enough for real relationship. Relationship happens when we open ourself to the other. In every case of authentic relationship, we do this directly. If we stay with the story, then we have fallen in love with the story—not with the One who tells the story.

To fall in love with the Creator, we must leave the story behind, and open ourselves to the storyteller. In this way, the apophatic way builds on the base developed through the cataphatic meditations. This way of negation takes us out of the world of the senses, and moves us directly into the world of the spirit...into the heavenly kingdom where dwells our God.

The Author of *The Cloud*

There are a number of remarkable features about the author of *The Cloud*. There is this extraordinary anonymity. His identity is a true puzzle. There are very few truly anonymous authors in Christendom. Our author's insistence on anonymity, and his removal of virtually all identifying information bespeaks of a great humility. Here is a man who did not believe himself to be so mightily important. A man who has truly left behind the false self that pretends to be the center of the universe. Here is one whose Christian journey has borne the sweet fruit of humility.

Our anonymous author wrote in the vernacular English, rather than Latin, the *lingua franca* of the Western church. He wrote for a particular individual. In these things, he stands apart from his contemporaries. He writes with a dazzling directness about spiritual experience, giving a wealth of practical advice. His *Cloud* is no abstract theoretical treatise meant to edify the masses. He is bent on communicating a particular method that can lead his friend to the most profound spiritual transformation. *The Cloud* is not a textbook, however. It is a compendium of personal experience that invites the reader to make a similar journey into the Divine Presence.

The author's sweet directness and gentle concern for his reader stands in marked contrast to the world in which he lived. England was just emerging from the thorough devastation of the Hundred

Years' War, which extended from 1337 to 1453. The bubonic plague had ravaged England in 1348/1349 and again in 1361. A third to a half of the population died during this time. The countryside was in chaos. Against such a backdrop of horror, this extraordinary soul writes to a spiritual friend on how he can open himself to the Presence of God.

The Theology of *The Cloud*

It is difficult to understand the method described in *The Cloud* without some prior understanding of the theology on which it rests. For our author, spiritual practice was inextricably intertwined with theology. He sets the stage for his apophatic approach to God by distinguishing between two types of power: the power of knowing and the power of loving. In his own words:

> All rational creatures, angels and men alike, have in them, each one individually, one chief working power, which is called a knowing power, and another chief working power called a loving power; and of these two powers, God, who is the maker of them, is always incomprehensible to the first, the knowing power. But to the second, which is the loving power, He is entirely comprehensible in each one individually, in so much that one loving soul of itself, because of love, would be able to comprehend Him who is entirely sufficient...to fill all the souls of men and angels that could ever exist. This is the everlasting wonderful miracle of love, which shall never have an end.[138]

Here, at the very beginning of his account, our author states his major premise, that intellectual knowing is an insufficient tool through which one might come to know God. Rather, God can be approached only through this "loving power."

Our author then goes on to describe how to engage this loving power in the task of knowing God. First, the practitioner "turns off" the intellectual knowing power as it strives to know God. This is accomplished by means of establishing the cloud of unknowing. Then the practitioner turns off the intellectual knowing power as it remembers the past by establishing the cloud of forgetting. Finally, the practitioner directs his heart to God by means of sudden impulses of love, not to get anything from God, but simply for the love of God alone.

The cloud of unknowing is first described by our author as the experience that happens when you first reach out to God with these sudden impulses of love. "This darkness and cloud is always between you and your God, no matter what you do, and it prevents you from seeing Him clearly by the light of understanding in your reason, and from experiencing Him in sweetness of love in your affection."[139] He describes a phenomenon that he believes everyone will experience, who tries to know God. We want to apprehend the Divine, but at our first approach there is only a darkness, which is like a cloud between us and God.

Later in his book, our author indicates that this darkness or cloud is not something substantial or objectively real like a cloud of water vapor or the absence of light. Rather, "when I say 'darkness,' I mean a privation of knowing, just as whatever you do not know or have forgotten is dark to you."[140] He also states that he locates this cloud above us, as a figure of speech only. "Take great care that you do not construe in a material way what is to be understood spiritually."[141]

For our author, it is vitally important to place this practice of the cloud of unknowing in the wider context of spiritual growth. He indicates, at the very beginning of his book, that these teachings should not be available to everyone. He states that these methods are not suitable for those who are new to the faith, or for those who have insufficient resolve or spiritual maturity.[142] He assumes that, prior to any practice of this prayer, one will engage in "certain preparatory exercises,"[143] namely the practice of Lectio Divina described in Part IV of the present volume. He warns that those who are not adequately prepared with the proper spiritual exercises may suffer various spiritual illusions.[144]

Once you have mentally created this cloud of unknowing between yourself and God, you are directed to establish "a cloud of forgetting between you and all the creatures that have ever been made."[145] This cloud of forgetting is to encompass everything that the practitioner has ever known.

> Whenever I say "all the creatures that have ever been made," I mean not only the creatures themselves, but also all their works and circumstances. I make no exceptions, whether they are bodily creatures or spiritual, nor for the state or activity of

any creature, whether these be good or evil. In short, I say that all should be hid under the cloud of forgetting.[146]

In a way that was utterly radical for his time, and even for our own time six hundred years later, our author included in this forgetting all our intellectual understandings of God. Whereas the practitioner in previous spiritual practice has reflected on the qualities of God using the sensory meditations, now he is enjoined to put the knowledge gained from these exercises under a cloud of forgetting.

The reason for this rigorous forgetting is a simple one. We cannot know, with certainty, whether the knowledge gained through the meditations is wishful thinking or the stark reality of God. So rather than risk a wrong understanding of something so important to us as God, the practitioner simply puts it all to the side. This forgetting includes not only our intellectual knowledge of God, but also includes any remembrance of our own sin. All of this remembering simply gets in the way of our encounter with God. When we are focused on our sin, we are not engaged in loving God. And the anonymous author of *The Cloud* is utterly ruthless in subordinating everything that might interfere with our active love of God.

Between the cloud of unknowing above and the cloud of forgetting beneath us, we are enjoined to aim our love at God in "sudden impulses of love." These are "nothing else than a sudden impulse, one that comes without warning, speedily flying up to God as the spark flies up from the burning coal."[147] In these matters, "a simple reaching out directly toward God is sufficient, without any other cause except Himself."[148]

As a device to assist the practitioner, our author suggests the use of a simple word to focus the attention.

Take just a little word, of one syllable rather than of two; for the shorter it is the better it is in agreement with this exercise of the spirit. Such a one is the word "God" or the word "love"....Fasten this word to your heart, so that whatever happens it will never go away....With this word you are to beat upon this cloud and this darkness above you. With this word you are to strike down every kind of thought under the cloud of forgetting.[149]

Our author understands this prayer to make a crucial difference in the life of the practitioner. "For it alone, of itself, destroys the root and the ground of sin."[150] By radically abandoning all of the things of this world, this prayer "crucifies the old self with Christ, so that the sinful body might be destroyed and we might be slaves to sin no longer."[151]

This fourteenth-century author has remarkable psychological insight. He understands that "virtue is nothing else than an ordered and controlled affection which has God for its single object, Himself alone."[152] To have God at the center of all things, we must take our precious self out of the central position. This process is accomplished by developing humility. For our author, humility is not a groveling in the dust as we commonly understand it today. Rather, "humility is nothing else but a man's true understanding and awareness of himself as he really is. It is certain that if a man could truly see and be conscious of himself as he really is, he would indeed be truly humble."[153]

For our author, the love of God is the central reality. His prayer is simply a means of ordering his unruly will and orienting himself in a consistent fashion toward the Divine. Here, pressing upon God with his "sudden impulses of love" and forgetting all else, our author has created a vehicle for the destruction of the old self and resurrection to new life in Christ.

The Practice of the Cloud of Unknowing

The author of *The Cloud* describes his spiritual exercise in bits and pieces, interweaving his description of the prayer with its theological underpinnings, and those results that are typical from sustained practice of this prayer. This is somewhat confusing for the modern reader. In order to simplify this jumble, and to make clear the essentials of the practice, I have rendered the prayer below.

SPIRITUAL EXERCISE 30
THE CLOUD OF UNKNOWING

1. Position your body comfortably, spine erect, on a chair or cushions.

2. Ground yourself in your physical sensations. Close your eyes and slowly become aware of the sensations of your

---

physical body. Feel the sensations as they flow through you. The sensations in your head...in your neck and shoulders...your elbows...your wrists and the palms of your hands...the sensations in your knees...your ankles and the soles of your feet.

3. Now create a cloud of unknowing that is between you and to your God. No matter how much you hope to know God, you can never know Him through the intellect. You can never hope to penetrate that cloud, that darkness. There is nothing that you can do to overcome this barrier. Consciously place this barrier between yourself and God.

4. Now put beneath yourself the cloud of forgetting. This is to be an active process at first, and only gradually quieting. Every time a memory or a thought or a feeling arises in your awareness, put it beneath your cloud of forgetting. Let nothing distract you. Every time a distraction arises, place it beneath this cloud.

5. Between the cloud of unknowing above you, and the cloud of forgetting beneath you, become aware of those sudden impulses of love for God. Lift your heart up to God, who "by his grace called you to this exercise. Have no other thought of God...a simple reaching out directly towards God is sufficient." [154]

6. If you find yourself having difficulty maintaining your focus on God, use a word to stabilize your attention. Choose a short word of one syllable such as "God" or "love." Repeat this word over and over again. "Fasten this word to your heart, so that whatever happens it will never go away.... With this word you are to beat upon this cloud and this darkness above you. With this word you are to strike down every kind of thought under the cloud of forgetting." [155]

7. When you find your attention wandering, don't scold yourself. Gently bring your attention back to the impulses of love which spring up in your heart. Direct these toward your God.

(To close your meditation)

8. When you are ready, let yourself come back to this place.
   Let the feeling return to your feet, your hands, and your
   face. Take a deep breath, and open your eyes.

The Results of Practice. The author of *The Cloud* has a number
of useful things to say about the practice that he describes. Of
great importance to us, living in a fast-paced time, he says that
this spiritual exercise "does not need a long time before it can be
truly done."[156] Rather, each impulse of the soul toward God is quite
short. We can learn this practice quickly and engage in it readily,
since it is so easy to do. Furthermore, our author indicates that
this practice can and should be repeated countless times every
day. By this means, we beat down all thoughts that come between
us and the Divine, and so stand more clearly in between the two
clouds. It is here that our purification occurs.

Of great significance is the parallel between the gift of tears
which the practitioners of the Jesus Prayer report, and "the sudden awarenesses and obscure feelings of [your] own wretchedness"
which the author of *The Cloud* reports. Our author devotes considerable space talking about how this spiritual exercise is the place
where our sin is transformed. He indicates that the practitioner
suddenly becomes aware of his sin, with concomitant feelings of
wretchedness. It appears, then, that both spiritual practices lead
to similar results, and to similar spiritual phenomena.

In addition, both this author and the writers who discuss the
Jesus Prayer indicate that these prayers should be done ceaselessly, even when eating or sleeping. The author of *The Cloud* says,
"work at this exercise without ceasing and without moderation,
and you will know where to begin and to end all your other activities with great discretion."[157] The results of this practice will be a
thoroughgoing behavior change which will resolve any "mistake in
[your] external activities."[158] This meditation practice, therefore,
has the beneficent result of purifying the practitioner from sin.

We begin to see, from the descriptions of the prayer of *The
Cloud* and the descriptions of the Jesus Prayer, some of the common threads that link monologistic prayers. There are phenomena
that both seem to evoke. There is an increased awareness of sin,
and a resolution of sinful behaviors through extensive practice.

of "praying ceaselessly" goes against common sense, both in four-teenth-century England and today, our author replies bluntly to his skeptics: "Understand it as best you can."[159] And there is, in both spiritual exercises, the insistence on going beyond the realm of discursive thought and into a deeper mode of being.

All of this is preparation for contemplative prayer, toward which monologistic prayer moves the practitioner. Monologistic prayer seems to be a vehicle where all that is extraneous to the pursuit of God is abandoned. To be perfect in the exercise of *The Cloud*, "all awareness and experience of one's own being must be done away with."[160] Thus, even self-awareness must be overcome, for the deepest success.

For us, embedded in a cultural matrix that values individuality over everything else, this is nothing short of shocking! We have placed the individual over every other value. This value is enshrined in our law and in our everyday practices. To hear that we must relinquish our precious individuality is, for us, cultural heresy. It is intriguing to look at what is gained by this, however. By following these humble stirrings of love in our hearts, we do nothing less than create a "good will...which is the substance of all perfection."[161] The result of this new will is "true decorum both of body and soul."[162] I suspect, as we look around at the landscape of violence and crime in which we live, that there might be some long-ing in our hearts for what our author describes as "true decorum." Whether we are willing to sacrifice our selves and our precious individuality to achieve this decorum, however, is another matter.

Toward the end of his work, our author discusses what happens in the later stages of practice. As we overcome our self-awareness by means of steady practice and God's gift of grace, we "leave aside this everywhere and this everything, in exchange for this nowhere and this nothing. Never mind at all if your senses have no under-standing of this nothing; it is for this reason that I love it so much the better."[163] In these words, our author prefigures Thomas Merton, who, in our own age has spoken of "the Palace of Nowhere" and of the God who whispers Her saving call to us: "Come with me to the Palace of Nowhere where all the many things are one."[164] We see in both authors the fullness of the apophatic tradition, speaking of God as totally hidden and fundamentally unknowable. Yet this unknowable One manifests to those who sacrifice the false self in order to draw closer to the Mystery.

In this process, the inner workings of the soul are

> remarkably changed in the spiritual experience of this noth-
> ing when it is achieved nowhere. For the first time that he
> looks upon it, he finds there imprinted all the particular sin-
> ful acts that he ever committed....It seems to him, sometimes,
> in his labour, that to look upon it is like looking upon hell. He
> despairs of ever winning, out of that pain, to the perfection of
> spiritual rest....
>
> He that has patience sometimes experiences consolation, and
> has some hope of perfection. For...many of the particular sins
> committed...are...rubbed away by the assistance of grace.
> Sometimes it seems to him that it is paradise or heaven,
> because of the many wonderful sweetnesses and consolations,
> joys and blessed virtues that he finds....Sometimes it seems
> to him that it is God....[165]

The spiritual exercise described by the author of *The Cloud of Unknowing* stands squarely in the apophatic tradition of the church. It is a prayer that is characteristic of the Western church. Those who practice this exercise as our author describes it will move into the great mystery of the Divine. Thus, it is a prayer of considerable power and effectiveness.

This prayer, like the Jesus Prayer, should not be used casually or lightly. The prerequisite for this spiritual exercise is the ability to quiet the mind and to rest comfortably with a single stimulus over a period of time. The practice of the sensory meditations and Lectio Divina are ways to achieve this concentrative ability. Depending on your ability to concentrate comfortably, a long peri-od of preparatory practice may be necessary before you are ready to embark upon this monologistic prayer.

Unlike the Jesus Prayer, this monologistic prayer has not enjoyed the same wide currency of practice. Thus, it has not been tested as thoroughly as the Jesus Prayer, by different generations and in different lands. The prayer of *The Cloud* is unique, howev-er, serving as the basis for a contemporary rendering in the center-ing prayer, which we will explore in the next chapter. Perhaps this is indicative of our age, that a traditional spiritual exercise has to be repackaged and made more acceptable to a modern audience.

Chapter 27

Centering Prayer

In the mid-1970s, monks at the Cistercian abbey of St. Joseph in Spencer, Massachusetts, began to talk together about the spiritual poverty of our times. They viewed with concern the exodus of sincere spiritual seekers within Christendom who were unable to connect with their own contemplative tradition. They wanted to find a way to make the riches of the contemplative life available to the lay person who could not spend a life in the monastery. The result of their conversations is centering prayer, a contemporary revision of the technique that was first presented in the fourteenth century, in *The Cloud of Unknowing*.

Responding to an invitation from Father Thomas Keating, abbot of the monastery in Spencer, Father William Meninger developed the initial form of centering prayer, and taught it within the walls of the monastery. Father Basil Pennington then began to offer classes outside the monastery, altering the prayer to fit in this new environment.[166] In 1981 Father Keating retired as abbot at St. Joseph's and began to teach centering prayer full time to the spiritually hungry. The practice was codified in 1986, with the publication of *Open Mind, Open Heart*.[167]

Like the Jesus Prayer, this form of prayer is not for the discursive intellect, and is not meant to be a forum for the creation of visual imagery or other forms of thinking. Rather, it is a technique that allows us to see what lies underneath all the busyness of the modern mind. It rests on the notion that, deep in our hearts, God is always with us.

Centering prayer rests on a much more developed and sophisticated theological base than does the technique of *The Cloud*. Centering prayer focuses on the incarnation of God: that God is always and everywhere present to us. Father Keating has given us a thoroughly developed understanding of the Pauline teaching of

229

"casting off the deeds of darkness and putting on the armor of light."[168] He not only explains the theology, but incorporates contemporary psychological understandings as well. As a result of these deeper understandings of the inner workings of the human mind, the authors of centering prayer revised several elements in the prayer technique. Because of these important differences, and because centering prayer is a true advance in the spiritual technology for inner transformation, we shall treat centering prayer as a separate form of monologistic prayer.

The Theological Basis of Centering Prayer

The basic theological underpinning on which centering prayer rests is that God is always with us. We find this understanding in the scriptures of both the Old and New Testaments. In the Old Testament, we hear in the book of first Kings that Elijah finds God in the "still small voice within."[169] The stories of the prophets are full of references of God being right there, in the midst of the people of Israel. This God, while being wholly other, is also the burning bush right in front of Moses. Not only is this God right here, He is named in the book of Isaiah, "Emmanuel," which means "God with us."[170]

In the New Testament, the incarnate aspect of God finds its fulfillment in the person of Jesus, God's Son, sent to redeem His people. Jesus, Himself, reaffirms this at crucial points in His ministry. In the gospel of John, Christ states, "I am the good shepherd."[171] The shepherd stands with his sheep; that is the nature of shepherding. A bit later in the gospel of John, our Lord says, "I am the vine, you are the branches."[172] In case we didn't understand the inseparable nature of the shepherd with the sheep, Christ gives us an elaboration of this notion with His vine image. There is no place in the vine where you can clearly say that the vine stops and the branches begin. Not only is God with us, He is indistinguishable from us except in the most general of generalizations. And at the very end of His incarnate time, in the last words of the book of Matthew, Jesus says, "know that I will be with you always, even to the end of time."[173]

The understanding which has come down to us through the church is that we are grafted onto Jesus by means of our baptism. Jesus, then, is always present in the soul of the one baptized. This theological understanding has been verified experientially by those who have devoted themselves to drawing closer to God. Generations of Christian contemplatives, those who have traveled the spiritual path before us, have indicated that Christ lives in the soul, and the soul is found in our hearts. Not the physical organ, but in our spiritual center which is located in the same general vicinity.

Perhaps the most dramatic example of this grafting and the transformation it can bring is found in the story of Saul of Tarsus, at the very beginning of the Christian era. Saul, the persecutor of Christians, the apostle who never knew Jesus in the flesh, was utterly transformed by his encounter with the risen Christ. Jesus even gave him a new name, Paul, to mark this transformation.

While much is made of his visionary experience on the road to Damascus, little attention is given to the quiet, yet more profound part of Paul's journey. Over the course of his remaining years, Paul changed and matured spiritually. As he gained knowledge of God's indwelling Presence, his connection with the Christ strengthened immeasurably. He was able to write from prison in Rome, just before his execution, "nothing can separate me from the love of God in Christ Jesus our Lord."[174] He is writing here, not from faith. His is not a strong hope in Christ. He writes like a man who "knows." He knows that nothing can separate him from the Lord because that has been his daily experience in prayer. Paul has seen and felt and listened to the Christ who dwells in his heart.

This is the close connection with Christ that we all long for. The basic understanding, which provides the basis of centering prayer, is that God is already with us, in our center. We are already redeemed; we are already participating in the Divine center. We are already with God, our Savior. There is nothing we have to do in order to come to our redeemer.

We don't "feel" like this though. These assertions of closeness to God run counter to our felt experience. Our felt experience of separation, however, is fundamentally untrue. Our felt experience is due to our dissociation—our disconnection from our true self. The authors of centering prayer are reiterating the same message that all of the deepest mystics of the church have given us: there is no fundamental separation between God and Her people. There is no abyss to cross, no journey that is necessary. What we hear from our spiritual fathers and mothers is something radically different. What they say is this: "God is closer to you than you are to your very self."

Our Felt Separation. Two thousand years ago, St. Paul wrestled with the same felt sense of separation that we wrestle with today. He complained, "I do the things that I don't want to do; and I don't do the things I want to do. What is wrong with me?!"[175] Paul explores this situation using the metaphor of the old man and the new man who lives in Christ. Paul's theological masterpiece, the book of Romans, conveys his understanding; an understanding reached in his spiritual maturity, after following the Lord Jesus in a disciplined manner for twenty years. Paul states that through Adam, sin came into the world. Adam stands as the old man, who was undone by a weakness of the flesh, by an undisciplined life that did not follow the commandments of God.

This old man is transformed, however, by the gift of Christ's righteousness. Humanity is given a new possibility through Christ's actions. We are invited to cast off the works of darkness and to put on the armor of light.[176] We are invited to become part of the resurrected body of our Lord and to participate in the new life that He gives.

Some modern psychological investigators have come to similar conclusions, although they use different language. The words they use to describe St. Paul's "old man" are the "false self."[177] From this perspective, each one of us creates a false self—a socially adapted ego—in response to the pressures of growing up. We learn very early that some parts of ourselves are not acceptable. Boys learn that it is not acceptable to cry. Girls learn that it is not acceptable to be rowdy and loud. So we cut these parts of ourselves off: we act like we are not these unacceptable parts.

The false self is our response to social pressure. None of us develops "naturally." That is, none of us is ever allowed to be just as we are. Rather, there is a constant process of shaping and conditioning, during which we learn to be acceptable to others. This socialization process is very important if we are to get along with one another in groups. However, it is achieved at a high cost. Our Lord indicates that, to return to our true nature and to return home to God, we must become like little children.[178]

In addition to pruning away parts of ourselves, our socialization in childhood also entails the creation of a variety of emotional programs, many of which are dysfunctional. As a culture, we are finally waking up to the social devastation in which we dwell. As a clinical psychologist, I see the horrid effect of these old emotional programs every day. I see women who have been sexually abused as children internalize this abuse and seek out men who abuse them as adults. I see children who grew up with abusive parents develop clusters of dysfunctional personality traits that are the perfect complement to their early abuse.

So you see, we are literally programmed for unhappiness. This happens in two ways: 1) by the pruning process of socialization, and 2) by the creation of dysfunctional emotional programs which then act to "control" the choices we make in our lives. All of this is absolutely contrary to the words of our Creator! After creation, God looked at Her work and said that it was good. Indeed, it was very good.[179] We act, however, as if parts of that creation were not good and have to be cut off. We have left that centered, balanced place where we are in tune with the Divine, with nature, with one another, and with our deepest selves. We are like Esau; we have sold our birthright for a mess of pottage.[180] We have abandoned our true self, created by God, and exchanged it for a maladaptive false self.

Father Keating rightly recognized that the meditation process is a direct attack upon this construct of the false self. During meditation, we attempt to focus and concentrate the attention. This is a process radically different from anything else we do. Instead of being plugged in to the old programming of the false self—instead of listening to the thoughts and feelings which are governed by this old programming—we disengage from it. We simply rest our attention in God.

From the perspective of the false self, we don't know how to get to the true self. We simply cannot see it. We are not even sure that it exists, at the start. We take its existence on faith, and begin our attempt to shed our old skin. Because we don't know how to get to the true self, we can't "do" anything other than unplug from the old. Most attempts to "do" something to get away from this false self are actually conditioned by that same false self. We cannot use it as a tool to cut itself.

All that we can do is to disengage our attention from the old, sinful person and from the false self. As we know from our experience in meditation, even this is incredibly difficult. We rest our attention in God, and a minute later become aware that we are wrapped up in our thinking again. Once more, even in meditation, we find ourselves following the dictates of the false self. Eventually, however, the false self will run out of fuel and die. Then the true self, which has been obscured within our deepest interior, will emerge. When the true self emerges, we become aware of our deep connection with God and with all Her creation.

This description of the destruction of the old self, and the emerging of the true self that God creates is taken from experience. It is not something made up or imagined. We first hear of this process in the letters of St. Paul. Paul, by means of much prayer over many years, accomplished this process in himself. With this perspective in mind, the lives of the saints become much clearer, and we see that the variety of disciplines that they used were attempts to disengage from the false self.

It is only from this perspective that certain passages of the gospels make any sense. Central to all the gospels is Jesus' command that we should love one another,[181] even to the extent of loving our enemy.[182] From the perspective of the false self, however, we cannot love our enemy. Our enemy, by definition, is one whom we hate. Only from the perspective of the true self—the self which knows that it is deeply interconnected with all beings—can one have an enemy and love that enemy!

From this understanding of the deep psychological dynamics that are involved in our journey toward God, our center, we begin to see why certain things are the way they are. Because our false self readily adjusts to every social situation, we see this falseness played out in every church community. From this perspective, we see that a conscious decision to choose Christ is not enough to lead a Christian life. Any conscious decision, including those pertaining to the spiritual life, does not really touch the deep unconscious programming of the false self. These decisions, well-intentioned though they may be, are regularly subverted by the false self. It is only through engagement in the regular disciplines of prayer, which accesses for us the power of God's grace, that these programs can be gradually drained of their energy and finally discarded.

Thus, the deep forms of prayer, such as those we are discussing here, function as a kind of divine therapy. Father Keating states that the process of meditation and contemplative prayer allows the old emotional programs to come to the surface and be discharged. In our meditation, there is a reduction of interior dialogue. This reduction removes the constant reinforcers of the false-self system. This quieting of the thoughts, the gross movements of the mind, allows the more subtle attributes to be seen. Ultimately, we disengage even from these. The energy which previously fueled the false self is withdrawn. As this occurs, the true self emerges. Finally, we realize that this true self has been in union with God all along. We simply could not be aware of this union from the perspective of the false self.

The Practice of Centering Prayer

Centering prayer is a modification of the prayer described in *The Cloud of Unknowing*. In centering prayer, there is no creation of a cloud of unknowing above you or a cloud of forgetting below you. These are mental creations; ideas that are artificial and not wholly real. Instead there is a resting of the attention in one's center, trusting that God is present to us there. There is no attempt made to "feel" God's Presence. Again, this would be seen as another mental effort; something that ultimately distorts our approach to God rather than something that facilitates our approach.

Finally, there is a different use of the "sudden impulses toward God" which the author of *The Cloud* describes. The author of *The Cloud* invites us to use a one-syllable word to help focus our attention, by "fasten[ing] the word to your heart"[183] and saying it over and over again. The authors of the centering prayer invite us to choose a word at the outset of our meditation, but to use it in a somewhat different way. Instead of repeating it constantly, as in the Jesus Prayer, we are to say it only when we become aware of distractions. We are to "touch distractions with the sacred word, like the light touch of a feather."[184]

Father Keating sums up this use of the sacred word with "the four R's." These are:

1) Resist no thought.

2) Retain no thought.

3) React emotionally to no thought.

4) Return to your sacred word when you notice you are thinking about some other thought.[185]

Centering prayer revolves around the use of a "sacred word." Before we begin our period of practice, we must choose a word or a sound or even a gesture. This symbol will serve as a tool to remind us of what we are doing—sitting in God's holy Presence—and to bring us back to that central reality. The sacred word is not sacred because of any intrinsic quality of the word. It is sacred because it expresses our *intent* to be in God's Presence and to yield to His action. Your sacred word may be one of the words used to refer to

God: Jesus, Lord, Kyrie (Greek for Lord), Abba, Amma (Aramaic for Father and Mother), etc. It may refer to a divine quality: love, one, still. It may be a gesture, made silently within yourself, such as raising the distracting thought up to the Divine. It may be totally devoid of intellectual content such as the sound of a pure tone, or a sigh like, "Ahhh."

Whatever you choose for your sacred word, it should be simple, short, and non-reflective. That is, you shouldn't go off on a ten-minute remembrance of Jesus' sermon on the mount if you use the name, "Jesus," as your sacred word. Furthermore, after you have chosen your sacred word, do not change it for the period of your meditation. Father Keating and the other leaders in the centering prayer movement recommend that you practice this method for at least twenty minutes at a sitting. They also recommend practicing twice a day: early in the morning when you arise, and in the afternoon or evening.

SPIRITUAL EXERCISE 31
CENTERING PRAYER

1. Position your body comfortably, spine erect, on a chair or cushions.

2. Choose a sacred word for this period of prayer. If you are uncertain about what sacred word to try first, try a word with no lexical meaning, such as a sigh like: "ahhh." This will prevent you from making discursive associations to your word.

3. Become aware of the physical sensations that flow through you. Close your eyes and experience the stream of sensations that course through your physical body. No need to change them. No need to judge them. Simply let yourself feel deeply the multitude of sensations that cascade through your body. Gently focus on the sensations in your head...in your neck and shoulders...your elbows...your wrists and the palms of your hands...the sensations in your knees...your ankles and the soles of your feet.

4. Now move your attention up to the region of your heart and establish your attention here. If you have trouble

establishing your attention in the heart, imagine that every inhalation pushes the sphere of energy around your head downward an inch or so along your spinal column, until your attention finally comes to rest in your heart.

5. Open yourself to the Presence of God. When your attention drifts away from God's Presence, say your sacred word gently, as if laying a feather on a fluff of cotton. As you say the sacred word, allow your intention to be with the Divine to move you back to your deepest center.

6. Let yourself rest here for the time you have set apart for your meditation.

(To close your meditation)

7. When you are ready, let yourself come back to this place. Let the feeling return to your feet...your hands...your face. Take a deep breath, and open your eyes.

Keating describes centering prayer as "a discipline designed to withdraw our attention from the ordinary flow of our thoughts. We tend to identify ourselves with that flow. But there is a deeper part of ourselves. This prayer opens our awareness to the spiritual level of our being...which is our participation in God's being."[186] Centering prayer is based upon cultivating a receptive attitude. The entrance into deep quiet is a mark of the power of our developing receptivity. We are not praying to have a spiritual "high," to have no thoughts, or to do or have anything. Our purpose, in centering prayer as in all of the exercises presented here, is to be with the Lord, to be open to His will, to be receptive to His movement in our hearts.

The reason why this discipline is so crucial in our coming to know God is simple. *"The chief thing that separates us from God is the thought that we are separated from Him. We fail to believe that we are always with God and that He is part of every reality."*[187] The obstacle that keeps us from knowing this fundamental reality is our thinking, our world view. "It needs to be exchanged for the mind of Christ, for His world view."[188] Centering prayer, then, can be best understood as an open-hearted consent to God.

Interior Movement during Centering Prayer. As you begin centering prayer, you may be disappointed as you become aware again of all the internal noise and distraction. The inner noise, however, is to be expected. You are loading the mind with less and less technique. As a result, your mind tends to wander more. Expect this, and gently bring the mind back to center with the sacred word.

After a time of practice, you will find your mind growing calmer and less distracted. The purpose of these deep forms of interior prayer is *hesychia*, or stillness. You may enter into a profound stillness during the time of your centering prayer. This is a place that has no words, thoughts, or images. When this occurs, rest yourself here at the center, and enter into the Mind of God. What we are doing, in our prayer, is letting go of our mental constructs, letting go of our ideas of our self and God so that we can experience our self and our God directly. This is the difference between experiencing the map and the territory that the map covers. While the map is helpful in many respects, we will never know the territory from the map.

You will have noticed, as we progress in our description of different kinds of monologistic prayer, that centering prayer is a relatively advanced technique. As we have sequenced the preceding prayers, from the Jesus Prayer to *The Cloud* to centering prayer, there is less and less to occupy the mind. As you progress in your practice, you will be able to hold your attention on God with less and less loading.

People usually expect to have fewer problems with interior prayer as they advance to the higher techniques. This seldom happens. Indeed, it seems sometimes like we are constantly starting over. In our subjective experience, it seems as if the more we practice, the more we become aware of our wandering mind. When we notice this at an advanced level, there may be some despair about making any real progress. We must understand this phenomenon of wandering mind in order to prevent despair. Father Keating likens this process to shining a light of progressively greater intensity on the surface of a carpet. Under dim light, the carpet looks clean. As we increase the intensity of the light, we begin to see big specks of dirt. When we put thousands of watts of light on a small patch of the same carpet, we see even the little tiny specks of dust. So it is with the mind and meditation. As we attempt to settle our wandering minds, at first only gross interruptions interfere with our concentration. The neighbor's dog barks, we compulsively think about an upsetting event: these are the sorts of things that disturb us. As we gain strength in our practice, we find that we no longer notice these things. Instead we notice that there is a subtle flow of thought in the back of our mind. This often seems like the same kind of interruption, but it is not.

As you continue with your practice, you will find progressively finer flows of thought. Each of these has always existed in you, flowing like a steady stream. But because of your occupation with the more gross events, you have never noticed them. When we can disengage from them, from our obsessive self-absorption, only then are we free to engage in the Divine.

The Results of Practice. Intensive practice of centering prayer serves as a kind of divine therapy, allowing the false self to surface and the compulsive, destructive patterns to resolve. While this process should never substitute for psychotherapy, it can have a remarkable impact in ways that are quite similar.

The power of this divine therapy is illustrated in the story of a colleague of mine. This woman, in her early forties, came from a dysfunctional family and was unable to affirm herself in any meaningful way. She found herself compulsively taking care of the needs of others, and sacrificing her own well-being in the process. Despite five years of psychotherapy with very skilled therapists, she was unable to resolve the false-self complexes which drove these behaviors in her. While she obtained some relief, there was no lasting behavior change, despite her best efforts and those of her therapists.

After learning meditation and practicing for some years, she went on a ten-day centering prayer intensive under the direction of Father Keating. During this time, she had a series of transformative experiences. After four days of intensive centering prayer practice, this is what happened:

While chanting, I became aware that all I need to do is to say "yes" and God will be a part of my life forever. It was so simple. I said "yes" and was immediately flooded with an intense feeling of love and the gift of tears. There are no words to describe what the tears are; they are not tears of grief, sorrow, pity. Perhaps the best way to describe them would be to say that they are tears of coming home, similar to the tears one has when one has been away from home for a long time and returns to the bosom of his/her family. They are not necessarily tears of joy or happiness, more a sense of overwhelming grace.

Later, while sitting in meditation, I felt as though God were gazing into my very being, flooding me with love. I have never been so tenderly loved, so completely loved, so totally accepted.

I sat down one night, determined to ask God to make changes in my life. I expected to wait quite a while before I got a sense of response, but this came instantaneously. I was overcome by a spiritual vomiting. One thing after another from my past came up. I no sooner recognized it, then another thing came up. These things that I was vomiting were the experiences of my false self: my pride, my self-pity, my preconceptions, my ideas about my self and the world. This kept up for hours, until I was exhausted. I went to bed, fully expecting to sleep because I was so emotionally drained.

Instead, as I lay there, I became engaged in wrestling with God. I know now that I was wrestling with my true self, but then it felt as though I were wrestling God. I kept holding onto all those things that I had vomited up earlier. I would not let go of them. They were how I defined and knew my self and my world. I knew that if I let go of them, my "I" would cease to be. It seemed as though there was a soft being with me, urging me gently to let go of my vomit. But I kept wrestling with that soft being, only I wasn't strong enough. I wrestled and fought, but still that being held on. I didn't sleep at all that night.

I was still wrestling as I walked to mass in the morning. Along the road, I was "debating" with God. I was asking God what would happen if I let go of myself. (As I write these words, now, the answer seems obvious. But you must remember that I was totally engaged in this tremendous struggle for my very being.) What would be left? Then I had a waking "vision." I'm still not sure what to call it. I was aware of myself looking into a mirror and seeing no reflection. I was aware of myself holding the mirror, but no reflection or anything else was coming back at me. There was just nothing in the mirror.

This, for some reason that I still don't understand, was very reassuring to me. It was as though I was still there, but I was nothing. So I said "Okay" to God, and let go of myself. The next sensation I had was the experience of free-floating. Then I just was, with no more sense of falling or floating. I did not know who I was. I did know where I was and what I was doing. But I had no sense of who I was. This continued for awhile. It was not bothersome. In fact, it was quite intriguing. I knew I still existed, but I did not know who this "I" was.

I spent the next few days exploring aspects of this "I," which was my true self, which had been hidden deep inside, below all the garbage that I had accumulated. It was like listening to an inner voice, instead of my usual thinking about things. My perception of reality shifted slightly. I became aware of the unity of all people and all things in God. This has stayed with me until today (a time period of several years).

This woman came back·from the ten-day intensive a changed person. Not only has her perception of reality shifted, as she indicates above, but her behavior has changed radically. She no longer feels compelled to take care of others, and to sacrifice herself for their needs. Yet, paradoxically, she seems more effective in her interactions with others, and is perceived as immensely compassionate. This woman even looks different. Her husband said, when he met her at the plane, that he didn't recognize her at first.

The account of this modern-day pilgrim describes what these forms of deep prayer are about. They are transformative tools that allow us to come into our true nature as children of God. The practice of meditation and contemplative prayer helps us to see ourselves as God sees us. More importantly, these practices help us to "be" ourselves. In the process, we come to know ourselves as participating in God's holy Presence. Here is where we find our deepest, truest nature.

Centering prayer is rooted in the apophatic mysticism of the Western church, and is based on the prayer described in *The Cloud of Unknowing*. Centering prayer is rooted in a profoundly incarnational theology. It rests on the understanding that God is always with us, that the Divine is always accessible to us in our deepest center. In addition, with the work of Father Keating, there is an expansion of the Pauline doctrine of "putting on the armor of light."[189] This theological expansion provides words for describing and understanding the transformations that occur in meditation and contemplative prayer. Thus, it allows for greater precision in description, and a greater understanding of the process.

One of my concerns as a teacher is the applicability of different meditations for different people. There is, for example, a clear developmental sequence in the meditations which I have tried to show in this book. But are there certain meditations that would work better for one kind of person than another? Since we all learn in different ways, it is likely that some people will learn better from one kind of technique than another.

Over the years, I have found some confirming evidence for this, as we compare the Jesus Prayer with centering prayer. In my experience with these two techniques, I have found that their efficacy is related to personality styles. For introverts, centering prayer seems to be more suitable. Introverts work better when they don't have to "talk," even when the talk is interior. Extroverts, on the other hand, seem to find the Jesus Prayer more compatible. The Jesus Prayer provides them with a way to go deeply into prayer, while still chatting away.

Centering prayer is an important technique for our spiritual transformation. It is not, however, a tool for beginners. The focus of centering prayer is too diffuse for most beginners. They have difficulty in concentrating their awareness on the inner center. Thus, centering prayer is for those who have developed some ability to focus attention and to rest their attention in God. In the next set of practices that we describe, in Part VI, we will take our developing ability to focus attention even further.

Chapter 28

Reflections on Monologistic Prayer

Monologistic forms of prayer serve as springboards to propel us into the deep quiet that is the Mind of God. These forms of prayer help us disengage from the discursive intellect. The monologistic prayers are vehicles that take us beyond the domain of the intellect and into that vast stillness of the Mind of God.

Thus, these forms of prayer involve the exploration of a part of the human mind that is usually closed off during childhood. This is the part that our culture deems non-productive; the part that used to spend hours when we were children sitting in sunbeams and drifting with the dust motes. This is the "being" part that lies deep within us, the true self that God created.

Our culture does not value this being-part highly. We seldom give ourselves the opportunity to explore it. Instead, we keep ourselves busy with all of our doing. We even have trouble with leisure, which is one of the prerequisites for exploring this being-part. Of the developed nations, the United States ranks among the lowest in vacation time per worker. In fact, our work week has been increasing in length over the past twenty years. This is symptomatic of our deeper malaise. We have overdeveloped our thinking, discursive intellect at the expense of other important parts of ourselves.

As a result, those things which come to us from our being-nature are rare in our culture. We do not, as a people, engage in artistic pursuits. We do not philosophize in a deep way. We make religious practices shallow and peripheral to our living. And we suffer the consequences of these actions. We find ourselves cut off from those deep roots within ourselves which give meaning and value to our lives.

The Movement of Monologistic Prayer

By using monologistic prayer, we move out of "doing" and into "being." There is virtually nothing to do in monologistic prayer. The repetition of a phrase is boring, and we quickly habituate to it. It is then that the real action of these prayers takes place. At just this point, we engage in a struggle of gigantic proportions; we fight our doing-part in order to go deeper within. With monologistic prayer, we fight to relinquish our doing in order to explore that which we, in faith, believe is more fundamental to us. Over and over again, our doing-part subtly regains control during our practice and takes us into discursive thinking. Over and over again, when we recognize this, we release the doing, to slip, once again, into our being.

It is quite difficult to stay here, in our being–nature. Our journey is not an easy one, because it seems, like Sisyphus, that we walk the same ground over and over. To root ourselves in our being-nature is difficult because we must walk away from everything our culture values: doing, activity, work, production. We leave behind those things that we know we will be rewarded for, in order to explore those things that we hope to be rewarded for. This is a huge sacrifice.

Not only is the sacrifice large beyond imagining, the process of making this sacrifice takes such a long time. It is not as if we can make up our minds to do this, and in a flash, it is accomplished. This sacrifice has to be engaged in time after time, over and over again. Our minds are so habituated to doing that we cannot relinquish it easily. We are like addicts; we keep going back to the doing that we crave. We cannot seem to let go of it.

As a result, we are like a people possessed. We are not free. As St. Paul would say, we are "slaves to sin."[190] But this is not our true nature. This is not what God created. This is what we have become, and it is not attractive. It is as if we were desperately trying to leave our deepest, most authentic, most beautiful being. It doesn't make any sense.

Spiritual Warfare

Monologistic prayer allows us to struggle directly with these issues. We begin this spiritual warfare with the sensory meditations. The sensory meditations focus our attention and are useful in helping us explore the wisdom of our God in a discursive manner. Often we get a taste of the non-discursive realm of Being as a result of our practice of these meditations. If you will, the sensory meditations use discursive thinking to prepare us to go beyond this way of thinking. Then the more advanced practices of monologistic prayer allow us to move more quickly into the non-discursive realm, the realm of Being. After we have learned the rudiments of controlling our attention, the monologistic prayers cut to the chase. They help us explore this vast pool of Being, and to take our rightful place within it.

Non-discursive prayer may in fact give us our first confirmation of the wonderful truth that Jesus alludes to, that we are already in union with God at our deepest level. Our felt separation, like the apparent separation of two neighboring islands, is an illusion of perspective. From the air above the islands, they look like two separate entities. When we go deep enough under the water, we see that the two islands are connected. Likewise, when we go deep enough into non-discursive awareness, we realize that God is the ground of our being.[191] We realize that our felt separation is only an illusion that is born of our limited perspective. We can begin to affirm, with St. Paul, that there is nothing that can separate us from the love of God in Christ Jesus our Lord.[192]

Moving On

Monologistic prayer, however, is not an end in itself. Even with this class of prayer there is some "doing." With each form that we have learned, there is some place for the discursive intellect to enter, make a judgment, and move us off track. The strength of monologistic prayer is the power with which it can move us into stillness. But there are stronger ways still.

Just as we nurture infants with milk and soft foods, we must nurture ourselves with forms of prayer that are easily digestible. But as we gain experience and strength, there are other forms of spiritual nourishment that are more suitable for our growth. We must learn how to match our ability to absorb nourishment with the vehicles that can provide that nourishment.

Unfortunately, our false self often gets in the way of this process. Instead of seeing that soft food is appropriate for the initial stages of the journey, the false self constructs a "good versus bad" situation. If solid food is more nourishing than soft food, then it must be "better." So the false self is constantly interfering with the process, trying to move us beyond our spiritual capabilities.

This tendency must be recognized and dealt with appropriately.

Because we are so easily fooled by our internal false self, it is most helpful to practice in a community. This does not need to be a monastic community. We can gather our spiritual friends into a community for regular group practice and discussion. When we have established such a community, we can go to other members of the community to receive assistance in spiritual discernment. "Am I really ready to move on to another form of prayer?"

What is crucial here is the match between our spiritual needs and the vehicle we choose to give nourishment. Every form of meditation and prayer described in this book works to nourish us. Some provide more than others. The richer vehicles for spiritual nourishment must not be used prematurely. If we try them before we are ready, they may cause illness, usually in the form of spiritual discouragement. We stop our practice because we feel it is too difficult, or maybe we feel that we are just not cut out to pray in this way. This is equivalent to saying that only a few are called to spiritual maturity. This is directly contrary to the gospel of our Lord. Christ invites each of us to grow into spiritual maturity, and to take our place as children of our Father/Mother in heaven.

So there is still more to learn in our prayer journey. After the monologistic prayers are practiced and mastered—something that may take several years or several decades, depending on the intensity of our practice—then there are even deeper ways of being in God. These are the contemplative prayers.

Contemplative prayer, in its highest forms, is completely non-discursive. Thus, to engage in contemplative prayer, we must first have developed our attention to such a fine focus that we can rest it in one place for a substantial period of time. We need a familiarity with the non-discursive realm, so that we don't fly away into discursive thinking as is our habit. By means of contemplative prayer we find our deepest fulfillment in Christ. Here we can rest fully in the love of God. Here we can come to know the true self, whom God created. And here we come to know God, entering into union with the Divine.

In this section on monologistic prayer, we have not been able to survey all of its multiplicity of forms. We have not explored, for example, the prayers of Dom John Main [193] or his successor, Father Lawrence Freeman. [194] We have not examined the delightful method for personalizing monologistic prayer which Father Ron DelBene originated. [195] We have not even looked at St. John of the Cross, [196] who stands in the apophatic tradition of *The Cloud of Unknowing*. John wrote some two hundred years after *The Cloud*, and expresses his vision of God in ways that are even more poetic and profound than the anonymous author of *The Cloud.*

The guidelines which governed the selection of monologistic prayers for this volume revolved around several axes. I was more interested in prayers from different branches of the church, prayers that had a longer history of usage, and prayers that demonstrated particular forms. My interest in these variables should not be interpreted as placing a lesser value on other monologistic prayers. We simply have limited space in which to introduce you to this great form of deep praying.

Moving to Contemplative Prayer. There are several signs which indicate readiness for the contemplative forms of prayer. Since it is unwise to move to these more difficult and rewarding prayers before you are ready, you may wish to consider these marks quite carefully.

The most sure way to decide your readiness is not to decide at all. Go to one who is spiritually more advanced, one who is familiar with meditation and contemplative prayer, one in whom you feel the power of God's Spirit, and ask that person. This is probably the safest, most conservative approach. It is sometimes difficult, however, to find such a person in our spiritually impoverished times. If a more spiritually mature person is not available, then go to your spiritual friends. Go to those intimates with whom you converse about spiritual matters, and begin to talk with them about your concerns. Lay open the thoughts of your heart, and ask for their perceptions of your journey. To help with this, let me give you some of the marks which indicate readiness.

First, if you are concerned about promotion and spiritual advancement, you are probably not ready. There is still too much of the false self active. In this circumstance, you are still concerned about external signs rather than internal change. You feel you would be "better" if you were more advanced—which is simply not true. You are already God's child; how could anything make you better? So if you have concerns about advancement, stay with the monologistic prayers for a few more years. This is probably the clearest mark that you are not ready to go on to contemplative prayer quite yet.

On the other hand, a lack of interest in promotion, may be a sign that you are ready to go on. The difficulty that arises comes from the cleverness of the false self. The false self, on reading these words, may adopt the posture that spiritual advancement is no longer important. It incorporates all sources of information and bends them to its own purposes. As a result, it can be very difficult to decide this on your own. You will notice the "Catch–22" element in this reasoning. It runs like this: "If you are ready to go on, you won't care about going on; but if you are concerned about advancement, you are probably not ready for it." I wish that things could be clearer and more direct in this area. Unfortunately, the false self is a wily opponent who is fighting to survive. This makes discernment a difficult task.

A second reliable method of discernment has to do with spontaneous contemplative prayer. If you find yourself repeatedly praying in a contemplative manner spontaneously, for extended periods of time (say five to ten minutes without distractions) then you are probably ready to move on to the formal practice of contemplation. This spontaneous movement occurs during monologistic prayer. During your practice, you repeatedly go into that vast stillness of God and rest there. There is no action of the discursive intellect. If the discursive intellect stirs, it does not engage you. You will first find that your will is absorbed in God. Later, your memory and imagination will be virtually suspended. When you recognize these occurrences, you will note that you have already moved on. Our movement in these matters is not by choice. That is what the false self does. Rather, when the false self is attenuated as a natural result of your practice, then God will guide you and move you where He wishes.

Finally, if you find yourself praying the monologistic prayers throughout the day, or if you find yourself cultivating the Presence of God on a regular daily basis, then you may be ready for contemplative prayer. This is the process of infused recollection. God is giving you a sense of His Presence. If you participate in this on a daily basis, so that you remain aware of God's Presence, then you may be ready for contemplation.

While warning you about the difficulties inherent in premature advancement, I do not mean that you should not finish reading this book, or that you should not learn anything about contemplation. It will be useful for your current practice if you have a map of the territory that lies ahead. Continue on, so that you have some understanding of the course yet to run. Read other books on contemplation as well. Read the lives of the saints who have enjoyed these modes of prayer, so that you have some understanding of the transformative power of these great tools.

Part VI
Contemplative Prayer

In this section, we will explore the tools of contemplative prayer. These are the most powerful tools that the church has developed to facilitate our union with God.[197] These tools are designed to release us from the last vestiges of the discursive mind and move us completely into the non-discursive realm, that great realm of Being where the Lord dwells. These tools can be the vehicle through which we enter into a spiritual union with God, realizing in our own flesh the illustration of the vine: that we participate in Christ just as Christ participates in the Father.[198] Once we have found our true self, our true identity in the Divine, then we can reenter the discursive world. But our point of view is forever changed. We now know our true nature, and are no longer confused by the changing shapes and shadows around us.

It is not easy, however, to talk about these tools of contemplative prayer. The language that we use is built to handle the concepts of the discursive mind and the false self, and does not easily lend itself to the discussion or explication of that which goes beyond these limits. When we use language to talk of the ultimate realities, it falls short in significant ways. It can only point mutely to the signs of these realities. To completely understand these deeper, more fundamental realities, we must first move into the non-discursive mind for ourselves.

How else than through actual experience can one who was born a slave describe what it is like to be free? Remember the example of the Israelites when they were freed from bondage in Egypt? Moses took them into the desert and into freedom, and all they could do was grumble and go back to their old ways as slaves, making images of God. Now, mind you, God does not exist any less in images. But we cannot experience the Divine fully within the constraints of images, because all images are created by the discursive mind. Our attempts are nothing more than attempts to capture God as an object.

The Definition of Contemplation. Up to this point in our practice, we have used the discursive mind in our efforts to disentangle our true self, which God created, from the false-self constraints

251

which we adopted in order to get along in the world. Up to this point, all of our thinking and all of our concepts about God have been created by the discursive mind and the false self. As a result, while these concepts may be very close to the mark, they are ultimately wrong. They miss the essence of the Divine. For this reason, we must find a way to go beyond the realm of discursive thinking.

Meditation consists of those techniques that make use of discursive thought to go beyond itself. Meditation, for example, encompasses all of the techniques which we have learned to this point: visualization, chant, lectio, and the monologistic prayers. In each of these practices, we focus our attention using discursive thought. Contemplation, on the other hand, does not use discursive thought at all. *Contemplative prayer is a radical abandonment of discursive thinking in order to experience that which lies beyond.* It is a radical effort to experience the stuff of life before we chop it up with our concepts and our words. It is totally different from anything we have ever done before.

Because contemplation involves going beyond conceptual thought, it is rather difficult to talk about. After all, what can you say if you can't use words or concepts? Because of this, you will find that the instructions for the spiritual exercises in this section will be more brief and less specific than before. This is an artifact that comes from moving out of the realm of discursive thought and into the realm of Being.

We make the transition from the meditative exercises into contemplation by exploring our passions, and learning to use them for our spiritual growth. Our passions are the raw emotional energies that drive us. This is the energy that we feel when we fall in love, or get excited about some new project. Until now we have focused on developing our attention. Now we need to learn about our passions, since they will provide the energy we need to continue our journey into contemplation. To make this transition, we must come to see our passions not as something negative which must be excised, but as an energy source which God has hidden from us until we were mature enough to use it properly.

Chapter 29

Harnessing the Passions for Union

Practicing the meditations described in this book will develop your attention into a strong tool, capable of focusing on a given stimulus for an extended time. You cannot successfully go on to contemplation until you can rest your attention on one stimulus and remain there for a period of five or ten minutes. This is the fundamental prerequisite for moving into contemplation. For most people, this process takes a period of years. Once this attentional focus has been accomplished, the next step is to bring your passions under control.

What Are the Passions?

The passions were identified by the early church fathers as our human appetites and desires. They are those passionate emotions which can dominate a person. There were two views about the origin of the passions. Some of the fathers, St. John of the Ladder [199] among them, felt that the passions were intrinsically evil—some alien thing that is grafted onto the soul by demons. Others, such as Evagrios[200] and Isaiah the Solitary[201] took a psychologically more sound view. They held that our passions have been perverted from their original nature. As something that is created by God, our passions are intrinsically good. But in our development into adulthood, we have misused our passions and become possessed by them into a kind of slavery.

The Western church has traditionally defined our passions as the great sins: things about ourselves that we need to excise. The three major passions are the sins of pride, greed, and lust. They are usually seen as destructive energies. And certainly there is evidence enough all around us to support this contention.

It is more appropriate, however, to think of our emotions simply as energy. When we are angry, when we are loving, when we are hurt or sad or joyful, we have a certain extra energy. This energy typically pushes us toward some expression of our feelings. If we are angry, we may shout at someone or something. Or we may exercise control and contain the expression of this emotion for the time being. The important point to note is that emotions are energy that pushes us toward some outward or inward expression of that energy.

God created us with these emotions. According to the account in Genesis, after God created us, He looked at us and pronounced His creation "good."[202] Thus, the passions that we have cannot be bad, as many in the church have taught over the centuries. Rather, like everything else about our humanity, they are deeply good, because they were created by God Himself. But, like any energy source, they are difficult to handle. And, if used improperly, the passions can be toxic to real life.

In virtually all of us, our passions have been expressed in a haphazard fashion, guided by the needs of the false-self system. As children, for example, we felt the passion which drives relationship. We wanted to be close to those who loved us, and whom we adored: most often our parents. This rudimentary passion drove our behavior. But our parents, perhaps, wanted time for themselves and so they pushed us away. As a result, we were hurt, and our passion for closeness had to be hidden. We tried to cut off the natural expression of this passion. Of course, it is not that easy. All that we did was succeed in driving it underground, into the unconscious.

A Parable of Distorted Passion. A psychologist colleague of mine, Dr. Elwin Nielsen, tells the following apocryphal story about this kind of coding. His story illustrates how the false self develops through a perversion of our natural passions.

There was a little girl who had a daddy who wasn't a very good daddy. He knew he wasn't a very good daddy, and he was uncomfortable about it, but he wasn't motivated enough to change. One day, while father was reading the newspaper, the little girl felt lonely. She asked her daddy, "Daddy, could I please sit in your lap and have you love me?" He looked at her sternly and said, "No. Can't you see that I'm reading?" So the little girl learned that it wasn't okay to ask directly to have her need for love met.

A little while later, the little girl asked, "Daddy, would you please play with me." She was really asking for love again, but she had learned by now that she had to code her request for love from daddy. Father answered the same as before. "No. Can't you see that I'm reading?" So the little girl learned that she had to code her requests even deeper, so that they could not be understood by her father as requests for love or attention.

Finally the little girl said, "Daddy, I'm hungry. Could you fix me some bread and jam?" The father, not recognizing this as another request for love, and feeling like he should take care of his child's physical needs, put down his paper and spread a piece of bread with jam for his daughter.

This story illustrates how we distort our passions. It shows how we code our passions to the point where we cannot recognize them. This is due to the false self, that part that we constructed to get along in the world. This child learned not to ask for love directly, but to ask for food. Is this process not present in all of us, in one way or another? We ask for one thing, but we really want something deeper and more important. So it is that all of our great passions are bent and distorted. We know these passions only in their pathological expression, because their natural expression, as functions of the true self, is virtually non-existent.

Pride, Greed, and Lust. The three major sins of pride, greed, and lust are the results of this distorting process. These sins are nothing but the distortion of the great passions that God created in us. These three passions encompass our entire world. Pride is our passion for our self; greed is our passion for things; and lust is our passion for other people. Everything in the phenomenal world can be found under this great tripartite division.

What is lust, but the energy which drives us toward union with one another. Is this bad or in some way evil? Certainly not. The energy that impels us toward union is the same energy that has driven you to read this book. It is the same energy that makes you fall in love. In and of itself, this energy is beautiful and holy. When distorted by the false self, however, it can be perverted and twisted into something that is unrecognizable. The false self takes that which is desired and turns it into an object whose only purpose is to serve our own pleasure. So we destroy what we profess to desire.

What is greed, except a deep desire for union with things, a passionate concern for getting more and more of something. Is this not the same energy that drives us spiritually? At the root of all our greed is the insatiable desire to be loved, and to give ourselves fully in love. The only place where we can satisfy these boundless desires is in God's arms. We are greedy for that love. We want to taste more and more of the sweetness of God. The more we taste, the more we want union with God. Is this evil?

Yet, certainly we see many perversions of this great passion that we call greed. For example, the relentless pursuit of more and more money drives people into becoming automatons: robotic money-generating machines. The relentless pursuit of any thing turns us into something less than human. When we are possessed by the passion of greed, we subordinate everything to fulfilling this passion. Unfortunately, no thing or accumulation of things can ever fill this black hole inside of us. There is no end to this yawning chasm within us, because this passion cannot be fundamentally satisfied with things.

From the perspective of the true self, it is clear that the only satisfaction of this passion will be found in God, that which is wholly other, and which can never be possessed by us. What we conventionally label "greed" is, in fact, simply that great passion which longs for God, and which pushes us toward union with the Divine. This is not evil.

What is pride? From the perspective of the false self, pride is the passion which gives us an overly high opinion of ourselves, that places us at the very center of everything. Pride is that energy which leads us to believe that we are more than the limits which seem to constrain us.

Is this not fundamentally true? Are we not much more than these limits? Did not our Lord say, "I am the Vine, and you are the branches?"[203] Fundamentally, what we call pride in the false-self system is really a recognition, from the perspective of the true self which God created, that we are more than what we appear to be. We are, indeed, children of our Father and Mother in heaven. We do, indeed, participate in the risen Christ. We are the branches of our Lord.

Perversions of this passion abound, of course, from the misguided religious leader who says he is God, to the arrogant sales clerk in the department store. But in its fundamental nature, the passion of pride is the energy which helps us understand our true nature as children of the Divine. And this is simply good.

So we come to understand that the passions are not evil, or something that must be excised. They must, however, be transformed from their false-self expressions. The passions, as they are bent by the dictates of the false-self system, will poison any attempt to move toward the Divine. But, once they have been seen for what they truly are, once their expression is directed into spiritually useful channels, then they can become powerful engines which quickly move us into the Divine.

This transformation was described by the early fathers as *apatheia*, which is best translated as dispassion. It is not apathy, but rather "a state of reintegration and spiritual freedom (that could also be rendered as) purity of heart."[204] It is not a state of indifference, but rather a state in which the passions no longer possess and rule us. The development of dispassion is closely linked with the development of love and humility.

Historical Methods for Dealing with the Passions

Our passions are such powerful energy sources that we have considerable difficulty in handling them successfully. This is the problem inherent in any energy source. How do you handle molten steel? How do you contain a million volts of electricity? This problem is magnified with our passions because there is no outward container that we can use for this energy. We, ourselves, in our own flesh, must find ways to contain and direct these powerful forces.

Over the last two millennia, the church has experimented with many different methods for transforming the false-self perversions of our passions. Unfortunately, at its inception, there was an already existing strain of gnosticism within Judaism, which quickly made inroads in the thinking of church leaders.

Gnosticism is a dualistic belief. It is based on the notion that what is material is inherently bad, and what is spiritual is inherently good. Gnostics believed that human beings were a combination of both the material and spiritual. Our bodies and passions are material, and hence bad. Our intellect and spirit, on the other hand, were believed to have come from the Divine. In creation, God caused a shower of divine sparks to come down from heaven and give us life. Our task, as human beings, is to turn from the evil inherent in the material world, and to free this divine spark within us so that it can ascend once again, and be united with that great source in the heavens. In this gnostic account, God is only in heaven; the incarnation is a sham.

The remarkable thing about this brief account is how it resonates with us. The extent to which this account feels somehow right is the extent to which gnosticism is alive in each of our lives.

The gnostic system of belief is antithetical to Christian belief. As Christians, we hold that creation is inherently good because God created it. The distinction between the false self and true self may look similar to the gnostic dualism at first glance, but there is a significant point of departure. We do not hold that matter is inherently bad. The true self created by God did not become mired in the material world; it was put in the middle of this wonderful creation by God. Our task is not to get free of this wonderful world. Our task is to find our true nature as children of God in the midst of this world.

Unfortunately, this clarity of distinction has not always been maintained by exponents of the church. To combat this on-going denigration of our bodies and the world we live within, I believe we must return to the teachings of Jesus, St. Paul, and the Old Testament in order to understand these matters truly. In the Old Testament, as we have said before, God creates the world and all that is in it and pronounces it "very good."[205] Jesus continues in this tradition. He never speaks of the body or the material world as inherently evil. He consorts with prostitutes and tax-collectors: those who were believed to have given themselves over to the pleasures of the flesh. Jesus preaches love and forbearance, not hatred and the excision of the soul from the body.

St. Paul speaks clearly and repeatedly of the flesh. For Paul, the word "flesh," or *sarx* in the Greek, did not typically refer to the physical body, although many have misinterpreted him in this way.[206] For Paul, the flesh meant the evil, distorted aspect of the egocentric self, what we have referred to as the false self. For Paul, the flesh is the internal state where our undisciplined passions direct the body. This is the state we are in prior to our gaining control of our passions by rooting ourselves in the soul through contemplation. This can be clearly seen in Paul's description on the works of the flesh, which are "wickedness, evil, covetousness, malice, envy, murder, strife, (and) deceit,"[207] and so forth. These are the works of the false self, and have nothing to do with the material world, *per se*.

Unfortunately, a distortion of Pauline thinking based on the gnostic dualism has always been a part of the church. A strand of thought arose within the church which advocated extreme measures to control the desires of the flesh. Many of the ascetical practices that were first tried in the deserts of Egypt and Syria were based on the desire to renounce the flesh. This rigorous physical asceticism then migrated into the monastic traditions of both Eastern and Western Christianity. Because so much of our spiritual practice comes from these roots, physical asceticism is pervasive in the disciplines and practices of our spiritual fathers and mothers.

This has resulted in strange behaviors among some of those who have taken the spiritual disciplines seriously. A consequence of such practices is that most people have concluded that the deep life in the Spirit is not for them. They have rightly decided that such practices are too extreme. So they come to believe that the spiritual life is either too far removed from them, or too offensive to engage in.

These results are a travesty. This is the opposite of what should happen when people see true spirituality. Life in Christ makes our life more abundant, more rich. One who has come to live in the Spirit is marked by a deep joy, a rich sense of meaning and purpose; one who is in balance with his world. Such a one should make others hunger for these sweets, not turn away in disgust. But such is our misperception: that what is true and beautiful is often obscured by the false self.

The Road Less Traveled. There is another way than the austerities which degrade the body. This way invites us to observe our passions in all of their variety. From these observations, we develop a deeper understanding of them, a discernment of their true nature. Theophan the Recluse, a Russian saint of the nineteenth century, has written instructions to begin this method.[208] This is included as

---

**SPIRITUAL EXERCISE 32
USING OUR PASSIONS**

1. Be aware that everything you experience is given to you by God. You can either take delight in what is outwardly visible, or you can look within, in order to draw closer to the Creator and giver of these gifts. You can either focus your attention on Christ, who dwells within us, or on the outer world.

2. Let your awareness be grabbed by something in the world. Feel one of your passions as it stirs you. For example, fully experience:

> The beauty of a person, an object, or a natural phenomenon like a sunset.
> Your own sense of pride in an accomplishment, in who you are.
> Your desire to have more and more things.

3. Holding your passion in awareness, let yourself become aware of the Divine, as it shines through your passions:

> Feel the energy of it.
> Trace that energy back to its source in God. Do not try to express or contain that energy. Just let it flow through you. Let yourself look inwardly.

4. As you experience the Presence of God in the energy of this passion, mentally transfer that joy to all created things. For example, as you come to feel the Presence of God in the beauty of another person, focus on that Presence. Take that sense of Presence and mentally transfer it to other things that are visible around you. Feel that Presence in these things as well.

5. Let yourself come to see God's Presence in everything. Observe not only the outward beauty, but also the inward beauty that is in every created thing.

6. Let yourself rest in this beauty in all things.

a spiritual exercise, but it is not necessarily one to be practiced only during our periods of formal sitting. This exercise can be done at any time, in any circumstance.

We live in a wonderland of beauty. It is all around us. It is not expensive. It is free for everyone who has the eyes to see it and the heart to experience it. This wonderland is the creation of our Father. We participate in this beauty—all of us. Even that which the world judges as unsightly or evil participates in this beauty. There is no end to it.

As you begin to focus in these ways, as you begin to use your passions to tap into the energy flow that streams through us, you will begin to feel more energized. You will begin to see the inward beauty that is all around you more easily, without effort. You will begin to feel the vibrant energy with which we are imbued by God. This energy will fuel your journey into union with God.

Chapter 30

The Orthodox Practice of Watchfulness

There is an ancient antecedent to the practice of utilizing our passions for spiritual growth. It was developed during the time of the desert fathers, and is known as the practice of "watchfulness." It is a method of observing and changing the passions and their expression. The successful practice of watchfulness will give us the energy we need for deep and extended contemplation.

Watchfulness is a technique of fixing our attention in our heart in order to observe and halt the flow of discursive thought. This technique originated with the desert fathers during that great exploratory time in the deserts of Egypt and Syria. It was first described in a systematic fashion by St. Evagrios,[209] an eighth-century abbot of the monastery of the Mother of God of the Burning Bush in the Sinai desert.

The practice of watchfulness is not a commonly known technique of prayer, because not many have practiced the meditative disciplines long enough to come to need this technique. Successful practice of this prayer technique is possible only for those who are considerably advanced along the spiritual path. This practice will be profitable only when the practitioner: 1) has developed the facility for moving attention into the heart center and rooting it there, and 2) can focus attention for sustained periods of time.

The Rationale for Watchfulness. The thrust of the disciplined spiritual life is to confront the false-self system, learning gradually to relinquish it in favor of the true self within us which God created. As we know by our practice, this is not an easy or a comfortable task. The false self is constantly originating thoughts which are designed to suck us back into the false-self system. These thoughts come to us as the passions: as pride, greed, and lust. In order to combat these "demons," Evagrios suggested keeping watch over the heart, where our desires arise. From this need, the practice of watchfulness has arisen. The practice of watchfulness purifies the passions, that "desiring–part" of the soul.

The Practice of Watchfulness

The practice of watchfulness is useful in stilling the actions of the discursive mind and the false self. This stilling can occur in the last stages of monologistic prayer, or here, at the outset of contemplative prayer. In either case, true contemplative prayer can take place only as the passions are purified and discursive thinking brought to an end.

The practice of watchfulness is an initial contemplative practice that allows us to bend the power of the passions to spiritual attainment. Watchfulness is based on the classical Christian understanding that the soul, which contains our desiring part, is located in the heart. In our natural state, coming from the true self that was created by God, our desires flow toward God. Ultimately we want nothing more than union with the Divine. But under the constraints of the false self, our desires are wrongly directed toward things in the outer world.

Watchfulness is a method for containing our desires by not expressing them in thoughts. At the beginning of our spiritual practice, we disengaged from the behavioral expression of these thoughts. Now we move to a more subtle expression of the same principle. At this level of practice, we constrain even the thoughts, because expressing a desire in thought tends naturally toward the expression of that thought in some sort of action. At the beginning of our journey, we constrained our outward behaviors, without really understanding the significance of what we were doing. Now, we constrain the thoughts from which these behaviors originated. This process allows the passions to flow in the purity which God created. The energy of these passions will serve as the vehicle which will move us into full awareness of the Divine.

During watchfulness, we disengage our thinking from our passions. The passions stay bottled up in the heart. The passions are our desiring part, so by holding on to the force of our desires, we can begin to direct this great force toward God. It is really God that we long for, when we long for all created things. With watchfulness, we experience the full force of our longing, and redirect it toward its proper object—the Lord. In so doing, we go back into the inner purity which God created in us, deep in our hearts. That purity resonates with the Divine. By diving into this natural purity, we are quickly transported home.

The practice of watchfulness is also a method for confronting the false-self system directly. Engaged in this practice, we observe the flow of thought. Rather than making decisions about which thoughts come from the false self and which come from the true self, we simply let go of all thoughts, allowing them to flow by without running after them. We do not have the expertise, from our entrapment within the false self, to discern which thoughts arise from the true self at this point. As we come to disengage from our thinking, our desiring part moves naturally toward the Divine. As we practice, we rest in God. There is simply a great quiet and a deep inner stillness. Here we can be assured that the true self is functioning as it should.

Watchfulness centers around observing and then disengaging from the flow of thoughts that stream through awareness. By the time you begin this practice, the flow should be rather sparse. If it is not, your practice will be much more strenuous and active than is appropriate for this point in the spectrum of practice.

There are two ways of observing and disengaging. The first is the ancient way, described by St. Hesychios, involving the "continual fixing and halting of thought at the entrance of the heart."[210] There is an active quality in this, however, that is somewhat contrary to the intent of the practice. A second and more psychologically sound way is to simply disengage from the thought. Withdraw your emotion from the thought, thus robbing the thought of any power over you. Simply contain the emotion within your heart.

SPIRITUAL EXERCISE 33
WATCHFULNESS

1. Position your body comfortably, spine erect, on a chair or cushions.

2. Ground yourself in your physical sensations. Close your eyes and slowly become aware of the sensations of your

physical body. Feel the sensations as they flow through you. The sensations in your head...in your neck and shoulders...your elbows...your wrists and the palms of your hands...the sensations in your knees...your ankles and the soles of your feet.

3. Move your attention up to the region of your heart and establish yourself there.

4. Observe the flow of thoughts from your heart center.

5. As you become aware of the flow of thoughts, disengage from each thought. Withdraw your emotion from the thought, and contain the emotion within your heart.

6. Continue this process of disengaging from thoughts for the period of your practice. Over time, you will notice that the flow of thought decreases. When you are blessed with stillness, rest there, close to God.

(To close your period of practice)

7. When you are ready, let yourself come back to this place. Let the feeling return to your feet...your hands...your face. Take a deep breath, and open your eyes.

The Interior Movement of Watchfulness. This prayer is quite different from most that we have practiced. In the beginning of your work with this technique, you may find it quite difficult. I began practicing watchfulness before I was ready. I had to exercise great effort when I practiced, because there were so many thoughts that were constantly arising. Later, after I realized that I was not yet ready for this prayer, I went back to the Jesus Prayer.

You are not ready to begin the practice of watchfulness until the flow of thoughts from your heart has been greatly reduced by the monologistic prayers. If you have difficulty with watchfulness at the outset, and find yourself having to exert great effort to maintain the practice, then you may not yet be ready for it. Be kind to yourself, and go back to the monologistic prayers.

The practice of watchfulness is difficult enough, even when we are ready. It is hard to see our constant reaching outward for things, our constant grasping. It is not flattering to see this constant grasping so clearly in ourselves.

As you become skilled in watchfulness, you will find in yourself an increasing amount of energy. You become more and more filled with energy as you refrain from throwing it away. It may be difficult to contain all of this, simply because you are not used to it. If you peg your "normal" false-self level of energy at an arbitrary 100, you are likely to find yourself accumulating energy in the 1000's. You will find yourself gradually filling up with energy, and then slipping in your practice of watchfulness and throwing all of it away. This is disheartening, to say the least, and can easily lead to the old self-blaming patterns.

These are the last-ditch efforts of the false-self system as it struggles to maintain itself. The false self is literally fighting for its life. The power with which it struggles is your own substantial power. As a friend of mine put it, "This is not a fun time!" While not particularly pleasant, nevertheless, the rewards of watchfulness are sweet. It is easier and easier to enter into stillness. Your sense of God's Presence throughout the day increases. You find yourself practicing more and more, in the little intervals that your day permits. You are more and more focused on the Lord.

The Results of Practice. The practice of watchfulness produces a continuity of attention in the practitioner. As we become skilled in our practice, we find that our attention is no longer broken by passing thoughts. We begin to attain control over the process which underlies and produces our thinking.

This internal continuity allows us to rest in the deep stillness of God. In monologistic prayers, despite our best intentions and despite loading our awareness with all the elements of our practice, our thoughts still wandered. This happened because our hearts were not pure. The pure passion within our souls was still directed by the false self in an outward direction, toward the things of the world. Our passion was not free to follow its natural inclination, to go within toward the source of all things. By means of the practice of watchfulness, our hearts will find peace. From the foundation of this deep stillness and peace, we can go on to contemplate the wonder and goodness of our God.

Chapter 31

Contemplating the Qualities of God

Contemplation is the movement of awareness beyond concepts and discursive thinking into that realm where the Divine is perceived and experienced directly. Only in this way can we get totally free from the illusions of the false self.

Because contemplation is a vehicle which takes us beyond the domain of thinking and concepts, it is rather difficult to use concepts and thinking to describe this process and the effects it produces. As a result, the next few chapters are rather scanty on words. In itself, this is quite illusory. While few words will be used here, entering fully into these exercises will result in a wealth of experience in the realm that is beyond words.

The Qualities of God

At this stage of our practice, we have plenty of experience entering into the Presence of the Divine. We have begun to feel that Presence on a regular basis outside of the times of formal practice. We are no longer strangers here. So now it is time to deepen our experience of the Divine Presence by focusing on the particular qualities of God. In the past, we have felt a generalized Presence. Now it is time to focus on particular aspects of that Presence, so that we can come to know our Creator more precisely, more fully.

We do this in our formal practice by entering deeply into the meditative state, and experiencing that Presence of God. Then we focus on a single aspect of the Divine. Do this by feeling God's Presence and differentiating the qualities that you feel most strongly. Identify them by feeling them, and then labeling them. For example, you may feel God's compassion, sweetness, kindness, nurturing, or any of the other wonderful qualities that flow from the Divine. Take the quality which you feel most strongly and focus your practice on that quality. Simply sit in the midst of this aspect of God and rest here. Learn about this quality by experiencing it. Feel it resonate in yourself, evoking parts of you that perhaps you did not know existed so completely and so strongly.

To help you learn the less structured practice of contemplation, our first contemplative exercise focuses on a quality of Christ from which all of us can learn and benefit. This exercise is presented for heuristic purposes only, in order to walk you through a beginning contemplative exercise. This way you will know, more precisely, what to do and how to work with this kind of exercise. Ordinarily, you would allow God to present to you the quality that you need to work on. Initially, however, this may give rise to some misunderstandings about contemplation, so we will begin our contemplative work with more structure than is ordinary.

SPIRITUAL EXERCISE 34
CONTEMPLATING THE KINDNESS OF CHRIST

1. Position your body comfortably, spine erect, on a chair or cushions.

2. Ground yourself in your physical sensations. Close your eyes and slowly become aware of the sensations of your physical body. Feel the sensations as they flow through you. The sensations in your head...in your neck and shoulders...your elbows...your wrists and the palms of your hands...the sensations in your knees...your ankles and the soles of your feet.

3. Move your attention up to the region of your heart and establish yourself there.

4. Open your heart and experience God's holy Presence. Feel Christ's holy Presence. Sit for a time in this Presence and feel the energy that radiates from our Lord.

5. Then focus on the loving-kindness which radiates from Jesus. You may also feel other qualities and energies. For this exercise, label them and refocus on Christ's loving-

kindness. Remember, this is not an exercise in thinking about a quality. Rather, it is a resting in that quality, that energy, without words or thoughts.

6. Sit in the midst of Christ's loving-kindness and rest here. Learn about this quality by experiencing it. Feel this energy as it radiates from our Lord. Feel the sweetness and gentleness of it, the power of it. Rest here during the period of your prayer.

(To close your period of practice)

7. When you are ready, let yourself come back to this place. Let the feeling return to your feet...your hands...your face. Take a deep breath, and open your eyes.

As you can see from this exercise, contemplation is much less structured than meditation. Without a well-developed attentional focus, the practice of contemplation is impossible. The subject matter of a contemplative exercise is too vague to provide the necessary structure to maintain your attention. Only when your attention is transformed into a stable tool can you begin to engage in contemplative work.

The next spiritual exercise is a generic contemplation which focuses on the qualities of God. This is contemplation in its true form. Here, God chooses the subject matter for us, and shapes His instruction to accord with our inner needs. This exercise can be repeated endlessly, and you will learn something new every time.

SPIRITUAL EXERCISE 35
CONTEMPLATING THE QUALITIES OF THE DIVINE

1. Position your body comfortably, spine erect, on a chair or cushions.

2. Ground yourself in your physical sensations. Close your eyes and slowly become aware of the sensations of your physical body. Feel the sensations as they flow through

you. The sensations in your head...in your neck and shoulders...your elbows...your wrists and the palms of your hands...the sensations in your knees...your ankles and the soles of your feet.

3. Move your attention up to the region of your heart and establish yourself there.

4. Open your heart and experience God's holy Presence. You may do this by visualizing or feeling that aspect of God with which you are most comfortable: the Father, Christ, the Divine Mother, the Holy Spirit. Sit for a time in this Presence and feel the energy that radiates from this holy One.

5. Then focus on a single aspect of this energy. Become aware of the many qualities which exist in these energies. Identify them by feeling them, and then labeling them. For example, you may feel compassion, sweetness, nurturing, wisdom, and so on.

6. Take the quality which you feel most strongly and focus your practice on that quality. Simply sit in the midst of this aspect of God and rest there. Learn about this quality by experiencing it. Rest here during the period of your prayer.

(To close your period of practice)

7. When you are ready, let yourself come back to this place. Let the feeling return to your feet...your hands...your face. Take a deep breath, and open your eyes.

After you have practiced this exercise for a considerable period, you may wish to enhance your contemplation with the following exercise. In this enhancement, you deepen your contemplation by feeling those pure qualities of the Divine resonating in your own being. In this process, you begin to explore the meaning of the creation story in Genesis: "in His own image He created them."[211] This enhancement is very similar to the previous exercise on which it is based. What we are doing in the exercise below is learning to experience a particular quality of God as it exists in ourselves. First we experience the quality as it exists in God. Then we feel that same quality in ourselves. We learn, through this, to conform ourselves more closely to the nature and will of God.

SPIRITUAL EXERCISE 36
DEEPENING YOUR CONTEMPLATION
OF GOD'S QUALITIES

1. Position your body comfortably, spine erect, on a chair or cushions.

2. Ground yourself in your physical sensations. Close your eyes and slowly become aware of the sensations of your physical body. Feel the sensations as they flow through you. The sensations in your head...in your neck and shoulders...your elbows...your wrists and the palms of your hands...the sensations in your knees...your ankles and the soles of your feet.

3. Now move your attention up to the region of your heart and establish your attention here.

4. Open your heart and experience God's holy Presence. You may do this by visualizing or feeling that aspect of God with which you are most comfortable: the Father, Christ, the Divine Mother, the Holy Spirit. Sit for a time in this Presence and feel the energy that radiates from this holy One.

5. Then focus on a single aspect of this energy. Become aware of the many qualities which exist in these energies. Identify them by feeling them, and then labeling them. For example, you may feel compassion, sweetness, nurturing, wisdom, and so on.

6. Take the quality which you feel most strongly and focus your practice on that quality. Simply sit in the midst of this aspect of God and rest here. Learn about this quality by experiencing it.

7. After you have spent considerable time contemplating this quality of our God, feel this same quality as it resonates within yourself. Feel how you, too, carry this quality. Let God's energy shape this quality in you so that it molds you even more closely to God's own image.

(To close your period of practice)

8. When you are ready, let yourself come back to this place. Let the feeling return to your feet...your hands...your face. Take a deep breath, and open your eyes.

After we gain some facility with this prayer in our formal practice, it is helpful to explore this prayer in our daily life as well. Open your heart to let this quality shine forth in yourself. Practice this quality, even in situations where it is difficult to remember. Our task is to completely reorder our lives, and to give ourselves fully to God. So let that which you learn in your heart flow outwardly, into your behavior, and into the lives of those around you.

Reflections on the Contemplative Process. With contemplative practice, we begin to journey into the vast depths of the Divine. This is a realm without limit; a realm where we can journey to find our true nature as God's children. This is the home to which He keeps calling us back; the home that we have always known was there but somehow could never find.

Because of the complexity contained within the simplicity of contemplation, these practices take time and dedication. The beginning disciplines of meditation are absolutely necessary to shape us so that we can reach the realm of contemplation. But once we can come and rest here, the beginning disciplines will hold little interest.

Here God instructs us, gently and continuously in our hearts. Here, we need the fuel of our passions to power us. And in this journey, our passions are cleansed, purified, and redeemed by God. We learn to see our true nature. We learn to be humble, not because we are supposed to, but because we recognize the rightness of this in our own flesh. We come to know what is true.

Here, faith is left behind. Faith is the hope that these practices will take us to God. As we enter into the contemplative disciplines, we come to know beyond doubting that we are in God. God Himself teaches us. We come to walk and talk with the Divine in ways that cannot be adequately expressed in words or contained in concepts. We learn that our true nature is the nature of love.

Chapter 32

Learning to Love

More than any other single theme, Jesus speaks to us of love. He teaches us about the centrality of love: that love is the *sine qua non* of existence. He shocks us with His teaching, saying that we should love our enemies, which goes contrary to common sense. Whatever we might conclude about our Lord Jesus, His ministry is inextricably bound up with loving in a new and radical way; a kind of loving which goes far beyond the bounds of what we conventionally know as love.

From this side of the fence, rooted as we are in the false self, it is difficult to understand this talk about love. It is incomprehensible that Jesus would give up His life on a cross for us. It is unfathomable to talk of loving your enemies. This talk is worse than nonsense; it hurts our heads when we really start to think this way.

In fact, from the position of the false self, love cannot be understood. From the false-self premise of "looking-out-for-number-one," such talk is gibberish. So if we are to understand what Jesus is trying to tell us, we must go beyond the parameters of the false self and see love from the perspective of the true self.

This means, of course, that we must go beyond words and concepts. We must move into contemplation to begin to understand what God is teaching us with all this emphasis on love. We must allow the Lord to speak to us directly, without the words and concepts, in the deep, dark recesses in our hearts. Only here will understanding gradually form and emerge.

Many people believe that they understand about love. They believe that anyone can understand the fundamentals of loving. Yet, when we look around at the brokenness of our world, it seems clear that we do not know how to implement love. This inability strongly suggests that we might not know what love really is. This state of affairs is perfectly reasonable, if you think about it. Most things that are fundamental to our existence take a while to understand. For example, trying to understand what makes the physical universe tick has occupied physical scientists for centuries. And they still have more questions than answers.

From the evidence around us, we must conclude that we do not know much about love. Our personal relationships are not characterized by love. Relationships between groups are not characterized by love. Relationships between nations are not characterized by love. Even relationships between those who profess to follow Christ are not characterized by love. Why?

I believe that our confusion about love stems from our rootedness in the false-self system. Each of us designed our false self to please other people; we designed it to help us survive, to help us get by in the world. "Getting by," however, is quite different from loving. Love is a direct connection between two people with each other. "Getting by" suggests some kind of peripheral, tangential contact.

From the perspective of the false self, love is an incomprehensible concept. Love is best defined as a caring for another person that is equal to our caring for ourself. This has no place in a survival mentality. From the perspective of the false self, we can never understand love, let alone practice it. The false self stands alone, at the center of the universe. It cannot, by its nature, love, because love would put someone else at the center. For the false self, this is anathema.

The realm where we can encounter love is in God, by means of contemplation. We do not go there to love God, because we do not know how to love. Our false self is interested in survival, not in giving up its own welfare for the welfare of another. So it cannot yet love. In contemplative prayer, however, we can sit with God and in God and receive His love directly. We can be filled up inside with that great goodness which flows so freely from the Divine. We can allow our mental structures to be softened and changed by the love of our Father. Only after we have been taught in this way, only after we have regularly been nurtured, can we then nurture others.

SPIRITUAL EXERCISE 37
RECEIVING GOD'S LOVE

1. Position your body comfortably, spine erect, on a chair or cushions.

2. Ground yourself in your physical sensations. Close your eyes and slowly become aware of the sensations of your physical body. Feel the sensations as they flow through you. The sensations in your head...in your neck and shoulders...your elbows...your wrists and the palms of your hands...the sensations in your knees...your ankles and the soles of your feet.

3. Now move your attention up to the region of your heart and establish your attention here.

4. Open your heart and experience God's holy Presence. You may do this by visualizing or feeling that aspect of God with which you are most comfortable: the Mother, the Father, the Christ, the Holy Spirit. Sit for a time in this Presence and feel the energy that radiates from this holy One.

5. Become aware of the love which flows from God. Feel it flowing around you. Feel its power, its texture, its light and warmth.

6. Let this love of God flow inside of you. Sometimes it seems to me that it is like an endless stream of light which floods into my darkness. It streams into my darkness, illumining and warming everything it touches. Be open to how the love of God comes into you. Rest here during the period of your prayer.

(To close your period of practice)

7. When you are ready, let yourself come back to this place. Let the feeling return to your feet...your hands...your face. Take a deep breath, and open your eyes.

After you have spent a long time here, perhaps years of receiving God's love and learning from Him, you may feel moved to focus your growing love outwardly, toward some person or event. While it is imperative that you do this, it is also crucial that you do not do it too soon. Too often, before we know how to love well, we feel moved to express our love to others. We give them something that we think is love, but that may not be. As we have found in our meditation practice, the false self is deeply rooted in our psyche. It continually puts up distractions to pull us off course as we journey toward the Divine. Until we transform the false self, we may end up giving those whom we wish to love something quite different. In scripture Jesus asks, "What father among you would give his child a stone, if he asked for bread?"[212] Unfortunately, we do this all the time. Worse yet, we do it to the ones we profess to love.

In contemplation, as we rest in God, we can learn about love. Only by experiencing it in our bodies and in our souls can we learn our lessons. Then when we love, we will do so truly, and with great benefit for those whom we love. Then our hearts will open like an ever-expanding conduit as we flow the love we have received from God into the world. This is the magic of the great saints among us. This is the magic of Mother Teresa of Calcutta and Padre Pio of our own time, the magic of John of the Cross and Teresa of Avila, of Francis of Assisi and Clare in times past. It is not their own love with which they endow the world. It is God's love flowing through them.

The difference is perceptible. We sense that there is some great difference in these people. They do not love as we do, meagerly. They roar love at us. They inundate us.

We, too, are all called to love in this manner. We are all called to sit with our Father/Mother in heaven and receive love fully. And slowly, as we see that there is nothing to fear, we can allow ourselves to approach our God and learn these deep lessons of the heart. As we have received this roaring torrent of love, so are we called to flood that love of God toward others. This is our purpose; this is what we were created for.

Chapter 33

Letting Go

The direction of our work has been to move from the cataphatic meditations to apophatic practice. We began with concrete images and references with which to focus our meditative practice. We have refined these stimuli over the course of our work together. With the monologistic prayers, we began to enter into the realm of the apophatic, leaving behind the sensory stimuli which served as our guides.

As we progressed to contemplative prayer, our focus has become even finer. We are in the process of leaving behind all of our comfortable guideposts, all of the concepts that we thought marked out the way. We do this not because it is novel, or interesting, or more challenging. We do this because we understand how pervasive the false self is in its self-deluding perceptions. Even the purest of our concepts can be twisted into something else by the workings of the false self. Even the notion of purity, itself, can be distorted beyond recognition. In our century, for example, we have seen the idea of ethnic purity used by racist groups around the world to justify beatings, rape, torture, murder, and wholesale genocide. We see this wonderful idea of purity twisted beyond recognition. This is the self-centeredness of the false self.

Up to this time in our meditation practice, however, even our purest apophatic practice has had a strain of the cataphatic within it. Even the practice of receiving God's love has a bit of the false self lurking in its depths. What, after all, is the experience that we feel as "love" in this practice? Does it truly come from God, or is it an emanation from our false self? Our concepts are operative in distinguishing between this sensation and that, between this feeling and that, in order to discern God's love in this practice. We must question how reliable our discernment is, given that we all come from a deep enmeshment in the false-self system.

278

That brings us to the final spiritual practice to be described in this book. In this practice, we abandon any dependence on the false self. We move forward in the faith and trust that any rigorous abandonment of *all* our concepts and thinking can only result in drawing closer to God. In this practice, we simply let go of any contents of our awareness. We relinquish even our sense of self.

Addressing Those Who Are Afraid. Somewhere in the dark recesses of American fundamentalism, a frightened soul came to believe that if you meditate and let your mind go blank, the devil will slip in and possess you. I cannot tell you how many times I have had to address this question from those whom I have taught. There is a deep fear, in individualistic America, of letting the mind go blank, of losing our precious self. This fear has been artificially attached to the fear of devil possession. None of this has any reality in fact.

First, your mind does not go "blank" in meditation or contemplative prayer. Typically, after you have wrestled with your wild thoughts and unruly attention, you *wish* it would go blank. But, unfortunately, wishing does not make it so. Second, this notion from fundamentalism attributes extraordinary power to the devil. Frankly, the devil is not powerful enough for these kinds of direct assaults. The devil does not need to be. Our sinful and broken nature, ruled by the false self, gives ample opportunity for entry by the devil.

Meditation is actually the opposite process. Meditation is the shutting of the door to the devil. It is one of the ways that we can address the false self directly and obtain release from its grasp. So to put this ancient spiritual discipline in the camp of the enemy is tantamount to sinning against the Holy Spirit. It takes the power of God and says that it is no power.

The third issue implied in this fear is that we lose our self when we meditate. In my experience, we cannot lose our true nature that God created. We can lose the false self, which we constructed to help us get along in the world. This does not seem like a very great loss for a Christian. The false self keeps us separated from God and from our own true nature. In fact, holy scripture enjoins this loss upon us from the Old Testament onward. We are asked by God, not for burnt offerings, but for "a broken and contrite heart."[213] In Ezekiel, God says that He wants to take from us our hearts of stone and give us hearts of living flesh.[214] He wants to help us restore our true nature.

In fact, we have now come to a spiritual practice in which you may let go of your sense of self or identity. This occurs very late in your journey into Christ. Many practitioners of meditation will never get this far. Many people who try this exercise before they are ready are simply unable to do it; their attention cannot sustain the focus for the period of time necessary for this practice.

As with everything in life, it is important not to engage in this practice until you are properly prepared. Those who have not gradually strengthened their attention can be very frightened if they somehow succeed in letting go for a short time. They find themselves in an amorphous sea of Being without any of the familiar landmarks. When we can no longer distinguish our self from the perceptions flowing through our awareness; when there is no longer any "I" to sort out things into categories like "good/bad," "up/down," and so on; a fragile ego can be frightened severely and even damaged by this fear. So this is not an exercise to try just to see if you can do it. Its effectiveness lies in being part of a series of exercises which will transform your awareness so that you can perceive the Divine.

Origins. This spiritual exercise came to me while I was meditating some years ago. Intuitively, I realized that this practice is the logical consummation of the contemplative journey. Only through this practice will the last traces of the false-self system release its power over us. I have never come across mention of this exercise in any of the texts which I have studied. It has either been carried in the oral tradition, or it is new to our Christian tradition.

In the twenty-five years that I have meditated, I have been graced, on a number of occasions, with "revelations" of practices that I needed. These occurred when I had gone as far as possible with one form of meditation, and did not know how to progress further. In times such as these, the Lord Jesus in His sweetness has provided guidance. I have either been led to a teacher, a book, or the Lord Himself has taught me.

It is this constant loving Presence which is so valuable to us as we walk the path back home. Within our false self, we feel alone and cut off. We shut our eyes to the warm light which constantly surrounds us. We stop up our ears to the murmuring of Christ in our hearts.

Our meditation really gains us nothing. That is to say, there is nothing new that is added to us. We are not listening to sounds that others cannot hear. We do not see things that are not there for everyone with eyes to see. All we do in our spiritual practice is strip away the thick coverings that are smothering us, isolating us. When we are finally free of our cocoons, what a realm of wonder we find in this place where we dwell!

SPIRITUAL EXERCISE 38
LETTING GO

1. Position your body comfortably, spine erect, on a chair or cushions.

2. Ground yourself in your physical sensations. Close your eyes and slowly become aware of the sensations of your physical body. Feel the sensations as they flow through you. The sensations in your head...in your neck and shoulders...your elbows...your wrists and the palms of your hands...the sensations in your knees...your ankles and the soles of your feet.

3. Move your awareness to the region of your heart and establish yourself here.

4. Observe the flow of thoughts and feelings from the perspective of your heart center.

5. As you become aware of each object-of-awareness, let it go. Simply release it, and refocus your attention in your heart center.

6. Continue this process of letting go. Let go of your thoughts over and over again. Let go of everything that comes into your field of awareness.

7. After doing this for some time, you may become aware of the "self" who has these contents of awareness. It is as if you step back from the moment-to-moment flow of data and become aware of the larger context in which this data flows.

This awareness will come to you naturally, in its own time. When it occurs, view the "self" as just another content of your awareness. Let go of your "self." And let go of what comes after the sense of self. And let go of what comes after that as well. Continue this process of letting go.

(To close your period of practice)

8. When you are ready, let yourself come back to this place. Let the feeling return to your feet...your hands...your face. Take a deep breath, and open your eyes.

As with the other contemplative practices in this section, this prayer may be repeated indefinitely with great benefit. The use of this prayer helps us release the last vestiges and traces of the false-self system. It allows us to realize our created nature as children of the most high. It is the road back home.

As you have been progressing in your contemplative practices, you have been experiencing more and more the Presence of God. These experiences will occur not just during periods of formal practice, but also during the mundane activities of your ordinary daily routine. You simply become aware of that abiding Presence within yourself, and in all creation. You begin to sense the unutterable holiness of creation.

This brings us full circle, back to the very first practice that we started with, the recollection of God. It is this fundamental Presence which is the heart of all spiritual practice. But where we had to struggle to feel His Presence in the beginning of our journey, now there is no effort required. This is the very life that we breathe. This is our own deepest Being. This is the great "I AM" who loves us.

Chapter 34

The Fruits of the Spiritual Life

Human beings are essentially goal oriented. We are motivated by goals. We change our behavior in order to achieve the goals that are important to us. So it is always useful to look at the results of a practice, since these results are also the goals for which we strive. What then are the results of these long, involved spiritual disciplines of meditation and contemplative prayer?

Presence. The first and most important result is an increasing sense of God's Presence in all things. Under ordinary circumstances, in a life which has little or no spiritual discipline, people sense God's Presence only rarely. Perhaps we sense that Presence when we attend church; perhaps when a tragedy hits us; perhaps at moments of extreme beauty. But for most of the time, we live a life that is without God. We do not sense this Presence.

When we begin our meditation practice, after we get used to the raging turmoil of our thoughts and emotions, we begin to have a few experiences of God's Presence. We feel something there, some of the time. When these gifts occur, we often give a whoop of joy inside. This destroys the experience and brings us fully back into the realm of the false self. Actually, our whoop of joy does not destroy the experience. It only refocuses our awareness back to the discursive mind and away from any sense of God's Presence. But subjectively, we feel like we have destroyed it.

The important thing to note is that, even in the beginning stages of meditation, the kingdom of heaven begins to open to us. The felt sense of God's Presence, however fleeting or faint, now becomes perceptible to us from time to time.

The process of meditation can be likened to tuning in a station on an old-fashioned radio. We are learning to tune ourselves so that we can receive God's signal. Since God has always been present to us, and since we have never learned to distinguish that Presence from all of our other experiences, God has been lost in the overwhelming noise of our lives. Now, as we learn to tune ourselves to God, we begin to pick up His signal. At first it comes in poorly, covered with static. The signal seems weak and we constantly lose it. It seems to fade in and out. Actually, it is our attention that is fading in and out, but subjectively it seems like we are having problems with the signal.

As we progress with our meditation practice, our ability to tune ourselves to God increases. As our attention strengthens, we are able to focus on the signal longer and more clearly. As we focus on the Divine, there is, bit by bit, a release from the dictates and compulsions of the false self. Our attention becomes even stronger. We begin to experience that Presence more easily in our periods of meditation practice. We even find ourselves experiencing the Divine outside of our meditation.

It is this increasing sense of God's nurturing Presence that is the first fruit of the disciplined spiritual life. As we continue our practice, we will find that the sense of God's Presence is something that is always with us. Even when we turn our backs on God, nevertheless He is faithful and present to us.

The taste of this fruit is so sweet, so compelling, that it alone is sufficient reason to devote ourselves to the spiritual life. Remember our Lord's parables? "The reign of God is like a buried treasure which a man found in a field. He hid it again, and rejoicing at his find went and sold all he had and bought the field."[215] The treasure of a full spiritual life is buried within us. We find it by disciplined work. And after our first taste, we find that it is worth everything we have to be able to live in this field.

Knowing Your True Nature. In addition to this first fruit, there are many others. Ranking high among these is the fact that, through Christ, we come to know our own true nature as children of the most high.

Many people walk around without any knowledge of this. Even those who believe in Christ and have thoroughly read the scriptures may have only an intellectual understanding of this. Because we do not understand our true nature, we do all sorts of things that are against our nature, against our very selves. We lie, steal, cheat, and kill: as if these actions are acceptable so long as we do not get caught.

Look at what happens when we do these things. Let's take the most extreme example for the purpose of illustration: killing others. We socially sanction going off to war to kill people. Many soldiers who actually engage in battle, however, get quite ill. Combatants develop a set of deep fears and anxieties that we now call post-traumatic stress disorder. It would be just as appropriate to say that their souls are sick.

Many of these veterans were placed in positions where they had to violate their true nature in order to survive. In a war zone, they had to kill others or be killed. Have you ever wondered why returning combat veterans seldom talk about their experiences? Because these experiences have made them ill. Not ill in a physical sense, but deeply wounded in their souls.

The consequences of other violations of our true nature are similar, but usually lesser in degree. There is a soul sickness that arises from lying, from stealing, and from the violation of all of the behavioral regulations embodied in the laws of God. The regulation of these particular behaviors is not arbitrary, although at the beginning of the spiritual journey it may appear so. Rather, these behaviors have to be stopped so that our souls can return to normalcy.

The need to engage in these soul-destructive behaviors is driven by the false self. The false self believes itself to be the center of the world—the most important entity in existence. Meditation is an antidote to the false self. It is a method that involves not responding to the promptings of this surface self, in order to discern and follow the promptings of a deeper, truer self. As we meditate, the driving compulsions of the false self begin to loosen their grip. We begin to have some intimation of who we really are, of what our purpose in this life might be. The more we meditate, the more we will experience God's love, and the clearer these perceptions will become.

We were created by God as His children. Jesus shares this with us over and over again. The story of the prodigal son is about each one of us. Each of us has been deluded by the dictates of the false self. As a result, we left our spiritual home, and we have wandered among strangers who have used us harshly. At any time during our sojourn into darkness, we can return home. There are two questions that are always before us. First, do we want to return home? Second, if we want to return, are we willing to walk the disciplined path that will take us there?

Our disciplined practice of meditation and contemplative prayer is a vehicle which can return us home. Through this vehicle, we come to know our true nature as God's children. Knowing who we are, our lives become full of meaning and purpose. For the first time, we know what we are supposed to do. We know why we are supposed to do these things. We stop acting like the ugly duckling of the fairy tale, having realized our own deep, innate beauty. We are set free!

Knowing the True Nature of Others. As we come to know our own true nature, we also come to understand something about the real nature of other people. We come to see others as our relatives, our family. We realize that we all have the same Father.

As we grasp the reality of our deep interconnectedness, our behavior begins to change. Our hearts open to others in compassion. It becomes less and less easy to hold extreme views: racism, homophobia, religious intolerance, and so on. It becomes harder to be harsh with those who do not agree with us. We find our own inner hardness softening and melting in God's love. Following God's commandments becomes easier and easier, since they are nothing but reflections of our true nature, sketches of our own true self.

Even the extreme commandments of Jesus become comprehensible and doable. The proposition, "Love your enemies"[216] becomes as obvious to us as "love your friends." They are fundamentally the same statement. We are fundamentally one people.

From the perspective of the false self—that frightened part that struggles for the approval of others, that struggles to get by—these concepts provoke terror. The false self needs an enemy. Without an external threat, there is no reason for its existence. This explains why we are so harsh with each other: the false self is simply busy creating enemies to react against. We are so possessed by the driving needs of the false self that we mistake its needs for our own.

As we grow in Christ, though, we learn compassion for others. Just as He loves us, so we are called to love one another. To our terror, Jesus responds, "Love one another, as I have loved you. There is no greater love than this: to lay down one's life for one's friends."[217] We begin to see this extended family of which we are members. We begin to participate with each other as God's children.

Understanding the Deep Holiness of Creation. As we are transformed by our practice, we also come to a deep reverence for the creation in which we are placed. Our compassion begins to extend to animals, plants, and even the rocks and air.

This movement is not another intellectual proposition. If we try to generate this by our own efforts, because we think we should, we will not be able to sustain it. This is a gift that comes from God and God alone. As we move more deeply into the Divine, we will begin to see the magic in the world: that all things are alive and conspiring with God to promote our mutual welfare. We come to realize that the air we breathe is there to nurture us; the ground we walk upon rises up to hold our feet. We become aware that everything pulsates with life and the Holy Spirit.

As with the other transformations described above, this awareness of the pulsating life in a supposedly inanimate world comes only slowly, as the result of long practice. First we catch little glimpses of it. Then, more and more, we realize the deep underlying reality of it. Finally, we become aware that all of us are walking in a living wonderland that is full of life. We are finally able "to see a world in a grain of sand and Heaven in a wild flower."[218]

These are some of the results of sustained meditation practice. We come to sense God in all things, and this results in a fundamental transformation of our selves. We understand ourselves differently; we are free, for the first time, to be ourselves fully and truly. We also come to understand the true nature of other people and the world in which we live. Our view of everything is changed.

All of the externals remain the same, of course. The ground beneath us is still made of dirt, our noisy neighbor still makes noise, our boss still acts like he has always acted. But *we* have changed. How we understand things has changed. What we hold to be important has changed. And so, everything is transformed for us.

Interior Gifts. There are many other changes, as well, which we may experience. The changes described above happen to everyone. Those changes that we will talk about below happen only to some. Unfortunately, there has been no scientific study of these phenomena yet, so we do not know what makes them happen or what prevents them from happening.

Infused prayer. Infused prayer is the experience of God giving us prayer; God, as it were, praying us from the inside. Speaking in tongues appears to be one kind of infused prayer. There are many other experiences of this kind that may come to us as we progress in our practice.

Infused prayer does not typically happen in the initial stages of our practice. Only after we have considerable attainment, only after our false self has been seriously weakened, can the Divine infuse us with prayer.

This experience may sound rather frightening to a novice, but in practice it is delightful. There is no effort needed from us. We simply allow the power of the Spirit to flow through us, praying us as it needs to do. There is a considerable element of trust here. To the extent that we are afraid and not trusting, to that extent we will not experience God's gift of infused prayer. To the extent that we have gained sufficient experience with the Divine to let go of our need to control, to that extent we are likely to experience infused prayer.

In all of these experiences, however, we must remember that these are gifts from God. They are not things that we can earn. They do not come to everyone. Rather, they flow from God, according to God's own wisdom. We do not control them in any way.

Visions and ecstasies. As we advance in our meditation, and as we engage in the other spiritual disciplines, we may have visions from God or fall into ecstasy. These experiences happen only to extremely advanced practitioners. They are not experiences to be sought after: seeking after them will only twist and distort our spiritual practice. Rather, they are gifts from God which come to those who have been greatly purified by their practice.

I personally believe that all of us have the capacity for visions and ecstasies. Under the pernicious influence of the false self, however, only a very few ever realize these capacities. St. Teresa of Avila indicates that these experiences happen only after the practitioner has many experiences of infused prayer. Only in the deep stillness of the Mind of God do we happen upon these great joys.

St. Teresa also cautions about seeking these experiences.[219] She talked about certain nuns who, through the powers of their overactive imaginations, believed that they had visions. Because these sisters did not have a firm foundation in God, and because they were not moving into their true self, they were further deluded by the false self. These so-called "visions from God" were simply another tool that the false self created to get approval from others. And of course, it did not last long. The fruit of the tree always gives the surest answer about the nature of the tree.

These experiences are not for us to search after. I mention them here for two reasons. First, as you read the spiritual literature, you will come across references to these things. You will need to under-

stand what they are about. Second, if you persevere in your meditation practice, these experiences may come to you. Knowing what is
happening may help you integrate these experiences into your life.

The resurrection body of Jesus. The great saints who have
continued their spiritual practice until they entered into union
with God sometimes share in the marks of Christ's resurrected
body. These are gifts given by God which are truly extraordinary,
and which are usually given the title of miracles. I will mention
just of few of them here.

St. Francis of Assisi, in an ecstasy with Christ, was given the
marks of Christ's stigmata: the wounds of our Lord in his hands
and feet and side. Since Francis, many others have received the
same sign. These are visible marks, created by unseen spiritual
forces, which come to only a very few of God's favored ones.

Similarly, there are reliable reports of levitation and bilocation
in the lives of the saints. St. Joseph of Cupertino[220] is one example
of the many who have demonstrated such gifts. As we have indicated previously, during the celebration of the mass, Joseph would
lose himself in prayer and levitate above the throng. There are
also reliable reports of St. Joseph being in two places at the same
time, a phenomenon called bilocation. This is something which we
hear in the life of Jesus, in Luke's story of the happenings on the
road to Emmaus.[221]

Finally, there are numerous examples of a great saint demon-
strating an incorruptible body after death. Their bodies do not decay
back into the earth, but remain whole and sweet smelling, even
after centuries. St. Teresa of Avila is one example of this phenomenon. Some years after her death, her incorruptible body was cut up
for relics, and these relics are now distributed throughout Europe.
But even in parts, her remains are sweet-smelling and incorruptible. There are other examples of this as well, St. Sergius[222]and St.
Seraphim[223] of Russia are two others that come to mind.

Again, this is not a gift to seek after. How would you try to find
it, in any case? These are the material results of a long and disciplined life of prayer. They are the miracles, which show us who do
not yet believe with our whole hearts, that Jesus is Lord of all.
They are, if you will, inducements to us for our own practice. They
are signs which indicate that there is more to understanding this
world than our intellect can know. Our hearts, however, can enter

into union with God. And in this way, we can come to know these mysteries directly.

Returning God's Gifts. As we progress in prayer, as we begin to realize these foretastes of the kingdom of heaven, we will find an even more extraordinary gift that awaits us. We will find that our level of energy increases. As the false self loosens its grip, we will no longer spend ourselves in internal conflicts. We will no longer waste our energy doing those things that are contrary to our nature. An extraordinary amount of energy will become available in the process.

It is crucial for our spiritual well-being that we direct some of this energy back into the world, that we let our actions flow with the same love as our hearts. When we are moved by a situation, we need to give ourselves permission to get involved in that situation and work to transform it. This is the path of compassionate service.

Most Americans are quite generous of heart. We are often moved by others less fortunate than ourselves, and we respond. But we are so tied up in the false-self system that the results of our actions are not always what we hope them to be. This occurs because we operate from the inadequate and biased understandings of the false self.

As we make progress in our spiritual work, as energy is released within us, it is important to spend this energy in caring for those around us. As we begin to really see, we have a greater responsibility to those in the family who do not yet see clearly. We need to act toward others in a more compassionate manner. We need to devote ourselves to helping our family in Christ come to a better understanding of our Lord.

There are two very practical reasons for this. First, as long as any one of the family is stuck in the false self, we are all diminished. We are so deeply linked to each other through the Body of Christ that we participate in each other's pain. In the long view, compassionate caring for others is nothing but enlightened self-interest.

Second, an extraordinary benefit will come to us as a result of serving others. This kind of service is a spiritual discipline in itself. As we give ourselves to others, we will be rewarded by God working within us, purifying our hearts. Mother Teresa of Calcutta is a wonderful contemporary example of this process. This rather ordinary Albanian nun became a saint by serving the poorest of the poor. Those who walk in her footsteps will also achieve sanctity through their spiritual discipline.

As we progress spiritually, we need to direct the flow of love that we are receiving toward others, outside of ourselves. If we try to hold on to God's love and contain it inside, we will get wrapped up in ourselves. We will pervert the Presence of God into a kind of private piety. The false self will have triumphed. Containing God's love is not possible. If we try to contain it, it will be as if, just as we are setting foot on the doorstep of our spiritual home, we are transported to hell, isolated once again within the false-self system.

A word of caution. While the discipline of compassionate service can be practiced at any time in our walk with the Lord, often we engage in some heroic act of love too soon. Notice that Mother Teresa did not immediately start off serving the poorest of the poor. She spent many years serving as a teaching nun in India first. Too often, we try to love before we know what love is. Too often, we give away the energy that God gives us to grow with, and no benefit results. Do not throw yourself away in some ill-conceived gesture of love. On close analysis, that gesture of love is probably the false self trying to get someone's approval. Rather, take the time to learn from the Lord; learn to discern between God's will and the alluring voice of your false self. Then you may, with wisdom, spend God's love in the service of others.

These are some of the benefits of the disciplined spiritual life, the fruits of our practice. The greatest of these fruits is a continual sense of God's Presence. It is the knowledge, in our own flesh, that God is truly with us.

From this Presence, other gifts arise. We come to know who we are and what our true nature really is. We come to know others just as deeply as we know ourselves. We, begin to see creation for the living wonderland that it is. Each of our days becomes a walk in holiness and beauty. For God is with us.

In addition, there are certain interior gifts which come to some. These are the gifts of infused prayer, and the visions and ecstasies that we read about in the lives of the great Christians who have gone before us. These are not bizarre hoaxes, perpetrated on an unsuspecting public. They are verified phenomena. We too, as we develop in our spiritual practice, may experience these same phenomena.

Finally, there is the gift of energy, and the avenue through which to express this gift: compassionate service. Compassionate service is itself a spiritual discipline. Engaging in this discipline brings benefits, not only to ourselves but also to the world around us. We allow ourselves to be conduits through which the love of God can flow into this broken world.

These are just a few of the things that happen as a result of deep prayer. I hope that you do not take my word for it. I hope that you practice until you, yourself, can verify what I say by means of your own experience. For God is truly with you. You have only to awaken to this wonderful Reality.

Part VII
Demons and Monsters

We spend our lives in an endless round of activity. We do things without ceasing. We get up early in the morning to go to work. We busy ourselves at work all day, and then come home and do our chores: the cooking and cleaning, and taking care of the kids, the house, and the car. Even in our play, we typically go off and "do" something. We go to the beach, or watch a ball game, or see a movie, or read a book. Our minds are constantly busy. This busyness is our life.

To enter into meditation, however, we must leave our busy doing behind, venturing into unknown territory. We do not know what is there; we do not know what to expect. Not only do we, ourselves, not know what it will be like, but very few of our friends have been to this strange land. So there is no first-hand information that we can gather before we enter. At best, we can perhaps find a guidebook like this one, or some tourist's memoirs.

Not only is there very little first-hand information, we also hear through the grapevine that this unknown land is filled with monsters and demons. As we discussed above, every meditator has heard the old fundamentalist fear, "If you meditate and empty your mind, Satan will come in and possess you!" Any meditator, even a beginner, has the necessary information to discredit this idea. Who, after all, can *empty* their mind? Yet we wonder whether meditation might open us to more evil in some way. After all, we do not know the territory ahead of us. And we wonder how we will find out before we make some mistake.

As you meditate, you will have strange and unusual experiences. These experiences are not "bad," but they will be strange to you because you have never experienced them before. You will constantly ask yourself, "Is this what I am supposed to be experiencing? What do others experience?" And because there is not a large body of experienced meditators who live down the street, you may not have anyone to talk to about your experiences. The chapters in this section are an attempt to give you that consultation. These chapters are a compendium of "road lore," a distillation of the experiences of others who have walked this way before you. These chapters explore the typical experiences that people have as they

begin to meditate. They address the common questions and difficulties that arise, to help you understand what is ahead.

We will also focus on typical problems that arise during meditation. There are some very predictable difficulties which arise during practice over which many people stumble. While we cannot
keep you from stumbling over them, we can give you practical
solutions for resolving these problems when they occur.

Our biggest problems revolve around our fears. We are afraid of
the unknown, and our fears drive us fiercely. When something
happens that we do not expect, we get frightened and upset.
Because we know next to nothing about the vast reaches within
us, next to nothing about the false self that floods us with compulsive thoughts and doing, next to nothing about the God who loves
us and saves us, we are vulnerable to our fears.

Our Lord Jesus constantly comes to us in the midst of our fears,
saying, "Fear not."[224] "I am the Way, the Truth, and the Life. All that
enter through me will find rest."[225] And when we hear this, some of
us (or even, some part in each of us) runs away howling, "Arrgh!
That's just what I was afraid of—what do you mean, 'rest'?!!"

There is really no help for us, is there? If we do not have real
monsters, slobbering to consume us on every side, then we create
our own. Notice that, once again, we have been successful in making
ourselves the center of attention. Our false self will make it so, even
if it has to stand in a pool of hungry crocodiles to accomplish it.

Since our false self will do anything to make itself the center of
the universe—even to the extent of imagining monsters waiting in
the dark to consume us, let us take heart and go forward. This is
just how we are; we do not have to be afraid of it. So let's go and
look more closely at these so–called monsters. What lies ahead of
us, in this uncharted territory within our own depths? What will
we face there?

Chapter 35

"Will I Have to Give Up My Chocolate?"

In our culture, many believe that meditation is a strange and unusual creature, from some exotic land. When you ask people what comes to mind when they think of meditation, they typically think of Eastern yogis wrapped in strange robes doing God-knows-what. Because we see meditation as something exotic, we have a number of fears about the whole process. Our fears are typically based on a lack of knowledge. We do not know what meditation is, so we do not know what to expect.

Will I Be Overwhelmed?

The most common fear facing the novice meditator is that you will be overwhelmed in some terrifying way. You will sit down to meditate the first time, and go so deep that you never come back. Or you will come back a totally changed person, unacceptable to your family and friends. Or you will renounce all your possessions, sex, and everything, and go to India to learn at the feet of some strange guru.

While we fear these things, a part of us secretly desires this kind of powerful magic that will transform us in an instant. But these things will not happen on our first attempt to meditate. They will probably not happen on the hundred-and-first, or on the hundred-thousand-and-first. In fact, they will not happen at all. I do not know of a single case in which these things have happened. Somehow, though, this has entered the folklore surrounding meditation. It has earned an enduring place, despite the total lack of evidence to support it.

We all have primal fears of being overwhelmed. The practice of meditation will give us the experience to chart this heretofore unknown land within us, these strange fears and imaginings. Remember that God never gives us more than we can handle in our meditation. We will not be overwhelmed. We may wish to be overwhelmed many times, but God will not do this to us.

Later, after we have developed our attention to a fine point, we may have unitive experiences in God. We cannot have these experiences, however, until we are ready for them. When we are ready, we will not have a sense of being overwhelmed. Rather, we will enter into the culmination of a long courtship; a sweet fulfillment of all that we have hoped and worked for. This culmination is diametrically opposed to the violation implicit in being "overwhelmed."

Despite these assurances, you may still retain your fears to some degree. Your fears will only be fully overcome by experience. I invite you to meditate, and to face your fears. Take courage, and move in the direction that your heart longs to go. You will find, as you meditate, that "overwhelm" is a word not heard in God's vocabulary.

"Outer" Problems Facing the Meditator

There are a number of problems for the meditator that are inherent in the outward direction of our culture. We do not live in an environment that values inner development. To understand this fully, it is helpful to contrast our culture's view of meditation with that of another culture. In Thailand, for example, an employee may ask for a leave of absence for up to six months to go meditate with a teacher. Typically, these requests are granted. If you asked for a similar leave in this country, your employer might question your suitability for employment of any kind!

As a people we have been taught not to value internal development. We value the outward things which we can see and hear and touch. While this focus has given us a wonderful material culture, we know little about the vast realm within us. This lack of familiarity gives rise to certain characteristic problems.

First, we do not know what to expect, as we journey within. Our friends and neighbors have likely not been there, so they cannot provide us with guidance. Imagine going to a foreign country without a map and a phrase book. That is what we have to do when we start our interior work. The only maps that exist are books like this. And no map sufficiently describes the terrain. Because of our culture's lack of inward-directedness, we do not have access to the anecdotal road lore that other travelers might have provided.

A second problem arises when we try to explain meditation to our family and friends. If we are fortunate, we will get polite interest. But some of our friends may look at us with big wide eyes and say, "You what??!!"

The cultural images that we have of meditation are mostly negative: images of Hare Krishna devotees selling flowers at the airport and the like. We have no sense of the history of meditation and contemplative prayer within Christianity. We are not likely to know anyone who regularly meditates. The whole thing seems foreign and perhaps even frightening. You, yourself, may have felt a bit frightened when you began to meditate. Having to explain what you are doing to others who do not understand and who are also frightened will often complicate matters for you. Their fears may feed your fears, inhibiting your confidence or even your practice.

This state of affairs is truly unfortunate. There is no remedy for it other than the slow creation of a significantly large body of people who meditate. Only then will the culture as a whole have enough information to feel comfortable with the concept of meditation. But what it means for us at this time is that we can expect to face fearful questioning and doubts, as we try to explain our spiritual practice to someone not familiar with the notion.

"Inner" Problems Facing the Meditator

In addition to the "outer" problems facing the meditator, there are also internal obstacles. These are the more significant obstacles; obstacles that our spiritual practice is designed to resolve. We may, in the course of our meditation practice, experience some or all of these. It's always nice to know what might happen, so that we can be prepared for the possibility.

Disciplined Attention. The first serious problem facing the novice meditator is the lack of a disciplined attention. This becomes painfully evident from the first moment that you try to meditate. Over and over again, you find your attention wandering from your desired focus. Over and over again, you have to drag your attention back to your meditation focus, only to watch it zip away again after just a moment. This can be extremely frustrating. You can get up from a period of meditation quite tired from all of the mental effort required to contain yourself. This can give rise to discouragement.

What is worse is that, as you deepen your practice, there seems to be no end to the distraction. Subjectively it feels like you are still wandering where you should not be. Actually, this is not true. But as you develop the ability to handle the gross distractions, distractions of a more subtle sort arise. The interface between levels of distraction is seamless, so it may feel like you are making no progress in containing and focusing your attention.

Actually, when you look at the content of your distractions over the period of several months of meditation practice, you will notice significant changes. You will find that the distractions that you are currently dealing with are much more subtle than the ones you previously dealt with. This is one of the markers by which you can gauge your progress.

Consistent Motivation. The second serious inner problem is the difficulty in sustaining a consistent motivation for your meditation practice. There was some reason that you began to practice: perhaps a friend got you excited, or you read a book, or went to a lecture. But over time, your motivation to practice will be seriously compromised. We usually think that this is the result of too many other things to do. Let me warn you, this is *not* the problem. The real problem is deeper and far more serious. The real problem lies with the false self mobilizing to preserve itself.

When you begin meditating, you embark on a journey that will thoroughly change you in ways that you cannot even imagine at the outset. You begin to dismantle the false-self system that has controlled your behavior for most of your life. As you continue, the false self "feels" what is going on, and reacts against it. It finds reasons for not meditating. If you will examine these reasons closely, you will see that they center around the preservation of the false self.

One of the inherent difficulties of meditation is the slowness of the process. The reward that we seek, union with God, is hard to obtain. We have to discipline ourselves thoroughly to achieve this reward. So there is a long interval between beginning meditation practice and the experience of the first unitive states. There is an important reason for the length of this interval. God is literally remaking us. This process does not take place overnight; our God does not rush us or overwhelm us. Rather, there is a slow, gentle transformation that gradually changes how we feel about ourselves.

But the length of the interval can cause us to lose heart and get discouraged. After all, in the land of instant everything, we have come to believe that we should be able to have "McSpiritual Experiences" for just $1.95 right now. And the minister down the street may, in fact, be offering just such a service. But God's transformation of us is gentle and slow. She does not force us or compel us. So when you see something fast or forceful in the spiritual arena, take care. Jesus reminds us that His yoke is easy, and that He is gentle and humble of heart.[226]

Unrealistic Expectations. A third inner problem that we will face is our unrealistic expectations about meditation. Because meditation is a virtually unknown practice, we do not know what to expect. We hear that meditation can bring us to see God face to face. That it can even bring us into union with the Divine. This is heady stuff, is it not? Furthermore, we apply our typical American time frame to it. After all, if it cannot be done in a year, it probably is impossible, isn't it? And in this way, unrealistic expectations about the results of our meditation practice multiply.

What many people do not understand is that meditation is a lifelong discipline. It is one of the few things that might take your entire life to master. If you expect to see God after a year of practice, you are likely to be disappointed. You will not see God because you have not developed your attention to a fine enough focus. Most people could probably develop this focus in a year's time, but they would have to sacrifice everything else to accomplish this end. Most are not willing to do so.

Most of us choose the longer route. We give twenty or thirty minutes to our meditation practice on those days that we are not too distracted. As a result, we do not progress with much speed. This is not the fault of the meditation; it is our fault for not practicing. Imagine trying to learn a profession like law or medicine, or trying to open a new business by devoting twenty or thirty minutes a day to the activity. You might graduate from law school, but you will take many, many years.

So, what can you realistically expect from a twenty-to-thirty-minute-a-day practice? You can expect lots of frustrations. You can expect to want to go faster, but not making the progress you desire. And you can expect the false self to throw up distractions and roadblocks at every turn.

You can also expect spiritual consolations from time to time. You can expect the slow dismantling of your false-self system. You can expect to spend years with no other visible result than an increasing sense of peace. You can expect your anxieties to gradually quiet. And, if you persevere, you can expect your entire life to change so slowly that the changes are almost imperceptible.

You can expect to experience the Divine in ways that you did not expect. If you continue, you can expect that God will bring you home again. Just remember, like the prodigal son, we have to do our part. We have to start the journey and persevere in it. Our Father cannot welcome us home until we have made the effort to get there. We cannot realistically expect Him to do His work and our work too.

Surfacing Repressed Memories. This brings us to the fourth inner problem that you are likely to encounter. As you meditate, you go deeply into the unconscious mind, and you begin to access the old pain that you have repressed and buried. This material surfaces as a natural result of meditation. This is part of the dismantling of the false self.

Father Keating calls meditation "divine therapy," the slow and gentle action of God in our hearts, healing our inner wounds and restoring our original nature.[227] But sometimes it does not feel very gentle. Sometimes it seems like we have unleashed a furious maelstrom. While this process can be uncomfortable, it is not unusual or unexpected. It can happen any time in your practice, and often happens several times. Recall the anecdote of my colleague who described her "spiritual vomiting." This was the process of releasing her old emotional programs. For her, the experience was most intense after she had journeyed for many years.

For others, this divine therapy happens at the start of the journey. For example, a student of mine who was attending a beginning meditation class quit after the fourth session. Later she returned and shared what had happened to her. She was in psychotherapy and had been at a plateau for over a year. She was stuck. Nothing new was coming up, but the old dysfunctional behavior patterns were still with her. As she meditated, however, the old emotional "stuff" that she needed to address began to surface during her meditations. The more she meditated, the more distressing were the old memories that came up. She finally felt that she could not handle any more, so she stopped meditating for about a year.

When this happens to you, there is no need to be frightened.

This is a known and expected part of the spiritual journey, albeit not the most pleasant part. When it occurs, it is a time for rejoicing, for now you begin to unload the false-self programming at an accelerated rate. You may wish, however, to consult a psychotherapist or a spiritual director who is familiar with this kind of eruption. Even God's therapy is not much fun, and it is difficult to go through if you have no support. So when this happens to you, seek out a counselor who can guide you through it and help you release these unhealthy programs.

As you continue in your practice, you will gain more and more experience in this spiritual way. Others will start to notice this and ask you for advice. And this brings us to another obstacle that we will address. The obstacle of spiritual inflation.

Spiritual Inflation. As a result of the disciplined practice of the exercises in this book, you may have unusual and exciting spiritual experiences. This will open you to the serious obstacle of spiritual inflation: the state of thinking that you know more than you really do. This is yet another ploy of the false self to reassert control. It constantly looks for ways to use what we do for its own benefit. The false self will always try to coopt your efforts. This is its nature.

Spiritual inflation is difficult to recognize if you are by yourself. To recognize it, you need to be practicing in a community. You need others around you who can give you feedback about your journey and your behavior. When you are by yourself, it is natural to think that you are important, and that special experiences are simply a mark of your importance. In community, however, others do not see you as you see yourself. They can give you a clearer perspective than would otherwise be possible.

Spiritual Materialism. This is a subtle trap that catches all of us from time to time. The trap of spiritual materialism[228] is the subversion of our spiritual practice by the false self. It appropriates elements of our spiritual development and uses them to strengthen the false-self system.

This subversion is not easy to identify or remediate. There are no clear patterns or clues that will readily identify this for us. We can simply expect that it will happen. Being on guard, we may catch this process earlier and contain the damage.

This subversion occurs when our desires interact with the meditative process. For example, *we want to attain our goal of union with God now*. If you look carefully at these words, you can see the false self at work. Words like "want" and "now" identify the grasping quality that drives these wishes, and they give the false self away. It is the false self that has these expectations; the false self that wants to be there now. And in a way that is so very clever, the false self has appropriated the apparently "good" desire to attain union with God, and perverted it.

Look at what results from this. With this desperate wanting, the false self has altered our course away from God and toward failure. The meditative process is slow, because the grip of the false self on us is extraordinarily tenacious. So we are unlikely to make quick progress. Then the false self whispers, "We aren't going anywhere with this meditation stuff. Maybe it won't work for us. I guess this is just another false promise. We just got suckered again."

With words like this, we become discouraged. With thoughts like these, we fail to see our real progress. Instead, we see where we think we should be, and compare it with where we think we are. When there is dissonance between these two places, as there will be due to the false self's carefully nurtured expectations, then we are disappointed. We lose heart. We find excuses not to practice in a disciplined way. And we have turned off the path again.

Meditation is a process that involves releasing our expectations. Meditation is a process that helps us to see ourselves as we truly are, developing within ourselves the virtue of humility. The false self, on the other hand, is the desiring part, the proud part. This is the part that pushes and drives us. By following its dictates, we are apt to lose our way.

The Value of Spiritual Community

How does a person who is near-sighted recognize their debility? You lose your vision gradually, imperceptibly. The near-sighted person thinks that everyone sees just as he does. It is only by going to the doctor, who has objective measuring equipment, that you learn about your near-sightedness. In a similar way, you need a spiritual community to help you address your spiritual inflation and the many traps of spiritual materialism. The community becomes both a measuring stick and a support for your journey.

Spiritual community does not just happen. It is the result of our intentions. Either we must seek out a spiritual community that has already formed, or we must gather a group of like-minded individuals and form one together.[229] Community is very important to the success of our long-term spiritual growth. A spiritual community gives us a group of like-minded people with whom to explore the difficulties of our journey. A community can give us encouragement when we are discouraged, counsel when we are confused.

Most importantly, in the community there is a clearer sense of Christ. Jesus promised that when two or three were gathered in His name, He would be in the midst of them.[230] This actually happens in spiritual communities. There is a kind of powerful discernment that goes beyond the capabilities of any of the group's members. Our meditation together seems to give us access to a depth in God that is otherwise very hard to achieve.

The oldest member of our OneHeart community, a woman in her middle seventies, talks of the loneliness of her practice for most of her life. "I was all alone, and I just couldn't talk to people about what was happening within me. Even the priests that I talked to didn't seem to understand." Since she has joined our community, her understanding and depth of practice have increased greatly. She says that not only have her adult children noticed a significant difference, but now when she goes for walks, complete strangers are drawn to her and pour out their pain. She has become a real force for healing in this world.

If you are serious about your journey into God, then begin to consider joining or forming a spiritual community. This is indispensable to the long-term success of your venture.

What can we conclude from this examination of the difficulties that face us in meditation? Will we, indeed, have to give up our chocolate? Will we have to renounce all the things that are most precious to us? The answer is a resounding "NO"! God will not make us give up our chocolate or anything else.

As we progress in our spiritual journey, we will find ourselves confronting aspects of the false self over and over again. We will want to give up those greedy, self-centered desires that have been driven by the false self. We will, in fact, engage in a continual process of repentance. We will turn from these things that have separated us from God and learn to walk in another way. Sometimes this process will be difficult; other times it will be easy. But in every case, as we walk more closely with our God, our repentance will be sweeter than any honey we could taste.

Our journey is to leave the false self behind. Our journey is to shed its constraints and to enter into the freedom that is God. This freedom is not license to do what we please. Rather, it is the profound freedom of doing what we were created for.

We were created for love. God created us to give and receive love. How sweet our life will be, when we can live from our true self, freely giving and receiving love...

Chapter 36

Spiritual Consolations and Nights of the Sense [231]

Many meditators, when they begin their practice, experience the blessing and sweet pleasure of God's Presence. This comes in different forms. One practitioner may feel a distinct sense of Presence. Another may have a sense of being wrapped in light. Still another goes so deeply into a visualization that it feels like she was really there. These are manifestations of God known as the spiritual consolations. They are part of the spiritual rewards of our practice. They consist of the good and pleasurable feelings that we experience in our meditation practice, and the felt sense of being close to God.

The spiritual consolations have a two-edged nature, however, so it is important to understand them thoroughly. On the one hand, the consolations are wonderful rewards that are marks of God's grace and love for us. On the other hand, our false self gets attached to these consolations and tries to incorporate them into the false-self system. You may find yourself meditating in order to "get" these rewards. When you notice this occurring, be aware that the false self is on the move.

There is, in addition, a subtle trap associated with the consolations. The trap is to fall into the mistaken belief that God is only present to us when we feel the consolation. Because this is when we feel God most clearly, we may come to the mistaken belief that God comes and goes in our lives. This is another case of projection. We project our human tendencies onto the Divine. The truth of the matter is that *we* are the ones who come and go. The assurance that we have from the saints, who are farther along the spiritual path than we are, and the assurance we have from God, Herself, is that She is always with us.

Spiritual Dryness. There can be no sense of spiritual consolation unless there is also some dry period between the consolations. We would not notice a reward as a reward if all that we experienced was reward. So, as you have no doubt discovered by now, there are periods of spiritual dryness in between the consolations. In these periods, you may meditate and feel absolutely nothing of God's Presence. This may lead you to believe that God has not been present to you. Not so! Rather, in those times of spiritual aridity, if you continue to be faithful in your disciplined practice, then God works much more strongly in your heart, preparing you to move even more deeply into the awareness of Her Presence.

Typically, you experience the consolations as you move into a new depth in the Divine. Just as traveling to a new place might excite and thrill you, so moving into a new spiritual depth will have a similar effect. But after a time, these things that were new become familiar. The excitement wears off. You no longer notice these new things. They become part of the familiar background.

So also we stop noticing God's Presence. We take that Presence for granted. We habituate to that Presence at each level of spiritual development. When God reveals Herself in a new way, we stand up and take notice. But after time passes this, too, is no longer new, so we no longer notice. We have become so accustomed to God on this level that we make Her invisible.

During these times of apparent dryness, God is working deep in our souls to move us even closer to Herself. Our tendency to habituate is actively utilized by our God. We are disturbed that we no longer feel Her Presence. So we begin to look even more deeply within. We begin to hone our attention to even finer levels, so that we might perceive more deeply. In a word, we are motivated. So our Mother makes even the dry periods work for the good. And in this way, our soul journeys more and more deeply into the Divine.

The Rhythmic Nature of Meditative Prayer. The course of our spiritual journey is most often an alternation between periods of spiritual consolation and periods of spiritual dryness. In the times of consolation, God's sweetness is utterly delightful. We are given a foretaste in these periods of what we can expect later in our journey. If we stay with our disciplines, we will experience a succession of unitive states with God that are successively more delightful. The final union of our souls with God is described as a permanent bliss of the most sublime nature.

These periods of consolation alternate with periods of dryness.

Rather than something to be feared or avoided, these periods of dryness are absolutely essential to our progress. They are times that drive us to strengthen and develop our practice. These periods enable us to develop control of our attention so that we can continue our spiritual progression.

We do not really understand this. We delight in the times of consolation but we dislike and even fear the times of dryness. This is another evidence of our false-self system at work. The false self wants the spiritual goodies, but none of the difficult work necessary to get them. After all, our false self is the center of the universe, is it not? So it is only right that all good things would flow toward it, and all bad things flow away.

When we put our fantasies in writing like this, so that we can see them and evaluate them objectively, their absurdity is immediately apparent. The whole process of our spiritual discipline is designed to expose these fantasies and to rupture the false-self system. Only then can our true nature emerge.

The Nights of Sense. Our initial periods of spiritual dryness prepare us for even more profound times of dryness, the nights of sense, which have been articulated by St. John of the Cross.[232] As the depth and intensity of our spiritual practice increases, so our satisfaction with our relationship with God and everything else decreases. This is a direct negative correlation.

As we move along the spiritual path, God constantly infuses into us the realization that only He can satisfy our desire for happiness. As we accept this infused knowledge, we become more and more dissatisfied with everything else. We even become dissatisfied with our spiritual exercises. And so we enter into the night of sense, and experience a terrible aridity. Everything around us loses its savor.

All too often, we misinterpret this phenomenon. We begin to doubt that God is here; perhaps we even think that God has abandoned us. None of this is true. We have entered into a night of sense, a spiritual phenomenon that is well documented in the lives of many saints. During these periods, God is making us understand that there is no true happiness except with Him.

During these times, you may fear that something is wrong in your relationship with God. You may feel considerable anxiety about your relationship, wondering if you are going backward rather than forwards. All the evidence of your senses points to the fact that something is terribly wrong.

To get through these nights, you have to learn to let go of your dependence on the senses for information. You have to trust even more in God; you have to faith more. You have to learn to relax and enter fully into the night, letting it teach you in its own strange way. In these nights, you will find yourself more and more strongly disinclined to practice the discursive forms of prayer. They will just dry up in you. You will be more inclined to interior solitude and quiet. Even though God seems miles away, you will feel the need to simply sit and be utterly still.

This is the way that God helps us grow. When we enter into a night of sense, we have come to the outer limits of our personal effectiveness. Our own efforts are no longer sufficient to move us deeper into God's Presence. From now on, God does the work in us. The only way that we can help is to continue our practice, to make sure that we stay with our spiritual discipline.

From this point forward, the spiritual journey is the path that we do not know. We are utterly dependent on God. This can be a time of severe personal disruption. Our false-self programs are breaking up. With many meditators, there are strong temptations to do what you know to be wrong or destructive. You can have a difficult time with this. But this, too, will pass. After you have gone through a night of sense, you will have a sense of an interior expansion. Your spiritual practice will stabilize once again, but it will be significantly deeper. Your interior horizons will broaden and you will come to very different understandings about your self and your relationship with God.

You may experience a number of these nights of sense. Each one will deal with a different aspect of the false self. Each night of sense will begin with a felt sense of God's absence, and a pervasive spiritual aridity. There is the sense that something is very wrong. Your previous spiritual practices will no longer satisfy or produce consolation. Your dependence on sensory data is interrupted and challenged.

Fruits of the Nights of Sense. Overall, there are several distinct fruits that come from these experiences. First, we come to understand the role of the false self more clearly. Ordinarily we do not notice that we think of ourselves as the center of the universe. We just act that way, as if it were self-evident. When we come up against opposition to our self-centeredness, we tend to discount it. We blame those who oppose us for our problems, carefully observing all of their deficiencies. In Jesus' language, we focus on the speck of dust in their eye, but totally ignore the plank in our own.[233]

As a result of a night of sense, however, we come to see the damage that we have done. We begin to see, perhaps for the first time, the havoc caused by the false-self system. As a result, our humility increases. Seeing ourselves as we truly are, we become less inclined to put ourselves at the center of everything. The false self cannot stand this scrutiny, and so it dissolves.

As a result of this process, we come, more and more, to faith in God, trusting ever more deeply in Her love for us and in the relationship. We have seen directly what relying on ourselves produces. It produces pain and separation, the hallmarks of the false self. As we come to reject the false-self system, we also come to trust that which is not the false self. We deepen our trust in God.

This is not simply a matter of faith, of trusting in the things that we cannot see or experience. As a result of the night of sense, we experience God's loving-kindness more clearly in everything we do; we experience the Divine Presence in everything that happens. It is as if we have been sensitized to God's Presence. With these newly sensitized eyes, we find that God is everywhere, even in those places that we thought She could not be.

Our perception of God's outpouring of grace is ever clearer. We see His action all around us. So it is much easier to trust in the Lord. It seems right to make Him truly our Lord, our boss. Now, as we enter into the great unknown that is God, we can do so without fear. We know that God is always with us. We even find ourselves entering the unknown with gladness, for it is here that God will meet us.

Our nights of sense are difficult to go through and to endure, but they produce such sweet fruit. Our nights of sense are like combat. We go into danger, and all of the customary supports that we have relied upon vanish. We grab for them, but they slip through our fingers. Only in this way can our God teach us to trust in Him. Only in this way will we learn to relinquish the false self. This is the way to go home.

There is a sweet alternation in meditation practice between the spiritual consolations and the arid periods. Neither aspect of the journey is to be feared or sought after. Both will come to us at the proper time. Both the consolations and the arid periods are like way-stations along the path we must travel. They mark our progress. It is important only that we trust in our God, and that we stay faithful to the discipline we have undertaken.

"Take my yoke upon you and learn from me, for I am humble and gentle of heart," says our Lord.[234] Sometimes that yoke will be easy, as if it were not really there. Other times, it will chafe us and constrain us. We will feel the weight of it. Yet remember, it is not the yoke itself that is difficult. The difficulty lies with the false self. When we feel the weight, it is the false self that feels it; the false self that is threatened by it; the false self that rails against it.

So when you find yourself fighting your practice, give thanks. You are frightening your false self. You are making good progress. Keep up the good work, and go with God.

Chapter 37

Inner Demons and Deeper Demons

Our culture has taken a peculiar stance toward evil. We have made a collective decision to relativize and ignore evil. In past generations, we were very clear about what constituted good behavior and what constituted bad. As a culture, we fought against evil as we perceived it. Our laws, our police, and our values were relatively congruent with each other in suppressing those acts that we deemed morally reprehensible. But in this age, we have taken another stance.

We seem to have given up on moral issues. We no longer are clear about what is right and what is wrong. We make excuses for those who do evil. We have taken our moral standards and said that they are relative to culture. So if someone does something that a previous generation would say was clearly wrong, we say that it is the norm for that person, so it is now acceptable behavior.

We say, for example, "This murder happened because Joey came from a bad home. He shouldn't be held responsible. The real culprit was the bad environment, which can't be punished." As a result, we ignore the evil in our midst.

Not only do we ignore evil in other people, we ignore it in ourselves. When we do something wrong, we quickly rush by it, as if to ignore that anything of note happened. We avoid looking at our own evil. On both the individual and corporate level, we deny that evil exists.

Conversely, there is a part of our psyche that is absolutely thrilled with evil. Witness the huge explosion in the popularity of horror movies since *The Exorcist*; the popularity of Stephen King and other horror writers. There is something that is so fascinating about the dark side of human nature that we must look at it. It compels us.

So we find ourselves in a most peculiar situation. On the one hand, we ignore the real evil in our lives. The real evil of people getting injured and killed, of the environment being poisoned, of small children not receiving what they need from their parents and other adults. On the other hand, we create a kind of sanitized evil for entertainment, where it cannot come off the page or the screen and hurt us, and are endlessly entranced by it. We have paralyzed ourselves. We ignore the real monsters around us and in us, but we make up sanitized monsters and play with them. This is a blueprint for disaster.

The Real Monsters. The real monsters are inside of us. These are the demons described by the early church fathers: pride, greed, lust, and all of the others. These are serious demons. If we do not take them seriously, if we do not acknowledge them as formidable adversaries, then they will possess us and rule us.

The discipline of meditation is one of the few successful ways of facing and fighting our inner demons. Meditation gives us a systematic method for fighting, where before we had nothing except our own weak will. The fighting, of course, has nothing to do with putting on armor and taking up the sword. It has to do with the slow tasks of recognizing and taking responsibility for our own evil. It has everything to do with rejecting our self-centeredness in favor of putting our God at the center.

Unfortunately, meditation is not nearly as flashy as a Jedi knight, nor as visually compelling as Yoda, the wise teacher in *Star Wars*. But these movies accurately dramatized the difficulties we face. Before Luke Skywalker could successfully face evil, he had to discipline himself. He had to give up his self-centeredness in favor of the deeper wisdom that dwelt within him. When he went out to fight evil before his training was finished, he was following the dictates of pride, following the false self. And he was defeated because he was operating from the wrong center. He was in his head when he should have been coming from his heart. So is the good vanquished in real life as well.

The evil Darth Vader is not some horrid satan. Rather, he is Luke Skywalker's father, seduced by the inner demons of pride and greed. But even though Vader had walked far with evil, he was able to choose another way at the end of his life.

The *Star Wars* movies depict with considerable accuracy what we go through in our spiritual struggles. We keep looking for quick, spectacular answers to problems that do not have such answers. We keep expecting easy-to-get, easy-to-digest McSpirit burgers, rather than the slow comprehensive change of heart that signals salvation.

> We want to be saved *now*. But our greedy desire for salvation keeps us from experiencing the salvation that is already ours.

> We want to see God *now*. But this desire keeps us from engaging in the disciplined practice that will bring us face-to-face with our Lord Jesus Christ. We do not want to work for it.

> We want to be heros and heroines in the battle with evil *now*. But how could we possibly hope to win a battle for which we have not prepared ourselves?

The early Christians had a profound understanding of evil, which they saw as passions run amok. When the passions have taken us over, then evil is the natural result. Our passions are demons then. They are the inner demons, and we are seldom free of them. Since most of our actions are driven by our undisciplined passions, we must conclude that most of our actions are tinged with evil. This is not a comforting thought.

Satan and the Demonic Host. In addition to the internal demons of our passions, Jesus and His followers talked about a satan, a person or being that was objectively real and hideously evil, who consistently rejected God's redemption. They understood that there were demons who were under the control of satan, and who constantly tempted humankind to betray God and their own true nature. Part of Jesus' spiritual power was the power to cast out demons. In scripture, Jesus and His disciples are in constant combat with satan and his minions.

As part of our cultural neurosis, we have refused to look at our own inner demons, and have focused exclusively on the deeper satanic demons instead. Our interest is misplaced. We have very little to fear from these demons. They are not very numerous and are not likely to even notice us. We are simply not pure enough to draw their attention.

Jesus and His disciples drew their notice because of their great purity. We are not such. We are stained through and through by our undisciplined passions. As a result, our actions are permeated with evil. From satan's perspective, we are not worthy of notice because we are already his. There are only a few who have disciplined themselves enough to warrant attention from this strange embodiment of evil that is satan. This demonic force is seldom, if ever, present to us, so it is not something that we need to worry about. satan is literally not important enough to spend any time worrying about.

On the other hand, our own inner demons are continually troublesome. This is important because we have to deal with these demons on a moment-to-moment basis. This is the primary source of evil in our lives. Yet very few of us take our own evil seriously. Even fewer will discipline their lives to resolve this evil. Instead, we seem to prefer the ersatz living of the false self.

Meditation and Evil. Meditation is one of the few tools that have been developed to fight the false self in a systematic fashion. Meditation is a kind of divine psychotherapy for the soul. It very gently allows us to see our scattered nature and the passions that disturb us. Meditation serves as a tool by which we gather our attention and learn to focus it. It serves as a vehicle, as our newly focused attention moves us deeply into the Divine Presence. It is a spiritual therapy, righting what is wrong in us.

Without the discipline of meditation, we are blown here and there by every passing wind of passion.[235] There is no freedom in this. We are at the mercy of our passions. We are enslaved to them. Where they move, we must follow. With the practice of meditation, we begin working toward real freedom. By observing and understanding our passions, we gain the knowledge to redirect them. At this point, we are no longer dominated by the passions. Rather, when we redirect the energy of our passions toward our spiritual growth, we escape from their domination. We are free to operate from the deepest levels of our being. We are finally free to be our true selves.

The matters that we have been speaking about are vital to our salvation. When we ignore them, we put our lives and our well-being at risk. This statement may seem histrionic, but it is not. When we ignore our own inner demons, our own unruly passions, then we condemn ourselves to living from the false self only. We continue, like Adam and Eve, to hide our faces from God. Hiding in this way does not bring happiness. It brings pain and separation.

God did not create Her children for suffering. We were created to love, and to love fully. We were created to have abundant life,[236] to live and move and have our being in God.[237] This is our lot in life. These are our true functions. The extent to which we do not enjoy these functions is the extent to which we are still identified with the false self.

To come into our own, to enjoy our inheritance as children of God, we need to work toward purifying our passions. We need to take responsibility for our own inner demons, and work to integrate this dark side. We need to let God's love shine in the darkest recesses of our souls.

To accomplish these ends, we must work toward completely surrendering our selves to God. We must work toward letting go of the "I" as the center of the universe, and allowing God to be our center. We need to connect our passions to the will of God. This will power our journey to salvation. This will give us the necessary strength to complete the journey.

Meditation is the means to this end. We cannot let go of our passions completely, once and for all. We are too attached to them. We are conditioned by a lifetime of experience to live from the false self. Instead, we need a slow, systematic method for addressing and resolving our passions, like the system we find in meditation and contemplative prayer. This brings us back into God's fold. This brings God's prodigal children home again.

Chapter 38

Technical Problems in Meditation

A number of difficulties can arise in meditation. These are technical problems and they can be resolved by applying specific remedial meditation techniques. They always signify some disturbance of the false self. The false self is trying to reassert control by disturbing our meditation practice. Therefore, it is crucial to recognize these problems for what they are and to apply the correct remedial techniques.

Anxiety

From time to time, you may find yourself growing anxious while you meditate. There are a number of possible causes for this phenomenon. In general, anxiety is not to be feared or avoided. Rather, it signifies that your false self is uneasy. This means that your efforts in meditation are having the positive effect for which you hoped and worked. Your false self is under attack and feels some real threat from that deeper part of you.

When anxious feelings come up during your meditation, ignore them. Always take this as your first approach. Most likely, your anxiety is transient. Simply treat these feelings as you would treat any other distraction. Refocus your attention back to the object of your meditation and continue. Do not pay attention to the anxiety unless it persists over several sessions.

Most of the enduring anxiety that you experience during meditation comes from the surfacing of previously repressed material. These are the old emotional tapes coming to the surface, bringing with them feelings of anxiety. So, when you experience anxiety persistently during your periods of meditation, look closely to see what the anxious feelings relate to. If you determine that these feelings come from your old emotional programs, begin to look at this anxiety-provoking material outside of meditation. It is crucial that you write down what you remember in a journal. In this way you can make the material objective, something outside of yourself. By making it objective, you can begin to work with it and transform it.

Let me give you an example of this process. A student of mine began to experience a deep and troubling anxiety during her meditations. The anxiety was quite severe and she began to experience it even outside of her meditation. She came to talk with me about it. As we explored these anxious feelings, she mentioned that she did not feel worthy to draw close to the Lord Jesus. As we explored where these feelings of unworthiness came from, she began to talk about how her family constantly ridiculed her as a child and made her feel she was not good enough to do anything.

As a result of this ridicule, she grew up constantly striving for others' approval. She never felt good enough. Now, as she went into meditation, she began to feel the spiritual consolations. When she felt God's sweetness, the anxiety came up. She did not feel worthy. She had not done anything for God, so she did not deserve anything good.

By talking about this material, this woman came to identify a destructive emotional tape from her past. She began to see how this heretofore invisible tape had controlled much of her life. It became clear just how destructive this tape had been. As she came to these understandings and confronted the falseness of this old mental construct, the anxiety vanished.

The process underlying this example is instructive. First, the meditator became aware of the anxiety. Second, when it was overwhelming, she went to talk with someone in her spiritual community about it. If there had been no one to talk to, similar results could have been accomplished by journaling this material. By writing it down or talking about it with someone, the material is transformed from subjective thinking into objective material. She made it have an existence apart from herself, so that she could look at it. If she had kept the material in her head, in a subjective fashion, it would run around in the same small circles hour after hour. In subjective form, these things cannot be changed. By objectifying this material, however, she changed it. The objectifying process changed her understanding, and with this, her anxiety vanished.

The anxiety was the false self's signal that she should stop meditating. Usually when you feel anxiety, you stop what you are doing. In this case, the woman was wise to the ways of the false self. She continued to explore her anxiety, even to the extent of running after it. By facing her anxious feelings, she learned about a destructive pattern and was able to resolve it.

There are other kinds of anxiety that you may encounter in meditation, though this is the most common. A related kind of anxiety may come up when you are doing a visualization. In these circumstances, you usually have come across another old tape from the false self. For example, you visualize God as very big and it brings you to the time when you were very small. Your constant failures during this time in your life may come up, along with a concomitant sense of unworthiness. If this occurs, it is likely to create some anxiety. Deal with this anxiety as you did before. Outside of your meditation, focus on what made you anxious. Journal your thoughts or talk with somebody you trust. Trace the anxiety to its source. Then it is likely to disappear.

Sometimes still another kind of anxiety occurs when you are engaged in one of the monologistic prayers. Often, when this happens, you will find that you have been repeating your prayer very quickly. When you notice this, deliberately slow down the pace of your prayer. Instead of "Lord-Jesus-Christ-have-mercy-on-me-Lord-Jesus-Christ-have-mercy-on-me," said as fast as you possibly can say it, slow down the pace. Take your time. Feel your anxiety like any other distracting object of awareness. Then refocus back to your prayer and continue. This will provide the remedy you need.

Finally, there is still another kind of anxiety that comes from going too deeply too quickly. This is quite rare and usually is transient. Sometimes when you meditate it seems as if you take a quick drop down into the stillness. On these rare occasions it may seem as if you were shot out of a rocket, you are going so fast. When this occurs, you may feel some anxiety.

This is nothing to be anxious about. This quick transit into the Divine is one of the consolations that God gives us from time to time. We are whisked into His Presence on a bolt of lightning. If this occurs with you simply rejoice and be glad of it. The Lord is with you.

Depression, Lethargy, and Lack of Motivation

In addition to anxiety, there is yet another axis around which problems collect in meditation. This is the axis of depression. By this, I do not mean out-and-out, down-in-the-dumps, deep depression, but rather a generalized low-grade sense of the "blues." The "down" feeling of having low energy, low interest, and low motivation. You do not have the energy to do a thing. Life has lost its savor. The things that used to please you no longer are enjoyable. The blues.

From time to time, you may experience these feelings before or during your meditation. The typical unschooled response would be to refrain from meditation. This is not necessary. On a spiritual level, you are "leaking" the energy that God has given you for life. Instead of containing and using your life-force, it is running through your fingers. There is no longer enough life-energy for you to go about the ordinary business of living.

Usually we adopt a helpless posture in the face of this kind of problem. If we do so, we miss a great opportunity to make a major advance against the false self. In every case, our depression will be accompanied by a pattern of negative thoughts. These are thoughts such as, "I'm no good," "no one could possibly like a person like me," "everything I touch turns bad," and so on. This is a golden opportunity to observe the false self in action and to confront it directly.

Outside of meditation, begin to journal these thought patterns. Think through them carefully. These thought patterns are wrong; they are attempts by the false self to reassert control and to turn you from your path. See if you can discern the inaccuracies in this pattern of thought and replace them with thoughts that are more accurate. If you have trouble here, talk to a psychologist and explore this matter further.[238] Do not let this opportunity pass you by.

It may sound peculiar to hear depression touted as a "golden opportunity" to make advances in your spiritual journey. Believe me, this is the case. When you are depressed, there is always a clear pattern of negative thinking running just below the surface. During your depression, it is relatively easy to access and work with these negative thought patterns. Depression can be a great gift if you are able to use it. It's like giving a builder the raw materials to make a building. Everything you need is right there in front of you.

You can also use certain meditative techniques to address the depression. If you are starting your meditation practice and using a visualization technique, visualize light streaming into your body. Imagine that God sees you in your darkness. His response is to flood you with light from above: "The light that shines in the darkness that the darkness cannot overcome."[239] Direct that light into those areas within you that are thick with darkness. Let the light gently penetrate and dissolve the darkness. Let the warmth that comes with this gentle light thaw out those cold parts in you. Let yourself sit in the light of God.

Other visualizations which are helpful in addressing depression are exercises nine and ten in this volume. Imagine God as quite large. Go to the Divine and ask to be held and loved. Or, if you are using a monologistic prayer, go to a repetitive prayer like the Jesus Prayer or the rosary. Increase the pace at which you ordinarily say the words. Be quite quick about it. This increase in pace tends to pick up your energy. You begin to pour into yourself more energy than you can leak out. As you do this, your depression will begin to lift.

Perhaps the most serious result of depression to your meditation practice is the tendency to lose the motivation to practice. When this occurs, you tend to attribute the lack of motivation to other causes. You have too much to do. You do not seem to be getting anywhere with your practice. Maybe it's all a waste of time.

This line of thinking is dangerous to our spiritual practice because it is so subtle. A direct assault we will recognize and address, but an indirect assault is not so easy to see. These indirect assaults are often more successful, because we do not notice them and we do not mount a defense.

There is always a larger spiritual issue behind the apparent desire to abandon our practice, yet we seldom look long enough to discern the issue. We are not, after all, abandoning our belief in God. We just do not have time for the most important part of our existence, our relationship with our Creator. We just cannot be bothered with discerning between what is real in our life and what is false.

Imagine driving down a street and making the decision that we do not have to bother with what is real or not real. We can do as we please. This is a recipe for instant chaos and disaster. Yet, when we make similar decisions about our spiritual life, we do not see the carnage that results.

When you notice that you have abandoned your disciplined practice, or that your practice is being seriously compromised, talk with a spiritual friend or someone in your spiritual community about this situation. It is sometimes difficult to discern, by yourself, what is going on. We have trouble seeing ourselves clearly. When we look at ourselves, we "pretty up" those things that are not nice to look at. We do not look into our blind spots.

To address this situation, talk with someone you trust and who you feel has some spiritual attainment. Sit down and lay out the difficulty as you understand it, and ask for help in seeing what is driving the problem. This way of handling the problem will give you the most success with the least effort.

Boredom

The final problem that regularly arises in meditation is boredom. In a peculiar way, boredom is a sign of your success in meditation. That you are experiencing boredom means that your false self is disturbed by your practice. It is throwing up into your conscious awareness reasons to stop meditating.

"I'm bored. This is getting me nowhere." These are not the thoughts of your true self. These thoughts reflect the grasping desires of the false self. The underlying reality here is one of grasping and desiring. These thoughts come from the part of you that constantly discriminates and says, "This is good and I want some. This is bad and I don't want it."

That you are experiencing boredom is evidence that the false self is disturbed and trying to reassert control. It does this by giving you reasons to abandon your practice and to get involved in the whole round of desires again. But there is no freedom here. You can never get enough approval, enough love, enough things. No matter how hard you try, no matter how clever you might be, you will never get enough approval, enough love, or enough things. Any attempt to do so is doomed from the start. So why continue running after these things that cannot satisfy?

Over and over again, it is apparent that our "problems" in meditation are really the activities of the false self trying to disrupt our practice. We are, after all, engaged in spiritual warfare. We are doing our best to vanquish the false self. In turn, the false self is fighting us fiercely.

Here are some general principles which will help you in your spiritual work. First, *do not take yourself too seriously*. Be aware that you will constantly be seduced by the false self's blandishments. This is okay. Recognize your own gullibility and do not be too hard on yourself. When you take yourself too seriously, you become full of self-importance. You lose perspective. You stop seeing yourself as you really are and identify with an idealized version of what you think you "should" be. When you do this, you are lost.

The important part of our work is not trying to avoid failure, but recognizing the patterns underlying our failure. Once we see the patterns and feel the pain they cause us, it is relatively easy to step out of these patterns. And this brings us to the next general principle.

Distinguish between the surface causes and the deeper causes. Typically, we do not have much experience in this. When something happens, we simply accept the cause that comes to mind as the real cause. When we are involved in spiritual work, however, things are not always that simple.

When we are engaged in the regular practice of meditation, the false self is under constant attack. We do not feel this, but the false self quickly comes to understand what is happening. As a result, the false self will respond by putting up all kinds of obstacles. If we accept these obstacles at face value, we have lost the struggle.

As we have seen in this chapter, each of the characteristic problems that comes up in meditation is due to the work of the false self. But it is never apparent from the start where the true origin of these problems lies. Anxiety or depression would seem to have little to do with the false self. Yet, when we look closely, we see that the false self originates these feelings, thereby misdirecting us and seducing us into abandoning our spiritual discipline.

Finally, *never forget that the false self is fighting for its life. And never underestimate the cleverness of the false self.* The false self is masterful at concealing and misdirecting. It has struggled to keep us from realizing our true nature, that we are sons and daughters of God. For the most part, it has been quite successful in this endeavor. Imagine an enemy that makes you forget who you are! How could you possibly fight such an enemy? This is the enemy who faces you, who lives inside of you, who knows you intimately.

The subtlety of our common enemy is the main reason why it is so useful to have a spiritual community with whom to share the journey. It is very hard to discern how we are fooling ourselves. It is always easier for someone who is sensitive to your journey to help you identify what is awry. For this reason, I encourage you to find others with whom you can share your spiritual practice. While it may be difficult to find these fellow-travelers, your efforts will be repaid one-hundred-fold.

Part VIII
Seeing Our True Nature

It is often instructive to look back over the path we have traveled. We see things differently from this perspective. When we are struggling up the mountain, our field of vision is often constricted to the next step of the arduous path in front of us. But as we look back, we can see the whole course of our journey, and the vast beauty of our God.

Looking back, it is possible to trace several threads which have run through this spiritual journey of ours. First, we see running through the entire course of our journey this gargantuan struggle between the true self and the false self. We see how we have compromised ourselves to secure the passing approval of others. How we abandoned our true nature. How we abandoned the love of God for the fleeting approval of our companions of the moment.

We also see the emergence of that pure nature which God created in each of us. We begin to recognize this true self as we learn to distinguish it from the false pretender. We begin to honor and follow this self, until finally it brings us home.

As we observe the struggle to allow the true self to emerge, we see a related battle. We see our constant need, during the course of our spiritual journey, to let go of our selfish attachments in order to step into the abundant life that God has given us. When we keep the belief that we are the center of the universe, we blind ourselves to God. Even though God is in front of us and all around us, we do not see. Only as we let go of our attachments do we begin to catch glimmers of the Divine. But it seems so hard to let go of this privileged position in the center. Our Lord warned us about this, saying that we would have to lose our life in order to find it.[240]

This battle to let go of our selfish attachments is the flip side of the struggle between the true self and the false self. These two struggles are really the same; we are just viewing them from different vantage points. Our grasping selfish nature is the substance of the false self, the self which tries to get enough, the self that does not trust in God or love or eternity. In every case, this part of our nature must be relinquished in order for God's abundant life to shine through.

Throughout all of these raging battles, we have wrestled with

327

the false self for control of our attention. Little progress can be made spiritually until we face this. Indeed, meditation practice can be understood as the disciplined effort to control our own attention. To the extent that we gain control, we disengage from discursive thinking and rest our attention in God. To the extent that we gain control, we let go of our precious false self and come to love fully.

Finally, as we look back over the way we have come, we begin to see the spectrum of meditative practices differently. The intricate connections between these practices begin to emerge. They no longer seem so independent or so disjointed. We have eyes, now, to see the flow from one practice to the next. Because we have more experience in this journey, we can understand better the flow from doing to being, from discursive thinking to non-discursive resting in God. And so we come to this place, where we can reflect together on the nature of our journey and on our own true nature.

We opened our spiritual exploration in this book with an inquiry. "What is real?" we asked. "What color is the snow?" As we have seen from our spiritual journeying, reality is not always what we think it is. From the perspective of the false self, the snow is always white, unless (tongue-in-cheek) it becomes politically incorrect to say this, in which case snow becomes any color that the group says it is.

From the perspective of the true self, however, what is real is what is grounded in the Divine. What is real is the true self, which knows itself to be in full union with God. What is real is the Lord, from whom all creation and all reality flow. What is real is truth and beauty and love.

These are measured objectively, in our souls. When we link up in the wonderful Body of Christ, when we realize our participation in each other, and Christ's participation in and through all of us, then these "subjective" phenomena can be understood for what they are. Then we can understand them to be emanations from God, rays of pure energy that enliven and thrill us. Then we enter into that abundant life to which Jesus so sweetly leads us.

Chapter 39

The Dynamics of the Contemplative Process

As we look back over the course of our spiritual journey, there have been several critical struggles. The first struggle that we experienced was the struggle to control our attention. The moment after we sat down to try our first meditation, we became aware of the unruly hyperactive nature of our attention. Most novice practitioners of meditation found themselves unable to concentrate even for a few seconds. But finally we began to control this wild thing.

The Main Event!

While the struggle to control attention is difficult, our second struggle has been even more complex, arduous, and demanding. This is the struggle that has only gradually been revealed to each of us. It has to do with the false self, and the ways we have forsaken our deepest nature in order to get the love and approval of others.

The false self comes to our attention only gradually. As we wrestle with controlling our attention, we notice that certain repetitive themes emerge. We try to disengage from the stream of inner chatter; we want to rest our attention in God. Instead we find ourselves making "to-do" lists, thinking over conversations with other people, thinking critically about our behaviors or those of others. These mental objects-of-awareness reveal to us what we are attached to, what the false self holds on to in order to bolster itself.

Thus, our meditation practice reveals the attachments of our false self. Our attachments, in turn, show us the nature of our false self. From the perspective of the false self, our selfish attachments seem only fair and right. Within the framework of the false self, we cannot see our inherent selfishness. It is only proper that our almighty "I" be considered the center of the known universe.

The Process of Dissociation. In clinical terms, we are dissociating from ourselves. When we were young, our deepest self could not bear the slings and arrows of the world. So the false self came into being to protect us. It protects by separating us, usually from our emotions and our bodies. We experience this dissociation by noting what we should feel but do not. Most of us are not aware of our physical body most of the time. Subjectively we float through space. We do not feel the physical sensations of our body until something drastic happens. And sometimes even then we maintain our dissociation.

The same holds true for other important parts of our experience. Most of us are disconnected from our emotions; we damp them down so that we hardly know they are there. We do not feel the connections that we have with others very strongly either. We certainly are not aware of God as an ongoing, ever-present constituent of our experience.

We have sacrificed the richness of all of this. Instead, we have identified our self with a small fraction of what we actually experience, a small portion of who we really are. If our sacrifice had purchased some sense of relief, some real surcease, then it might have been worth the price we paid. But look at what we get. Inside of us, there is a felt sense of emptiness, a sense that we are missing something vital. We have a deep need for love that is seldom filled. We act in ways that go against our own nature in order to get a brief sense of that love. But mostly, we just feel empty. Trying to fill our emptiness, we turn to drugs or violence, which provides a "high" that gives us the illusion of warmth and connection. Or we become so achievement-oriented that we work ourselves to death in order to get love and approval. These are all symptoms of our dissociated lives.

At the center of all this is God. Look at what we replace God with, look at what we replace our deepest self with. Instead of feeling the love which constantly flows to us from the Divine, we orient ourselves toward things. We become attached to a car, a job, a person, a role, a drug, an ability. We look to these things to replace the flow of love that we have cut off by turning away from God. And we are devastated when the love we get is a pale reflection of the love that we know we deserve.

Our passions, our attachments to people and things, conceal in themselves a marvelous secret, an ironic secret. The energy in us that naturally loves God and orients us toward Her is this same energy of our passions. This is the same energy that connects us with all our things, that gets us lost in all of our things. This energy comes from God. To feel love at its true amplitude, in the measure that we know we deserve, we need to complete the circuit and return that love to God.

It is our choice. We can channel what we receive from God into our attachment to things. This way leads to emptiness and loneliness. Or we can channel our passions back to the Divine. This completes the circuit and fills us with the most incredible love. This brings God's prodigal children back home again.

The mechanism for this homecoming is our attention. Here we finally understand the importance of controlling our attention. Left in its natural state, our attention gets lost in the multitude of things to play with. It gets involved with and then lost in the passions. We need to train our attention so that we can focus it on the Divine. Only in this way can we return home.

Meditation can be thought of as the method for gaining control of our attention. If there were just a few things that we were attached to, a few things that our attention got caught up in, then the process of meditation would be relatively simple and short. But we are so lost in our attachments, and we are attached to so many things, that the process of gaining control is rather lengthy for most of us.

What is more, we cannot gain control of our attention by a simple act of will. To be sure, our will is important. But despite our willing it and our best intentions, we find our attention wandering back to our attachments. A more subtle control is needed. This control is gained only by repeated practice. Over and over again we sit and focus our attention. Over and over again, when we find ourselves wandering, we come back to our meditation focus. Gradually our focusing becomes easier. As we are able to rest our attention in God for more than very brief times, we are blessed with an ever-increasing sense of His Presence. And so it is that we slowly make our way back home, leaving the pigs we have been herding, and the people who abused us,[241] to come and celebrate with our Father.

What Is Our Home Like? The increasing control that we establish over our attention leads us into already existing internal states which we had dissociated out of awareness. We have acted, for the most part, as if heaven was not present to us, as if God were dead. Meditation takes us back to those already-existing internal states where we learn otherwise.

Nothing is added to us by meditation practice. These states have always existed within us. Access to the Divine has always been available to us. But we have been so successful with our dissociation that we could not find the door, and if we happened to find the door, we could not find the handle to open the door. Many have scoffed at the notion that such a door even existed, calling it a fairy tale. Controlled attention, however, allows us to find that inner door and enter. Control of our attention allows us access to these deep interior states at will.

These states do not exist in only a privileged few. Rather, only a few have bothered to prepare themselves appropriately so that they can enter here. You do not prepare for an Olympic competition by living an unfocused dissipated life, filled with drinking and carousing, and short on exercise. You do not graduate from school by playing games and staying up late, not attending to your studies. In every case, success in an endeavor means that you focus your attention. These principles are true for finding God as well.

As we control our attention and gain access to these internal states, what we find at first is a vast stillness. Here there is tranquility and rest. Here we come to experience our center as something far deeper than we imagined. As we grow in comfort with these states and as we refine our attention further, we enter into the states that the mystics describe. Here we are with God, face-to-face. Here we begin to receive directly the extravagant love of God. Here our attachments are blown away in the hurricane of the Holy Spirit, God's holy wind. Here we are stripped bare and find in that bareness a richness that cannot be described in words.

This is the home to which our Father invites us to return. This is the promised land. It is closer to us than we are to our selves.

The Central Issue of Meditation

The central issue in any meditation practice is the control of our attention. Until we can forge our attention into an appropriate tool, until we can rest our attention in God, we are lost in the wilderness. And we all know how the wind howls out in that wild place. We know of the wild beasts that prey on people there.

As we begin our meditation practice, we make slow gains in controlling our focus. As we gain facility in this, we become aware of all of the things that our mind goes wandering off to. In this way, we begin to learn about our attachments. We learn about the ways that we have directed energy into things in order to get love.

Most of us have to experiment here for a time. We are convinced that we can get love from these things. So we try and try, but we continually come up empty. Eventually, however, we begin to let go of some of our attachments. As we do this, there is a subtle change in our dissociation. We begin to have an energy, previously locked up in the attachment, that is available to us. We explore this energy in meditation, tracing it back to its source, and find God there.

So the central issue of meditation, gaining control of the attention, leads to the identification of our attachments. Our next step, then, is to let go of our attachments to things in order to trace the energy back to its source in God. These are the inner dynamics of the spiritual journey.

The Spectrum of Practice. As we progress in our spiritual journey, we explore the broad spectrum of contemplative practice. The specific practices are arranged here in a developmental order, beginning with those that are easiest and most structured. We start with the sensory meditations: the practices of visualization, chant, and kinesthetic meditation. These practices enable us to get some control over our attention. We load our attention with familiar things, such as sights and sounds and feelings. We load our attention as if it were a restless mule, always wandering off the road to sniff out some attractive flower or munch some luscious bunch of grass. Finally, under enough weight, our mule begins to travel down the narrow way.[242] It is so heavily burdened that it stops running to investigate every little thing on the side of the road.

As our attention stabilizes, we can go on to more advanced practices. We begin the practice of Lectio Divina, learning to read scripture in a new way. We learn to read, not with our intellect as we were always taught, but with our hearts. We learn to sit still with our scriptures, waiting for God to teach us. We learn to stop running after knowledge, even spiritual knowledge.

Later, we begin the monologistic prayers, saying a short phrase over and over again. This takes us quickly into the vast stillness that is the Mind of God. Here, in this awesome and endless state of Being, we rest with God. Here, too, we may first experience the nights of sense. Here God is working in us to teach us to let go, even of our sensory experiences. We protest, we fight. Our false self struggles to survive. But as we stay faithful to our spiritual discipline, so God stays faithful to us. She teaches us in the depths of our being, sharing Her own depth with us.

It is likely that we will use the monologistic prayers for many years. Indeed, many of the saints who have gone this way before us have used the monologistic prayers exclusively. These prayers are sufficient to bring the experienced user into contemplative stillness and into union with God.

We may, however, wish to go on with the contemplative prayers. Here we begin by observing the passions and transforming them. Here we look at these fundamental energies which God has placed in our hearts and begin to use them as She ordains. We use the strength of our passions, now, to fuel our journey. Before, in our earlier stages, they were encumbrances which kept us from ourselves and our own true nature. Now we learn to free this energy so that it can drive us more quickly into the arms of the Divine.

In contemplative prayer, we sit in utter stillness. We rest with God, without trying to learn or do anything. We let go of everything so that we can be fully present to our God. We let go even of our self—that part of us that seems to be our identity and the organizing axis of our experience. We let go of our false self and cast ourselves on the Divine. And with this sacrifice, we come to know who we are, truly. We come into our heritage as God's sons and daughters. We come back home.

The Central Dynamic of Meditation

The spiritual discipline of meditation and contemplative prayer enables us to let go completely of everything that is not God. These disciplines enable us to let go of all the attachments and desires which give the illusion of satisfaction. It is as if we have been trying to fill our starving bellies with illusions, instead of with real food. But the illusions give us no lasting satisfaction; there is no nourishment in them. They are like modern supermarket apples: they look red and delicious all over, but they are mealy inside and have no taste.

Meditation allows us to let go of these things that do not satisfy. Meditation takes us through a long process of de-conditioning, where we learn to distinguish between the things that really satisfy and the things that don't. From the perspective of this true understanding, we learn that all our activity and doing have gained us nothing; our efforts are all for naught.

Meditation then takes us the further step. It teaches us to let go of our efforts, on the promise that God will be there to provide for us. It teaches us to stop our obsessive doing. It teaches us to open to the deep being that lies within each of us. "Seek first the kingdom of heaven, and all else shall be added to you."[243] Meditation is a spiritual discipline that teaches us to be whole.

In our broken and confused times, such a tool is of the greatest importance. We Americans live in a country that has been the dominant force in the world in this century. We have the highest material standard of living of any people that has ever lived. As a result, we would expect that Americans should be the most happy and contented people in the world. But we are not. We are, for the most part, a broken people. We live lives that are empty and meaningless. We increasingly turn to drugs to fill our inner emptiness. We have become the world's heaviest consumers of illegal, mind-altering drugs. We are a culture overcome by violence. It fills our television, our movies, and our lives. Gangs terrorize our streets and violence invades our home life. This is not a happy picture.

We have been free, as a people, to explore the full measure of emptiness that comes from reliance on the false self. We have each pursued our self-centered ends. These pursuits have brought us nothing but pain and emptiness. To have more than the pain of our self-centeredness, we must go beyond the limits of our false selves. We must let go of the false self and move into the true center which lies hidden in each heart. We must enter into the realm where our efforts to control and manipulate are useless. We must explore our true depths in the Divine.

For this, we need the spiritual disciplines. We need a systematic method for transforming the false self. We need a method to enter into God's truth. This is the dynamic of meditation. It is the tool which can restore us to our true nature, the tool that enables us to let go of our selfish attachment in order to embrace the Lord Jesus. Meditation brings God's prodigal children back home again.

Chapter 40

The Fundamental Promise of Christianity

Of all the revelations that humankind has received, the revelation of Jesus Christ is unique. Our Savior comes to us with a message that is absolutely startling. He tells us that we are already saved! He says that we are already whole at our deepest level. He says that our true self was created by God, and reminds us of that earlier message in Genesis, that we are made in the image of God. But, because of Adam's sin, we have forgotten our true nature. We have lost our way and left our home to herd swine, living as hired hands, always shut off from the good things of life.

Through God's sacrifice in Christ, we are made whole again. Through God's extraordinary efforts, His children are called to awaken from their misery, called to return to their home and take their rightful place in the family of God.

God calls us through His Son, Jesus. Through our Father's love, Christ has been grafted into our souls. If we take the trouble to look carefully, we will find that Christ is already enthroned there. He is already in our souls, hidden deeply in our hearts. Our Savior has always been with us, just as He promised.[244] He has always been whispering in our hearts, gently guiding and loving us, and encouraging us to begin the journey back home. He keeps reminding us of our true nature: we are heirs, not servants.

Meditation is the method for tuning in to our heart. It is a tool that is in evidence in Jesus' own life, as we see Him frequently leaving the crowds and going off to pray in the desert. The tools of meditation were further developed by our early fathers and mothers in the church as ways to listen to this heart channel. They are effective ways to tune in to the Divine who is constantly with us. Emmanuel!

The fundamental promise of Christianity is that we are already whole at our deepest level. We are already saved. There is no tower that we have to build into the sky to see God; there is no yawning abyss that we must bridge. The God who loves us has already resolved these difficulties. She has taken them away. We have only to listen closely in our hearts and we will hear that sweet music of our Mother.

And what do we hear when we finally tune in to this sweet music? We hear all the old familiar things, but they are no longer pious platitudes, empty of meaning. We hear, vibrantly, and we know that God is with us. We hear about the importance of loving and our hearts are opened by the power of this message. We learn that God has always loved us, even as we strayed farthest from Her. And in our deepest recesses, we know that we are coming home.

Our sin—all those attachments that have kept us from the love of God—sloughs off like an old skin. All those things that consumed our attention and kept us focused elsewhere are abandoned. We know our true nature now. There is no longer any need to occupy ourselves with the things that are false and empty. We know the way home. We know now that in our heart of hearts we have always been home. That Christ has always been with us. And we know that we have always been loved.

Being Right with God

Jesus tells us that we are already whole, already loved, already part of God's holy family. One of the strongest statements of Jesus' message is found in St. Paul's letter to the Romans, in chapters five through twelve. Paul speaks here of our being made right with God. St. Paul affirms that our faith in Christ makes us whole and brings us back into a right relationship with the Divine. This is possible only because of Christ's sacrifice of Himself on the cross. In Paul's language:

> Our old self (our false self) was crucified with Him so that the sinful body might be destroyed and we might be slaves to sin no longer. A man who is dead (whose false self is dead) has been freed from sin.[245]

Here Paul speaks about the old self as we have spoken about the false self. This is the part of us which, even desiring to do good, finds itself unable to do that same good. It is a separate self, a dissociated self that is apart from our deepest and truest nature. Yet, in the old life that was guided by our own selfish desires, it controlled us.

We can take charge of ourselves by allowing that old false self to be crucified with Christ. We can allow this false part of us to die by letting it wither on the vine, withdrawing our energy and attention from it. We do this by no longer following its promptings; we do this by refocusing our attention in God. We no longer listen to the secret urgings of this old false self. We turn from our old life so that we might really live.

This is the disciplined path down which meditation takes us. By means of our disciplined practice, we refrain from our old ways of doing, our old attachments and passions. We simply sit and focus on the Lord Jesus. As we do so, our old false self withers and finally dies. As it dies, we are reborn fully into a new life in Christ. In St. Paul's blessed words:

> If we have died in Christ, we believe that we are also to live with Him. We know that Christ, once raised from the dead, will never die again; death has no more power over Him. His death was death to sin, once for all; His life is life for God. In the same way, you must consider yourselves dead to sin but alive for God in Christ Jesus.[246]

Christian meditation can be considered as the amplification of this outline of St. Paul. Meditation is the detailed working out of this intricate process that Paul describes. It is the prescription for letting go of the false self. Meditation shows us, in exquisite detail, how we can "cast off the deeds of darkness" that flow from the false-self system, and how to "put on the armor of light."[247]

Is this not what we wish? Do we not deeply desire to put on this armor of light? Have we not longed for this all of our lives? Yet, trapped within the false-self system, our every attempt has met with failure. With meditation, though, we have a systematic, detailed method for putting on this glorious armor. Here we have a way to join with our Lord Jesus and achieve our heart's most intimate desire.

To accomplish this, there is nothing that we must do; there is nowhere that we must go. Our task is a simple one. But, mind you, this simple task is not easy. Our task is to just sit and be still. Our task is to let go of the false self, the "old self" of which Paul speaks, so that we can sink into that other, deeper self who is already with our God. Our task is to *remember* that we are already participating in the Divine.

Know the Tree by Its Fruits!

Our Lord Jesus has given us a very accurate compass, so that we can steer a course successfully through the repeated illusions thrown up by the false self. This compass is found by observing the fruits of our spiritual labors. If our efforts bring forth good fruit, then we are working in the right way. Our inner life is in accordance with God's will and our spiritual disciplines are being strengthened. If the fruits of our labor are suspect, if they are not sweet and nourishing, then something is wrong.

Yet, it is often difficult to make this simple distinction. Through a quiet spiritual materialism, our false self creeps in and whispers that sour is sweet, that bad is good. For this reason, as I have said before, it is most useful to be a part of an ongoing spiritual community that discusses these issues on a regular basis. The community allows us to test out our perceptions with others who are not so tied in to our particular false-self system. Community provides the antidote to self-centeredness and helps each of us to stay on course.

And what are the fruits of practice? They are subtle and quiet. We will probably not notice them at first. Most often, the people whom we live with are the first to notice these changes. They may comment on our growing peacefulness, the lessening of our anger. Over time, we will experience an increasing sense of peace and calm. The great passions that stir us—our anger and fear—will relax and resolve. Physically, we will notice that our muscles are more relaxed than usual.

As we continue our practice, we will have an increasing sense of purpose and meaning in our life. Even the ordinary things will take on a different dimension. We will begin to notice the Presence of the Lord in many small ways. This Presence has always been with us, but we did not have the eyes to see it before. Now, however, we are opening our eyes. We are seeing and hearing in new ways.

Ultimately, as we continue with our practice, we will enter into unitive states where we will see the Divine more and more clearly. Finally, we will enter into the deepest union with our God, so that we feel that Presence with us at all times. Our life will be utterly transformed and energized at this point. The sweetness of God's blessing will flow from us like water flows from tall mountains. The world around us will be graced and restored to wholeness by the love that flows through us. And we will know, beyond a shadow of a doubt, what is real and what is not. For we will be made whole in our God.

May the Peace of God
which passes all understanding
keep your hearts and minds
in the knowledge and love of God
and of His Son
Jesus Christ, our Lord.
And the Blessing of God Almighty
Father, Son, and Holy Spirit
be upon you
and remain with you
always.

Acknowledgments

Although I am responsible for the writing, this book is a corporate endeavor, reflecting the contributions of many people over the years. These contributions begin with the love of God in sending us our Lord Jesus Christ to remind us of our true nature. These contributions continue through the work of those great fathers and mothers of the church who went before us, transmitting from generation to generation knowledge of the great Mystery.

In my personal history, I have been blessed with many wonderful teachers. I wish to acknowledge the contributions of Mrs. Stohl, the fifth grade teacher who helped me to *see* for a time; Beth Kennedy, a wise old woman who helped me untangle some of my knots and get going with life; Dr. Elwin Nielsen, a dear friend whose nurture, good humor, and clear thinking helped me strike a new balance in my life; Father Thomas Keating, O.C.S.O., who is one of the great church fathers of our time; and Father Gregory Elmer, O.S.B., who has encouraged me during times of trial in my spiritual journey.

There are many others who helped in my spiritual formation. Several were professors in seminary: Dr. Max Pearce, whose nurture and gentle inquiry helped root me in the deep traditions of the church in those early years; the Rt. Rev. Fred Borsch, who presented the social agenda of the church rooted in a deep spirituality; Father Norm Mealy, whose joy was always in the Lord; and Father Edward Hobbes, the "master" of New Testament Greek, who taught us the language with which God would ravish our souls.

Others contributed to my spirituality by forming my pastorate. Most important among these was Father "Pete" Winder, who taught me that love was missing in the lives of most people, and that this precious love is what the church needs to provide. I also wish to thank all my parishioners through the years. They both nurtured and challenged me to go further in my understanding of God.

Much of the material in this book has been hammered into its present shape in OneHeart, our lay contemplative community in Southern California. I want to thank my fellow teachers in

342

OneHeart for their assistance and patience, as we have traveled together. They include: Paul Bowler, Beth Jahncke, Charles Julien, Suzanne Kaisch, Edythe Peters, Dr. Malcolm Schleh, Dr. Hal Simeroth, Carol Smith, and Dr. Deborah Spaine. I also wish to thank my colleagues in Contemplative Visions who have helped form and guide the OneHeart community: Linda Cushing, Bertha Dannemiller, Marleen Darras, Jeffrey Dondanville, Charles Julien, Dr. Jim Rogers, and Dr. Hal Simeroth.

Many people made direct and specific contributions to this book. My special thanks to Brigit Leonard. Because of a conversation that we had one afternoon, during the course of a long car ride, this book came into being. Without her encouragement and support, I would not have begun the task of writing. Thanks also to Michael Katz, who helped refine this book to its present state; and to my editor, Doug Fisher, who has been encouraging and unfailingly kind throughout the process of publication.

A number of people were generous in reading the text and making comments to strengthen the work. Their comments helped me to see my biases and strengthen the text greatly. My deep thanks to Adrienne Barnes, Bertha Dannemiller, Marleen Darras, Beth Jahncke, Suzanne Kaisch, Dr. Bobbi Nesheim, Dr. Hal Simeroth, and Dr. Deborah Spaine. My gratitude also to Lynn Edwards who was my technical editor for this project and to Linda Cushing and Tom Marcotte for their graphics support.

I especially want to thank the monks at St. Andrew's Abbey in Valyermo, for their gracious hospitality in providing a place for solitude, stillness, and spiritual refreshment.

Finally, my thanks to my wife, Suzanne, and our son, Sam. They sacrificed enormously to support my writing. There are not words enough for me to thank them properly for their love and support.

Notes

1. Ezekiel 36:26.

2. Winnecott. D.W. Ego distortion in terms of true and false self. In D.W. Winnecott, *The Maturational Processes and the Facilitating Environment*. New York: New York International University Press, 1960, pp. 140–152.

3. I am indebted to the poet, Robert Bly, for this image of the radiant light which surrounds children, and the subsequent "cutting off" of this light through the process of socialization. Bly's description, in his book *A Little Book of the Human Shadow*, speaks of this process as the method by which the shadow is formed. It is equally useful in illustrating the creation of the false self, as I have used it here.

4. This cutting off process is described by the Swiss psychiatrist, Carl Jung, as the process which creates the shadow, that dark side of our personality which contains all of our latent abilities and impulses.

5. Tillich, P. *Systematic Theology, Volume II*. Chicago: University of Chicago Press, 1957, pp. 29–39.

6. cf. Genesis 1:27.

7. In Genesis, the earliest written record accepted as authoritative in the Christian tradition, the person of God seems to have both a male and female nature: "God created man in his image; in the divine image he created him; male and female he created them" (Genesis 1:27). In the Christian revelation of God, on the other hand, Jesus refers to God as "Father" in all four gospels. Contemporary theologians have rightly raised the issue of what this signifies about the nature of God. The church currently is exploring this

matter. Unfortunately, until it is resolved, there are no universally agreed upon principles to guide our language about God.

One solution is to use gender-neutral terms for the Divine. I do not believe that it is possible for a Christian to use gender-neutral terms exclusively and remain true to our revelation in Christ. Through Jesus, God incarnates into flesh, and our flesh comes in either male or female packages. To avoid gender-specific language is to deny an important aspect of the incarnation. Avoiding gender-specific language with regard to God leads to a conception of God who is utterly transcendent and far away. This is contrary to God's continual self-revelation as the church has received it.

On the other hand, the exclusive use of masculine language for God seems misleading and inappropriate. The first authoritative words that we have about the nature of God indicate that God has both masculine and feminine natures. Thus, to limit the Divine to one or the other is inappropriately narrow.

In response to this dilemma, I use gender-neutral terms such as God and the Divine when possible in this book. Where gender seems appropriate, I have deliberately used either Father or Mother to describe aspects of the Divine which seem to partake more of one nature or the other. When I am quoting another author, I have quoted directly and make no attempt to change the author's words to conform to my usage here.

8. John 15:5.

9. John 14:23.

10. cf. John 15:4–8.

11. Willard, D. *The Spirit of the Disciplines*. San Francisco: Harper-Collins, 1992.

12. 1 Peter 2:11.

13. Willard, D. *The Spirit of the Disciplines*. San Francisco: Harper-Collins, 1992, p. 159.

14. Matthew 11:29.

15. Many people have tried to start meditation before they were ready, before they had gone through these first steps which

include behavioral regulation. Typically, they have great difficulty with meditation. If you cannot regulate something as tangible and obvious as an outward behavior, then you will not be able to regulate successfully something as subtle as your thinking or, even more subtle, your attention. Meditation is not a practice for someone just starting on the spiritual journey. To be successful in this, as in any endeavor, you need to begin at the beginning.

16. Shapiro, D. *Meditation*. New York: Aldine, 1980, p. 14.

17. Romans 6: 6–11.

18. When I speak of the church in this way, I am referring to the whole body of Christendom, the church universal. I capitalize when referring to a specific denomination, as in the Roman Catholic Church.

19. See footnote 7 for a discussion of the use of gender in this book.

20. 1 Kings 19:12–13.

21. Simeroth, H.H. *Living in Grace: How to Participate in the Divine Life of God*. work in progress.

22. Wolff, H.W. *Anthropology of the Old Testament*. Philadelphia: Fortress Press, 1974, p. 40.

23. Kittel, W. *Theological Dictionary of the New Testament, Vol III*. (G.W. Bromily, ed. & transl.) Grand Rapids, MI: Eerdman's, 1965, p. 610.

24. Romans 5:5.

25. Assagioli, R. *Psychosynthesis*. New York: Viking, 1965.

26. Genesis 25:27–34.

27. Matthew 28:20; John 14:21; Luke 11:9–10.

28. Matthew 28:20.

29. St. Isaac of Nineveh. *Mystical Treatises by Isaac of Nineveh*. (A.

Wensinck, ed. & transl.) Wiesbaden: Dr. Martin Sandig oHG, 1969, p. 38.

30. Meister Eckhart. *Meister Eckhart: The Essential Sermons, Commentaries, Treatises, and Defense.* (E. Colledge and B. McGinn, eds. & transls.) New York: Paulist Press, 1981, p. 187.

31. Genesis 1:27.

32. Br. Lawrence. *The Practice of the Presence of God.* Orleans, MA: Paraclete Press, 1985, p. 61.

33. Br. Lawrence. *The Practice of the Presence of God.* Orleans, MA: Paraclete Press, 1985, p. 109–10.

34. Romans 13:12; Ephesians 6:13.

35. 1 Thessalonians 5:17.

36. St. Irenaeus. *Against Heresies,* in *Ante–Nicene Fathers, Vol. I.* (A. Roberts & J. Donaldson, eds.) Grand Rapids, MI: Eerdmans, 1989, p. 448.

37. St. Gregory of Nyssa. *Against Eunomius*, in *Nicene and Post–Nicene Fathers, Vol. V.* (P. Schaff, ed.) Grand Rapids, MI: Eerdmans, 1979, p. 149.

38. St. Teresa of Avila. *Teresa of Avila: The Interior Castle.* (K. Kavanaugh & O. Rodriguez, transls.) New York: Paulist Press, 1979.

39. Bradshaw, J. *Healing the Shame That Binds You.* Deerfield Beach, FL: Health Communications, 1988; Kaufman, G. *The Psychology of Shame.* New York: Springer Publishing, 1989; Harper, J.M., & Hoopes, M.H. *Uncovering Shame.* New York: W.W. Norton, 1990.

40. Genesis 1:31.

41. Psalm 51:1–2, 11, 18.

42. Roberts, B. *The Experience of No-Self.* Boston: Shambhala, 1985.

43. Peck, M.S. *The Road Less Traveled*. New York: Simon & Schuster, 1978.

44. St. Ignatius of Loyola. *Ignatius of Loyola: The Spiritual Exercises and Selected Works*. (G. Ganss, ed.) New York: Paulist Press, 1991.

44a. Miller, G.A. The magical number seven plus or minus two: some limits on our capacity for processing information. *Psychological Review*, 1956, *63*, 81-97.

45. By the phrase "Mind of God" I am pointing to a particular experience. This experience, which occurs in meditation, is one of great inner vastness, of immense space. In this experience, there is a falling away of the usual constraints of time and space, and an entrance into the boundless infinite Mind of God. By this I do not mean the place where God "thinks." This is not a busy intellectual place. But there seems to be no term to describe adequately this vast still place.

Unfortunately, the English language has not developed an adequate language of the soul by which we can represent these experiences to each other. At this juncture, we do not have a sufficient spiritual vocabulary to describe these things.

46. Tart, C. *Waking Up: Overcoming the Obstacles to Human Potential*. Boston: Shambhala, 1986.

47. Personal communication, Claire Etheridge, Ph.D., 1986.

48. Pastrovicchi, A. *St. Joseph of Cupertino*. Rockford, IL: Tan Books, 1980.

49. I would refer you to Herman Hesse's *Journey to the East* for more on this. Hesse presents a thinly fictionalized account of the difficulties involved when you separate from your spiritual companions that is very illuminating.

50. Matthew 13:44.

51. Personal communication with Morton Kelsey during a retreat he led for the Episcopal Diocese of Utah in the late 1970's.

52. St. Ignatius of Loyola. *Ignatius of Loyola: The Spiritual Exercises and Selected Works*. (G. Ganss, ed.) New York: Paulist Press, 1991.

53. Genesis 1:27.

54. Luke 24:13–35.

55. Colossians 1:15.

56. St. John of Damascus. *Exposition of the Orthodox Faith*, in *The Nicene and Post-Nicene Fathers, Vol. IX*. (P. Schaff & H. Wace, eds.) Grand Rapids, MI: Eerdmans, 1989.

57. For those interested in purchasing icon prints for meditation, let me suggest two sources: 1) St. Vladimir's Seminary Press, 575 Scarsdale Rd, Crestwood, NY 10707-1699; and 2) St. Isaac of Syria Skete, Rt 1, Box 168, Boscobel, WI 53805.

58. For other references on using icons for spiritual growth, let me refer you to two books. The first, by Henri Nouwen, titled *Behold the Beauty of Icons*, and published by Ave Maria Press, is an excellent and more extensive introduction to praying with icons than is possible within the constraints of this volume. The second book, Richard Temple's *Icons and the Mystical Origins of Christianity*, is published by Element Press. Temple's book is a very deep and rich goldmine for those who want to discover their mystical heritage as Christians.

59. Zander, V. *St. Seraphim of Sarov*. Crestwood, NY: St. Vladimir's Seminary Press, 1975.

60. Johnson, R. A. *Inner Work*. New York: Harper San Francisco, 1986.

61. For more on the process of initiated symbol projection, let me refer you to R. Assagioli's book, *Psychosynthesis*. New York: Viking Press, pp. 287–303.

62. Bunyan, J. *The Pilgrim's Progress*. New York: Collier, 1956.

63. Matthew 28:5.

64. Richardson, C.C. *Early Christian Fathers*. New York: Macmillan, 1975, pp. 149–158.

65. Pastrovicchi, A. *St. Joseph of Cupertino*. Rockford, IL: Tan Books, 1980.

66. A lovely and stirring example of Byzantine chant can be found on the compact disk *Grande Liturgie Orthodoxe Slave*, released by Harmonia Mundi, number HMC 90101. A typical example of Gregorian chant can be heard on the compact disk, *Feasts of Our Lady*, released by Paraclete Records.
   When buying chant for spiritual reasons, I recommend recordings of monks or nuns for the quality in their chant that comes from living the chants for years. These recordings differ significantly from those produced by secular choirs.

67. I prefer using chants in a language other than English, since this inhibits the discursive intellect to some degree. The Kyrie is Greek and means: Lord have mercy upon us; Christ have mercy upon us; Lord have mercy upon us.

68. Taize Canons and Litanies. GIA Publications, 7404 S. Mason Ave, Chicago, IL 60638.

69. For more on this, consult Nyanaponika Thera's valuable book, *The Heart of Buddhist Meditation*. New York: Samuel Weiser, 1975. Here Thera translates *vipassana* as mindfulness.

70. Because Western Christians are used to crossing themselves from left to right, we will preserve that usage here. My apologies to Orthodoxy, for appropriating a spiritual practice of theirs without following fully the form they prescribe.

71. Ward, B. *The Sayings of the Desert Fathers*. Kalamazoo, MI: Cistercian Publications, 1975, p. 103; Maloney, G. *Why Not Become Totally Fire?* New York: Paulist Press, 1989.

72. Ephesians 4:7–16.

73. If you are interested in gathering people into a meditation group, write OneHeart, P.O. Box 5915, Fullerton, CA 92635. In OneHeart, people interested in Christian meditation have come

together to form an ecumenical community to learn these deep forms of prayer. We have been quite successful in this endeavor. The depth of our joint practice is extraordinary, and the mutual support that we give one another in sustaining our practice is life-giving. OneHeart is now a powerful component of our spiritual work.

Having done this successfully, we can help you start a similar community in your own area. Write us, if you want further information. In addition, teachers from OneHeart are available for workshops, seminars, and retreats. We would be happy to talk with you about the possibility of having such a gathering in your area.

Our long-range goal is to create a network of Christians interested in contemplative work. I do not know what can come of such a network, but the possibilities are striking!

74. Matthew 18:20.

75. Joshua 1:8.

76. John 5:39.

77. Luke 24:13–35.

78. Guigo II, quoted in S. Tugwell's *Ways of Imperfection*. Springfield, IL: Templegate Publishers, 1985, p. 94.

79. Personal communication with Dr. H.H. Simeroth, September, 1993.

80. Matthew 5:1–7:29.

81. Mark 2:4.

82. Luke 15:11–32.

83. John 8:3–12.

84. John 10:30.

85. St. Nikodimos & St. Makarios. *The Philokalia, Volumes 1–3*. (G.E.H. Palmer, P. Sherrard, & K. Ware, eds. & transls.) Boston: Faber and Faber, 1979.

86. St. Nikodimos & St. Makarios. *The Philokalia, Volume 1.* (G.E.H. Palmer, P. Sherrard, & K. Ware, eds. & transls.) Boston: Faber and Faber, 1979, pp. 29–71.

87. Evagrios of Ponticus. *Texts on Discrimination in Respect of Passions and Thoughts.* In St. Nikodimos and St. Makarios, *The Philokalia, Volume 1.* Boston: Faber & Faber, 1979, p. 38.

88. Ward, B. *The Sayings of the Desert Fathers.* Kalamazoo, MI: Cistercian Publications, 1975.

89. I use the term "fathers" here following the lead of Douglas Burton-Christie. While there were a few women who also went into the desert to pray, the overwhelming majority were male. An attempt to use a gender-balanced nomenclature would thus be misleading. Furthermore, almost all of the written documents were produced by or written about the men in the desert. For these reasons, I have chosen to use the more traditional nomenclature, the desert fathers. For a further discussion of this, I refer you to Burton-Christie's work, *The Word in the Desert*, published by Oxford University Press, 1993, page 24.

90. Let me encourage you to keep a record of what happens in your spiritual practice. Write down what you do in your meditations and record what happens. Also, as you begin to notice your perceptions and behavior changing, keep a record of this. Many of the changes which we experience are so subtle that we barely notice them. It is as if we change direction by a hair's breadth. Yet after years of practice, these tiny changes mount up. Journaling will give you a place to collect these changes. It is a wonderful way to validate what is happening to you by means of your practice.

91. Father Michael, the Recluse of Uusi Valamo, quoted in S. Bolshakoff's *Russian Mystics*. Kalamazoo, MI: Cistercian Publications, 1980, pp. 267–8.

92. Romans 8:38–39.

93. For further reading on Lectio Divina, let me suggest: Hall, T. *Too Deep for Words.* New York: Paulist Press, 1988. Panimolle, S. (ed.) *Like the Deer that Yearns.* Middlegreen, England: St. Paul Publications, 1990.

94. Deuteronomy 6:4–5.

95. Deuteronomy 4:39.

96. Deuteronomy 11:18–19.

97. Exodus 3:14.

98. St. Athanasius. *The Life and Affairs of Our Holy Father Anthony* in R. Gregg's (ed.) *Athanasius*. New York: Paulist Press, 1980.

99. St. Athanasius. *The Life and Affairs of Our Holy Father Anthony* in R. Gregg's (ed.) *Athanasius*. New York: Paulist Press, 1980, p. 31.

100. Psalm 51:19.

101. Ware, K. *The Origins of the Jesus Prayer*, in C. Jones, G. Wainwright, & E. Yarnold (eds.) *The Study of Spirituality*. New York: Oxford University Press, 1986, p. 176.

102. Arrow prayers are quick verbal ejaculations that are shot up to God like arrows. Examples of these verbal ejaculations are: "God be with me" or "God is Love." They are usually used in a repetitive manner in the manner of monologistic prayers.

103. St. John Cassian. *John Cassian: Conferences*. (C. Luibheid, ed. & transl.) New York: Paulist Press, 1985.

104. Salinger, J.D. *Franny and Zooey*. Boston: Little, Brown, & Co., 1961.

105. Anonymous. *The Way of a Pilgrim*. (R.M. French, transl.) Minneapolis: Seabury, 1952.

106. Philippians 2:9–10.

107. John 16:23.

108. 1 Thessalonians 5:17.

109. Evagrios of Ponticus. *On Prayer*, in St. Nikodimos and St. Makarios (eds.) *The Philokalia, Volume 1*. Boston: Faber & Faber, 1979, Text 71, p. 64.

110. Evagrius Ponticus. *The Praktikos and Chapters on Prayer*. (J.E. Bamberger, ed. & transl.) Kalamazoo, MI: Cistercian Publications, 1981, p. 66.

111. St. Diadochus of Photiki. *On Spiritual Knowledge and Discrimination*, in St. Nikodimos and St. Makarios (eds.) *The Philokalia, Volume 1*. Boston: Faber & Faber, 1979, Text 59, p. 270.

112. Ware, K. *The Origins of the Jesus Prayer*, in C. Jones, G. Wainwright, & E. Yarnold (eds.) *The Study of Spirituality*. New York: Oxford University Press, 1986, p. 178.

113. St. John Climacus. *The Ladder of Divine Ascent*. Boston: Holy Transfiguration Monastery, 1978.

114. St. Hesychius the Priest. *On Watchfulness and Holiness*, in St. Nikodimos and St. Makarios (eds.) *The Philokalia, Volume 1*. Boston: Faber & Faber, 1979, pp. 161–198.

115. St. Philotheos of Sinai. *Forty Texts on Watchfulness*, in St. Nikodimos and St. Makarios (eds.), *The Philokalia, Volume 3*. Boston: Faber & Faber, 1984, pp. 15–31.

116. Anonymous. *The Way of a Pilgrim*. (R.M. French, ed. and trans.) San Francisco: Harper & Row, 1965.

117. 1 Thessalonians 5:17.

118. Anonymous. *The Way of a Pilgrim*. (R.M. French, ed.) New York: Seabury, 1952, pp. 8–9.

119. Anonymous. *The Way of a Pilgrim*. (R.M. French, ed.) New York: Seabury, 1952, p. 9.

120. Anonymous. *The Way of a Pilgrim*. (R.M. French, ed.) New York: Seabury, 1952, p. 16.

121. References for the three essential operations of the Jesus Prayer can be found in many places. Prominent among these references are R.M. French's *The Way of the Pilgrim*, p. 8; and I. Chariton's *The Art of Prayer*, p. 89.

All too often the Jesus Prayer has been taught as if it has only one operation, that of saying the words. This is the most misunderstood point in the practice of this great prayer. The spiritual giants who have used this prayer are unanimous in stating that the words are the least important of the three operations of the Jesus Prayer.

122. Chariton, I. *The Art of Prayer*. London: Faber & Faber, 1966, p. 94.

123. Theophan the Recluse, in I. Chariton's *The Art of Prayer*. London: Faber and Faber, 1966, p. 98.

124. Theophan the Recluse, in I. Chariton's *The Art of Prayer*. London: Faber and Faber, 1966, p. 100.

125. For a more complete discussion of the gift of tears, I refer you to Irenee Hauscherr, S.J., *Penthos: The Doctrine of Compunction in the Christian East*, published by Cistercian Publications in 1982.

126. Matthew 6:33.

127. Anonymous. *The Way of a Pilgrim*. (R.M. French, ed.) New York: Seabury, 1952, p. 105–6.

128. Marcucci, D. *Through the Rosary with Fra Angelico*. New York: Alba House, 1992.

129. Luke 1:38.

130 Ward, J.N. *Five for Sorrow, Ten for Joy*. Cambridge, MA: Cowley Publications, 1985.

131. This is a custom in the liturgical churches: the Roman Catholic, Eastern Orthodox, and Anglican Churches. The intention of signing one's self with the cross is to purify the body, mind, and soul. It is accomplished by bunching together the thumb, forefinger, and middle finger of the right hand, and touching in succes-

sion the center of your forehead, your stomach, the left shoulder, and then the right shoulder. This makes the sign of the cross over your body. For the purpose of saying the rosary, it is not necessary to engage in swaying your body, as we did in the kinesthetic meditation above which also used the activity of crossing.

132. For those unfamiliar with identifying the Lord's Prayer with *Our Father*, you say the complete Lord's Prayer here, and every place that you see an *Our Father* indicated.

133. For further reading on the use of the rosary, let me suggest J. Neville Ward. *Five for Sorrow, Ten for Joy*. Cambridge, MA: Cowley Publications, 1985. A Protestant minister describes the meditations which go with saying the rosary.

134. Anonymous. *The Cloud of Unknowing*. New York: Paulist Press, 1981.

135. *Richard of St. Victor*. Richard of St. Victor. (G.A. Zinn, ed. & transl.) New York: Paulist Press, 1979.

136. St. John of the Cross. *The Collected Works of St. John of the Cross*. (K. Kavanaugh & O. Rodriguez, eds. & transls.) Washington, D.C.: ICS Publications, 1979.

137. Pseudo-Dionysius. *Pseudo-Dionysius: The Complete Works*. (C. Luibheid, ed. & transl.) New York: Paulist Press, 1987.

138. Anonymous. *The Cloud of Unknowing*. New York: Paulist Press, 1981, p. 123.

139. Anonymous. *The Cloud of Unknowing*. New York: Paulist Press, 1981, pp. 121-2.

140. Anonymous. *The Cloud of Unknowing*. New York: Paulist Press, 1981, p. 128.

141. Anonymous. *The Cloud of Unknowing*. New York: Paulist Press, 1981, p. 218.

142. Anonymous. *The Cloud of Unknowing*. New York: Paulist Press, 1981, cf pp. 101-2, 221-3.

143. Anonymous. *The Cloud of Unknowing*. New York: Paulist Press, 1981, p. 187.

144. Anonymous. *The Cloud of Unknowing*. New York: Paulist Press, 1981, p. 205.

145. Anonymous. *The Cloud of Unknowing*. New York: Paulist Press, 1981, p. 128.

146. Anonymous. *The Cloud of Unknowing*. New York: Paulist Press, 1981, p. 128.

147. Anonymous. *The Cloud of Unknowing*. New York: Paulist Press, 1981, p. 126.

148. Anonymous. *The Cloud of Unknowing*. New York: Paulist Press, 1981, p. 133.

149. Anonymous. *The Cloud of Unknowing*. New York: Paulist Press, 1981, p. 134.

150. Anonymous. *The Cloud of Unknowing*. New York: Paulist Press, 1981, p. 145.

151. Romans 6:6.

152. Anonymous. *The Cloud of Unknowing*. New York: Paulist Press, 1981, p. 147.

153. Anonymous. *The Cloud of Unknowing*. New York: Paulist Press, 1981, p. 148.

154. Anonymous. *The Cloud of Unknowing*. New York: Paulist Press, 1981, p. 133.

155. Anonymous. *The Cloud of Unknowing*. New York: Paulist Press, 1981, p. 134.

156. Anonymous. *The Cloud of Unknowing*. New York: Paulist Press, 1981, p. 121.

157. Anonymous. *The Cloud of Unknowing*. New York: Paulist Press, 1981, p. 200.

158. Anonymous. *The Cloud of Unknowing*. New York: Paulist Press, 1981, p. 200.

159. Anonymous. *The Cloud of Unknowing*. New York: Paulist Press, 1981, p. 200.

160. Anonymous. *The Cloud of Unknowing*. New York: Paulist Press, 1981, p. 201.

161. Anonymous. *The Cloud of Unknowing*. New York: Paulist Press, 1981, p. 215.

162. Anonymous. *The Cloud of Unknowing*. New York: Paulist Press, 1981, p. 224.

163. Anonymous. *The Cloud of Unknowing*. New York: Paulist Press, 1981, p. 252.

164. Thomas Merton, quoted in J. Finley, *Merton's Palace of Nowhere*. Notre Dame, IN: Ave Maria Press, 1978.

165. Anonymous. *The Cloud of Unknowing*. New York: Paulist Press, 1981, p. 254.

166. Personal communication from William Howell, who interviewed Fr. Keating about these matters, May, 1993.

167. Keating, T. *Open Mind, Open Heart*. Warwick, NY: Amity House, 1986.

168. Romans 13:12.

169. 1 Kings 19:12.

170. Isaiah 7:14.

171. John 10:11.

172. John 15:5.

173. Matthew 28:20.

174. Romans 8:39.

175. Romans 7:15.

176. Romans 13:12.

177. Winnecott, D.W. Ego distortion in terms of true and false self. In D.W. Winnecott, *The Maturational Processes and the Facilitating Environment*. New York: New York International University Press, 1960, pp. 140-152.

178. Matthew 18:3.

179. Genesis 1:31.

180. Genesis 25:33.

181. Matthew 22:39; Mark 12:31; Luke 10:27; John 13:34.

182. Matthew 5:44.

183. Anonymous. *The Cloud of Unknowing*. New York: Paulist Press, 1981, p. 134.

184. Personal communication with Fr. Keating, April, 1990.

185. Keating, T. *The Spiritual Journey*. Snowmass, CO: St. Benedict's Monastery, 1987, p. 16.

186. Keating, T. *Open Mind, Open Heart*. Warwick, NY: Amity House, 1986, p. 35.

187. Keating, T. *Open Mind, Open Heart*. Warwick, NY: Amity House, 1986, p. 44.

188. Keating, T. *Open Mind, Open Heart*. Warwick, NY: Amity House, 1986, p. 45.

189. Romans 13:12-14.

190. Romans 6:17.

191. Tillich, P. *Systematic Theology, Vol 1*. Chicago: University of Chicago Press, 1951, pp. 155–159.

192. Romans 8:39.

193. Main, J. *Word into Silence*. Ramsey, NJ: Paulist Press, 1981.

194. Freeman, L. *Light Within: The Inner Path of Meditation*. New York: Crossroad, 1987.

195. DelBene, R., & Montgomery, H. *The Breath of Life: Discovering Your Breath Prayer*. San Francisco: Harper & Row, 1981.

196. St. John of the Cross. *The Collected Works of St. John of the Cross*. (K. Kavanaugh & O. Rodriguez, eds. & transls.) Washington, D.C.: ICS Publications, 1979.

197. In the contemplative part of the spiritual journey, those who have preceded us describe their experiences as primarily receptive in nature. That is, God does the action, and we receive God's action. When sexual imagery is used, Christ is typically described as the bridegroom and we human beings as the bride. The overwhelming body of evidence from our forebears is that God is present in masculine form here. To be faithful to this, I will use either masculine images for God, or gender-neutral terms in this section on contemplative prayer.

198. John 15:1–8.

199. St. John Climacus. *The Ladder of Divine Ascent*. Boston: Holy Transfiguration Monastery, 1978.

200. Evagrios of Ponticus. *The Philokalia, Volume 1*. (St. Nikodimos and St. Makarios, eds.) Boston: Faber & Faber, 1979, pp. 29-71.

201. St. Isaiah the Solitary. *The Philokalia, Volume 1*. (St. Nikodimos and St. Makarios, eds.) Boston: Faber & Faber, 1979, pp. 21–28.

202. Genesis 1:31.

203. John 15:5.

204. St. Nikodimos and St. Makarios. *The Philokalia, Volume 1.* Boston: Faber & Faber, 1979, p. 359.

205. Genesis 1:31.

206. I am grateful to Dr. Hal Simeroth for his help in clarifying these matters.

207. Romans 1:29.

208. Theophan the Recluse. *Unseen Warfare.* Crestwood, NY: St. Vladimir's Seminary Press, 1987, p. 130.

209. Evagrios of Ponticus. *The Philokalia, Volume 1.* (St. Nikodimos and St. Makarios, eds.) Boston: Faber & Faber, 1979, pp. 29–71. See also pp. 16–31 in Volume 3 of *The Philokalia.*

210. St. Hesychios the Priest. *On Watchfulness and Holiness*, in St. Nikodimos and St. Makarios, eds. *The Philokalia, Volume 1.* Boston: Faber & Faber, 1979, p. 163.

211. Genesis 1:27.

212. Matthew 7:9.

213. Psalm 51.

214. Ezekiel 36:26.

215. Matthew 13:44.

216. Matthew 5:44.

217. John 15:12–13.

218. Blake, W. *Selected Poetry and Prose of William Blake.* New York: Random House, 1953, p. 90. ("Auguries of Innocence")

219. St. Teresa of Avila. *Teresa of Avila: The Interior Castle.* (K.

Kavanaugh & O. Rodriguez, transls.) New York: Paulist Press, 1979.

220. Pastrovicchi, A. *St. Joseph of Cupertino*. Rockford, IL: Tan Books, 1980.

221. Luke 24:13–35. A careful reading of Luke indicates that Jesus was in Jerusalem and on the road to Emmaus at the same time.

222. I have viewed the remains of St. Sergius and can testify that they appear to be intact and incorruptible.

223. Zander, V. *St. Seraphim of Sarov*. Crestwood, NY: St. Vladimir's Seminary Press, 1975.

224. Matthew 10:31; Luke 12:32; John 12:15.

225. John 14:6; Matthew 11:28.

226. Matthew 11:29–30.

227. Father Keating calls meditation the "divine therapy" in *The Spiritual Journey*. Snowmass, CO: St. Benedict's Monastery, 1987.

228. Trungpa, C. *Cutting Through Spiritual Materialism*. Berkeley: Shambhala, 1973.

229. See note 73.

230. Matthew 18:20.

231. I am indebted to Father Thomas Keating for much of the material in this chapter.

232. St. John of the Cross. *The Collected Works of St. John of the Cross*. (K. Kavanaugh & O. Rodriguez, eds. & transl.) Washington, DC: ICS Publications, 1979.

233. Matthew 7:3–5.

234. Matthew 11:29–30.

235. Ephesians 4:14.

236. John 10:10.

237. Acts 17:28.

238. If you are depressed and have difficulty identifying your pattern of negative thinking, you may wish to go to a psychotherapist who is skilled in the cognitive-behavioral treatment of depression. Your therapist can quickly show you how to work with these thoughts and change them.

239. John 1:5.

240. Matthew 10:39.

241. Luke 15:11–32.

242. Matthew 7:13–14.

243. Luke 12:31.

244. Matthew 28:20.

245. Romans 6:6–7.

246. Romans 6:8–11.

247. Romans 13:12.

A Select Bibliography

Introductory Texts to the Spiritual Life

Underhill, E. *The Spiritual Life*. New York: Harper & Row (no date given).

> Takes the practice of mysticism out of the realm of the ethereal, and places it at the center of all human growth.

Dallas, W. *The Spirit of the Disciplines*. San Francisco: Harper-Collins, 1992.

> Provides the context within which Christian spiritual growth takes place. This is a key book for understanding the place of meditation and contemplative prayer in the array of Christian spiritual disciplines.

Finley, J. *Merton's Palace of Nowhere*. Notre Dame, IN: Ave Maria Press, 1978.

> This book is an excellent study of the religious search from a Christian perspective and contains valuable insights into the false self.

Sinetar, M. *Ordinary People as Monks and Mystics: Lifestyles for Self Discovery*. New York: Paulist Press, 1986.

> A delightful book that talks about integrating the contemplative way with ordinary life.

Johnston, W. *Silent Music: The Science of Meditation*. San Francisco: Harper and Row, 1979.

> A book by a Jesuit who lives in Japan detailing some of the research by Western scientists into what happens during meditation.

Spiritual Practices by Primary Authors

Br. Lawrence. *The Practice of the Presence of God*. (H.M. Helms, ed. & R.J. Edmonson, transl.) Orleans, MA: Paraclete Press, 1985.
  This book presents the basic teaching of Br. Lawrence for the practice of recollection in God and is very important.

St. Ignatius of Loyola. *The Spiritual Exercises and Selected Works*. (G. Ganss, ed.) New York: Paulist Press, 1991.
  The master of visualization in his major work.

Nouwen, H. *Behold the Beauty of the Lord: Praying with Icons*. Notre Dame, IN: Ave Maria Press, 1987.
  An exquisite introduction to the use of icons in prayer.

DeMello, A. *Taking Flight: A Book of Story Meditations*. New York: Doubleday, 1988.
  This book of story meditations invites the reader to use visualization and to plunge deeply into our Lord with this means.

Hall, T. *Too Deep for Words: Rediscovering* Lectio Divina. New York: Paulist Press, 1988.
  A basic introduction to Lectio, the traditional meditation on scriptures that is central to Christianity.

Anonymous. *The Way of a Pilgrim*. (R.M. French, ed. & transl.) San Francisco: Harper & Row, 1965.
  A classic of Russian spirituality which describes the practice of the Jesus Prayer by a religious mendicant in Russia.

Chariton, I. *The Art of Prayer*. London: Faber & Faber, 1966.
  This is a fascinating compendium of wisdom that has grown up around the Jesus Prayer. It is, at the same time, both readily accessible and will take you years to fully understand.

Marcucci, D. *Through the Rosary with Fra Angelico*. New York: Alba House, 1992.
  An introductory book to the rosary, giving an account of its history and practice.

Anonymous. *The Cloud of Unknowing*. New York: Paulist Press, 1981.
> A "how to" book from the fourteenth century, describing one way of entering into union with the Divine.

Keating, T. *Open Mind, Open Heart*. Warwick, New York: Amity House, 1986.
> This book is the basic text describing Centering Prayer. A marvelous introduction to Christian contemplation, this book must be carefully read.

St. Teresa of Avila. *The Interior Castle*. (K. Kavanaugh & O. Rodriguez, eds. and transls.) New York: Paulist Press, 1979.
> Describes contemplation in stages, to the end point of union with God. Considerable instruction on the latter stages.

St. John of the Cross. *The Collected Works of St. John of the Cross*. (K. Kavanaugh & O. Rodriguez, ed. & transl.) Washington, D.C.: ICS Publications, 1979.
> The standard English translation of John of the Cross.

DelBene, R., & Montgomery, H. *The Breath of Life: Discovering Your Breath Prayer*. San Francisco: Harper & Row, 1981.
> Describes a method for personalizing monologistic prayer. This is a very powerful method that is readily accessible.

Theophan the Recluse. *Unseen Warfare*. (Nicodemus of the Holy Mountain, ed. & E. Kadloubovsky and G.E.H. Palmer, transl.) Crestwood, NY: St. Vladimir's Seminary Press, 1987.
> This book is perhaps the most extraordinary document in this collection, for the depth of Theophan's spiritual insight, and his wisdom about the struggles inherent in undertaking any spiritual discipline.

Lives of the Saints

Underhill, E. *The Mystics of the Church*. New York: Schocken, 1971.
> This brief book is a history of the Western church from the perspective of its great mystics.

Bolshakoff, S. *Russian Mystics*. Kalamazoo, MI: Cistercian Publications, 1980.

This is a survey of mystics of the Russian church. There are great spiritual heros here, that remain unknown to the West.

Pastrovicchi, A. *St. Joseph of Cupertino*. Rockford IL: Tan Books, 1980.

The life of a wonderful saint in the Roman Catholic Church, who was blessed with many of the manifestations of Christ's resurrected body.

Zander, V. *St. Seraphim of Sarov*. Crestwood, NY: St. Vladimir's Seminary Press, 1975.

A delightful book about a nineteenth-century Christian mystic. Seraphim displayed many of the powers claimed by Eastern yogis.

Auclair, M. *St. Teresa of Avila*. Petersham, MA: St. Bede's Publications, 1988.

Perhaps the best biography of this great saint. The language is somewhat stilted, due to the translation from the French, but the power of Teresa's life is captured and revealed to us.

The History of Christian Spirituality

Holmes, H. *A History of Christian Spirituality*. San Francisco: Harper and Row, 1980.

This book summarizes the history of Christian spirituality in 161 pages and does a wonderful job. I still don't know how he did it but it's an extraordinary book and everyone should read it.

Jones, C., Wainwright, G., & Yarnold, E. (eds.) *The Study of Spirituality*. New York: Oxford, 1986.

A collection of learned essays that marvelously illumine the spirituality of the Christian church in its many facets, throughout its rich and varied history.

Writings from the Ancient Christian Tradition

Ward, B. *The Wisdom of the Desert Fathers*. Oxford: SLG Press, 1986.
> An exquisitely rendered translation of the sayings from the desert fathers. These writings reveal a revolutionary perception of the world of the Spirit.

Ward, B. *The Sayings of the Desert Fathers*. Kalamazoo, MI: Cistercian Publications, 1975.
> An alphabetical compendium of the sayings of the fathers that is a "must read" for everyone serious about contemplative prayer.

Ward, B. *The Lives of the Desert Fathers*. Kalamazoo, MI: Cistercian Publications, 1981.
A book complementary to *The Sayings*, this volume translates some of the more personal observations of a pilgrim who toured Egypt in the fourth century.

Maloney, G. A. *Pilgrimage of the Heart*. San Francisco: Harper & Row, 1983.
> A compendium of Eastern Orthodox spirituality. There is much of value in this little book.

St. Nikodimos of the Holy Mountain & St. Makarios of Corinth (eds.) *The Philokalia, Volumes I, II & III*. (G. Palmer, P. Sherrard & K. Ware, transl.) Boston: Faber & Faber, 1979 and 1981.
> A compendium of over one thousand years of practical Christian spirituality.

St. John Climacus. *The Ladder of Divine Ascent*. (Archimandrite Lazarus, ed. & transl.) Boston: Holy Transfiguration Monastery, 1978.
> Describes the beginning of the contemplative journey in terms of behavior changes that allow one to draw closer to the Divine. A good companion to Teresa.

Evagrius Ponticus. *The Praktikos and Chapters on Prayer*. (J.E. Bamberger, ed. & transl.) Kalamazoo, MI: Cistercian Publications, 1981.

A most penetrating analysis of the human spirit written by a Christian mystic of the early church.

St. Isaac the Syrian. *The Ascetical Homilies of Saint Isaac the Syrian*. (Holy Transfiguration Monastery, transl.) Boston: Holy Transfiguration Monastery, 1984.
St. Isaac is one of the Syriac fathers, and is little-known in the West. His early and penetrating insights into the process of deep prayer and its effects on our souls is very useful.

Useful Theological Texts

MacQuarrie, J. *Principles of Christian Theology*. New York: Charles Scribners, 1966.
A basic text in Christian theology that is helpful to anyone walking the path.

Lossky, V. *The Mystical Theology of the Eastern Church*. Crestwood, NY: St. Vladimir's Seminary Press, 1976.
This volume will plunge you deeply into the great mystical traditions of the Orthodox Church. A "must read."

Fox, M. *Original Blessing*. Santa Fe, NM: Bear and Company, 1983.
A somewhat strident book but valuable nevertheless for the important reclaiming of a strand of the Christian tradition that has been, for the most part, lost.

Tillich, P. *Systematic Theology, Vols. 1–3*. Chicago: University of Chicago Press, 1951.
Somewhat formidable in length, but a very accessible discussion of the major issues of Christian theology by a man deeply concerned with the spiritual journey.

List of Spiritual Exercises

Exercise

List of Illustrations

Index

Fr. Ken and the OneHeart teachers give workshops, lectures, and retreats throughout the country in the area of spiritual development and Christian meditation. We also assist individuals in forming meditation groups. Please contact:

Fr. Ken Kaisch, Ph.D.
OneHeart
P.O. Box 5915
Fullerton, CA 92635-0915